# EXPLORING MILITARY AMERICA

**Also by the same authors**

*The Persuaders*

**also by Marcella Thum**

*Exploring Black America*
*Exploring Literary America*

# EXPLORING MILITARY AMERICA

by Marcella Thum
& Gladys Thum

ILLUSTRATED WITH PHOTOGRAPHS

Atheneum   1982   New York

*Library of Congress Cataloging in Publication Data*

Thum, Gladys.
Exploring military America.

Includes index.
SUMMARY. A travel guidebook that annotates military sites and museums in the United States from Colonial times to the war in Vietnam, on a state by state basis.
1. United States—Description and travel—1960—Guide-books. 2. United States—History, Military.
3. Historic sites—United States—Guide-books.
[1. United States—Description and travel—Guides.
2. United States—History, Military] I. Thum, Marcella.
II. Title.

E158.T49    917.3    81-10832
ISBN 0-689-30894-9    AACR2

Copyright © 1982 by Gladys and Marcella Thum
All Rights Reserved
Published simultaneously in Canada by McClelland & Stewart, Ltd.
Composition by American Book-Stratford Graphics,
Brattleboro, Vermont
Printed and bound by Fairfield Graphics,
Fairfield, Pennsylvania
Designed by Mary M. Ahern
First Edition

DEDICATED TO
*Arville Thum*

# CONTENTS

## PART I

*Summary of American Military History from Colonial Era to Vietnam War*

Colonial Era (1521–1574)   3
French and Indian War (1754–1763)   4
American Revolution (1776–1783)   6
The War of 1812 (1812–1815)   9
Texas Rebellion of 1836   11
The Mexican War (1846–1848)   11
Civil War (1861–1865)   13
Indian Wars   16
The Spanish-American War of 1898   20
World War I (1917–1918)   21
World War II (1941–1945)   22
Korean War (1950–1953)   24
Vietnam War (1961–1975)   25

## CONTENTS

# PART II

Military Sites in the United States  27
(EXPLORED BY STATES)

INDEX  319

# INTRODUCTION

Captain John Parker led about 60 armed Massachusetts farmers facing several hundred advancing British Redcoats on the Green at Lexington, April 19, 1775.

He said, "Stand your ground. Don't fire unless fired upon. But if they mean to have a war, let it begin here."

A shot rang out—whether British or American, no one will ever know. Eight Americans were killed, ten wounded. The Revolutionary War was begun and the United States was born. The American Revolution, however, was not the first important fighting on American soil, nor, unhappily, would it be the last.

In its more than two centuries of existence, the United States has fought in ten major wars, at home and abroad, not counting the colonial wars and numerous small military conflicts in which civilian militia or regular forces have been engaged.

The Americans who fought these wars were not all white Caucasian males as it might appear from pages of books on America's military history. All races have been present. Black soldiers have taken part in almost every major war, from Colonial to Vietnam, as have Hispanic-American soldiers. American Indians fought for as well as against the United States forces. American women

## INTRODUCTION

grabbed muskets and fought and died in Indian wars, nursed wounded on battlefields of every war and performed daring acts of espionage.

Today, in every state of the Union, there are battle sites, actual forts, reconstructed forts, military museums, historic naval vessels and airplanes, as well as statues to war heroes and monuments to war dead. A great many battle sites have been destroyed and forgotten; others are not open to the public; some are acknowledged only by plaque or monument; but there are a number of places where actual battlefields can be visited, with redoubts, trenches and earthworks still visible. Each branch of military service has its museums, honoring its valiant deeds and heroes. In addition, there are dozens of military museums maintained by organizations, communities, states and the nation.

It would be impossible in one short book to include every known site in the United States commemorating military struggle. Whenever possible, sites have been chosen that have visitors centers and exhibits—or, in some cases, descriptive markers. Many museums include some military items; we have tried to choose those museums that specialize in military history. All of the sites and museums included in this book may be viewed by the public for a small fee or no fee at all.

Since hours, days and months of the year during which exhibits are open are always subject to change, it is essential to write or call ahead and make sure of opening and closing times. All sites or museums listed should be considered as open the year round unless otherwise indicated. However, even year-round sites may

## INTRODUCTION

be open only by appointment. Also, in summer, additional programs are often available at major sites. Operating military installations are included in the listings only if they contain a museum or exhibit area open to the public. But most military installations will arrange group tours of their facilities if called in advance.

*Exploring Military America* was not written to glorify war. As General Sherman wrote of war, "Its glory is all moonshine . . . war is hell." Yet it is important for both young and old Americans to be aware of their military heritage. Visiting the sites where Americans fought and died in well-known and not-so-well-known battles makes these people and battles cease to be only dull names and dates in a history book. We can feel for what these people were and what they endured, the heroes and the villains and the ordinary soldiers who helped shape the United States. We can regard the record of military struggles on American soil and overseas as badges of honor or as wounds. Usually, they are both. For those visiting these sites and museums, both the pride and the hurt can be felt and better understood.

# PART I

*Summary of American Military History from Colonial Era to Vietnam War*

## COLONIAL ERA, 1521–1754

Chief Joseph of Nez Perce tribe said on October 5, 1877, "Hear me, my chiefs, I am tired; my heart is sick and sad. From where the sun now stands, I will fight no more forever."

From the sixteenth to the late nineteenth century, the Indians of mainland America had fought a valiant, if losing, battle against European invaders. The first military forces to arrive in what is now the United States were the Spaniards, who came to Puerto Rico in the fifteenth century, reached Florida in 1521, then spread into what is now southwestern United States and California. The French arrived in Canada in the sixteenth century, but planted their first colony, at Quebec, at the same time the English began their colony in Virginia in the early seventeenth century. The French extended their control into the Great Lakes and down into the present state of Louisiana. The English—with brief interventions by the Dutch, Spanish and French—colonized the eastern seaboard from New England to Georgia. In Alaska in the late eighteenth century, Tlingit tribesmen fought and eventually lost against Russian and American traders, while in Hawaii, Kamehameha I combined all of the Hawaiian Islands under his control, a royal control that slipped away as Mainland Americans descended on the islands in the 1820s.

The early Europeans came to the North American

continent in search of precious minerals, furs, land and religious freedom, but they came well-armed. Although the American Indian was a hard and ruthless fighter, his weapons were primitive, and in the first full-scale battle between English colonists and Mohegan Indians in 1637, called the Pequot War, the Pequots were virtually wiped out. In King Philip's War in Massachusetts and the Tuscarora and Yamassee War in the Carolinas, again the Indians fought fiercely, and again they were crushed.

In time, as the European settlers began to fight among themselves, various Indian tribes joined forces with the Spanish, French and English. Iroquois Indians allied themselves with the British against the French; Algonquin and Hurons with the French against the English. No matter which side won though, the Indians lost.

By the early eighteenth century, Spanish strength had declined in Europe and thus in its colonies, and the conflict over who should control eastern North America narrowed down to France and England. Each side claimed territories also claimed by the other. A final clash was inevitable, and the first major war on American soil resulted: the French and Indian War.

## FRENCH AND INDIAN WAR, 1754–1763

The war should have been called the French and English War, since Indians fought on both sides of the conflict. From 1748 to 1754, French forts multiplied in the Great Lakes area and in the Ohio Valley. When the French built Fort Duquesne, where Pittsburgh now stands, on territory claimed by England, a young Colonel George Washington was sent by the British royal governor of Virginia to demand that the French withdraw. Washington's small force was defeated by the French. A second attempt by British General Braddock to take Fort Duquesne brought an even more disastrous defeat in 1755, when his troops were massacred in a French and Indian ambush. Then French General Montcalm mounted an attack from Fort Carillon, later Fort Ticonderoga, on British Fort William Henry. Again, the British were defeated and massacred by the Indians, despite Montcalm's protests.

Now the British, who had a larger navy than the French, sent to America more than 20,000 regulars, as well as large sums of money for equipping Colonial volunteers. In 1758, the tide of battle turned. The British navy defeated the French at Louisburg; the French were finally driven from Fort Duquesne and Fort Ticonderoga. British General Wolfe captured Quebec. The Treaty of Paris in 1763 ended the French and Indian War. England took possession of Canada and all of eastern North America from Atlantic Ocean to the Mississippi River, with the exception of the area around New Orleans, which remained French.

Perhaps the most important result of the war was its effect upon the American colonists. Such future Revolutionary War leaders as Philip Schuyler, Israel Putnam, Horatio Gates—and George Washington—served their military apprenticeship in the French and Indian War. Further, the need for protection against the French was removed from the colonies. Though the menace from Indian attacks remained—Pontiac's War, 1763–1766, in the Great Lakes area, was the greatest Indian uprising of the time—nonetheless, the French and Indian War's ending lessened colonial dependence upon England. The colonies began to turn more to each other to solve their mutual problems. A common resentment arose against British taxation without representation and against the tightening of British control over the colonies' economic interests. In effect, the French and Indian War set the stage for the American Revolution.

## AMERICAN REVOLUTION, 1776–1783

On a March evening in 1770, a group of angry Bostonians yelled "Lobster-backs!" and threw rocks at a squad of British Redcoats stationed in their city. The squad shot into the protestors. Five Americans were killed. In the years that followed, from 1771 through 1774, American colonials fought the British at Alamance Creek, North Carolina; off Providence, Rhode Island; in Boston harbor, Massachusetts; and at Portsmouth, New Hampshire. All of these engagements took place before the famous Battle of Lexington and Concord in Massachusetts and the "shot heard 'round the world."

The shot certainly was heard and repeated in a wider area than is generally realized. There were only thirteen colonies at the time of the Revolution. Military action, however, took place also in what are now the states of Maine, West Virginia, Vermont, Alabama, Illinois,

# HISTORY OF THE AMERICAN WARS

Indiana, Kentucky, Tennessee and Ohio—as well as Florida and Louisiana, both colonies claimed by Spain. Additionally, American colonists attacked Canadian strongholds, and the fledgling American navy carried on a war at sea with the powerful British fleet.

Even before the Declaration of Independence was signed in July, 1776, such battles as Bunker Hill, in Massachusetts, and Ninety-Six and Moores Creek, in the Carolinas, had taken place. Also, Benedict Arnold had marched through Maine and on Quebec, without success. But the Revolutionary War's basic action settled into three stages: the war in the north, the war in the middle colonies and the west, and, the final stage, the war in the south.

In the north, the British held New York City and Newport, Rhode Island. Lord Howe so successfully routed General Washington in battles around New York that the war seemed over before it had scarcely begun. Then, Washington's forces crossed the icy Delaware River from Pennsylvania on Christmas, 1776, surprised the British-paid Hessian troops, and took Trenton. Following that brilliant stroke, Washington defeated the British at Princeton a few days later.

From Canada, in the summer of 1777, British General Burgoyne marched south, confidently planning to separate New England from the rest of the colonies. Floundering in the forests of Vermont and New York, he was defeated by colonial militia at Fort Stanwix, Oriskany, and Bennington. His supplies exhausted, Burgoyne surrendered at Saratoga in October, 1777. Saratoga proved to be a decisive battle in the war, because it brought France into the conflict on the side of the American colonies.

At the same time, however, Lord Howe had occupied Philadelphia. And after defeats at Brandywine Creek and Germantown, Washington and his discouraged troops had settled down for the long cruel winter of 1777-78 at Valley Forge. The powerful British navy was also busy, destroying 44 American ships in Delaware Bay. Nevertheless, fearing a blockade by French ships, the British troops withdrew from Philadelphia in the summer of 1778. Washington tried to stop Howe at Monmouth, New Jersey, but the British managed to slip away and settle in New York. Monmouth was the last big battle in the northern colonies.

In the middle colonies and the west, the British with their Indian allies massacred pioneers at Cherry Valley, New York, and at Wyoming Valley, Pennsylvania. The Battle of Kettle Creek was fought on frontiers of Georgia; and in the wilderness of Indiana, George Rogers Clark's frontier fighters took Fort Sackville from the British at Vincennes.

With the war stalemated in the north, the British turned south in December, 1778, seizing Savannah, Georgia, and Charleston, South Carolina, then marching across the Carolinas and Virginia, continually harassed by the Americans in a guerrilla form of warfare. Lord Cornwallis, commanding the British Army in the South, was defeated in 1780 at Kings Mountain, South Carolina, and then was maneuvered by Lafayette into an indefensible position on the Yorktown peninsula. Washington's army, along with the French fleet and French troops, cut off escape. On October 19, 1781, Cornwallis surrendered. While major fighting was over, the Battle of Blue Licks on the Kentucky frontier was fought almost a year later.

Officially, the American Revolution ended with the Treaty of Paris on September 3, 1783. The American colonies were now a nation.

## THE WAR OF 1812: 1812–1815

This "Second War for American Independence" was a confused struggle. The peace treaty did not even mention the problems that began the war, including the British navy's impressment of about 20,000 American seamen into the British navy between 1793 and 1812. Furthermore, when war seemed imminent, and then was declared, New England threatened to leave the Union, more angry at Presidents Jefferson and Madison than at the English, because the American government's action had halted a profitable trade with England. But there was anger enough against the British, too.

American pioneers in the Old Northwest Territory—which included the present states of Ohio, Indiana, Illinois, Michigan, Wisconsin and parts of Minnesota—accused the British of encouraging the raids of the brilliant Shawnee chief, Tecumseh. The British still held, illegally, several forts in the area. Tecumseh, who strove to unite Indians in both north and south against the intruding American pioneers, was finally defeated by General William Henry Harrison at the Battle of Tippecanoe on the eve of the War of 1812.

Though American attempts, with ill-prepared troops,

to invade British-held Canada were disasters, the small American navy performed heroically. Commodore Oliver Hazard Perry's defeat of the British at the Battle of Lake Erie allowed General Harrison to recapture Detroit, which had been lost. Commodore MacDonough's defeat of the British fleet on Lake Champlain forced the British army to retreat from Plattsburgh. On the high seas, American privateers captured over 1,300 British ships, and the United States ship *Constitution,* known today as "Old Ironsides," destroyed a half-dozen proud British warships. In spite of all this, the British fleet still blockaded the East Coast, however, and raided Eastport and Castine in Maine, a reminder that the Maine-Canada border was yet another issue in the war.

In 1814, the British were stopped from invading the United States at Lundy's Lane, near Niagara, New York, but were successful in marching on Washington, D.C. Retaliating for the American burning of York, present-day Toronto, in Canada, the British burned the White House and other government buildings. When the triumphant British moved on Baltimore, however, Fort McHenry and the Maryland militia stood firm. That attack still lives in the words of the "Star Spangled Banner" written by Francis Scott Key.

When the British attacked New Orleans, trying to seize control of the Mississippi River, they were driven back in utter defeat by General Andrew Jackson, frontiersman-soldier, at the Battle of Chalmette. But that battle was fought January 8, 1815, two weeks after the peace treaty at Ghent, ending the war, had already been signed.

## TEXAS REBELLLION OF 1836

As early as 1821, American settlers trickled into Spanish-owned Texas, and the Spanish government welcomed them. By 1836, however, Mexico had become independent of Spain. The new ruler of Mexico, Antonio de Lopez Santa Anna, regarded the Texans as a danger and determined to disarm them. With an army of several thousand, he laid siege to the Alamo, a walled mission-fortress, defended by 187 Texans. The defenders died rather than surrender. That same month, February, 1836, Santa Anna brutally executed 300 prisoners captured after the Battle of Goliad. The Alamo and Goliad fired the Texas Rebellion. On March 1, Texas declared her independence, and in April, Sam Houston, leading a hastily trained Texas army, decisively defeated Santa Anna at San Jacinto. The Republic of Texas was born.

The young Republic lasted almost ten years, until 1845, when Texas was annexed by the United States. Mexico refused to accept the independence of Texas and considered the American annexation an act of war. When American troops were attacked by Mexican dragoons in May, 1846, along the disputed Texas border, the Mexican War was begun.

## THE MEXICAN WAR, 1846–1848

Some voices in the United States protested the Mexican War, calling it "unjust and rapacious." But volunteers flocked to enlist. Though they often brawled among themselves, most of them proved, nonetheless, to be resourceful soldiers for General Zachary Taylor. They defeated the Mexican army at Monterey in September, 1846, and at Buena Vista in February, 1847.

On the western coast of Mexico, General Winfield Scott captured the port of Vera Cruz in March, 1847. With the able assistance of such young West Point officers as Robert E. Lee and Ulysses S. Grant, Scott fought 250 miles inland, defeating Santa Anna in the mountain passes near Cerro Gordo. Despite brave Mexican resistance, Scott reached and captured Mexico City, the capital, in September, 1847.

Meanwhile, General Stephen Kearny at Fort Leavenworth, Kansas, had been ordered by President Polk to occupy Mexican-held New Mexico and California. After securing New Mexico without a fight, Kearny's men reached California in December, 1846. A group of Americans in California, encouraged by the ambitious Captain John C. Fremont, had earlier revolted against Mexican rule in what is known as the Bear Flag Rebellion. In fact, the American flag had been raised over Monterey by the American navy six months before Kearny's arrival.

Combining forces with the navy, General Kearny defeated the small Mexican army in a battle outside of Los Angeles, which ended Californian-Mexican resistance. The Treaty of Guadalupe-Hidalgo, which ended the Mexican War, added to the United States the areas of California, Nevada, Utah, most of Arizona and New Mexico, and parts of Colorado and Wyoming.

# HISTORY OF THE AMERICAN WARS

## CIVIL WAR, 1861–1865

For many years, northern and southern United States had been growing farther and farther apart, philosophically, politically and economically. The North was becoming an industrialized society, with immigrants from abroad providing the inexpensive labor for the factories; the South was still an agricultural society, relying on slave labor. Fearing the North's political and economical domination and its growing anti-slavery movement, several southern states threatened to leave the Union. After Abraham Lincoln, a northerner and an anti-slavery man, was elected President in November, 1860, South Carolina seceded the next month, followed by ten other states. They established their own country: the Confederate States of America.

In April, 1861, the Confederates fired upon and captured Fort Sumter in South Carolina, the opening volley of the Civil War. In July, Confederate troops marched on Washington, D.C., meeting the Union army at Manassas, Virginia. The soldiers on both sides were untrained, and each had only a handful of experienced officers who had served in the Indian Wars and the Mexican War. The South won what came to be called the first Battle of Bull Run, but its invasion of the North failed, a pattern that was to be repeated throughout the war.

The Union armies did little better in their attempts to take Richmond, Virginia, the capital of the Confederacy. President Lincoln was unable to find a Union general who could invade the South and defeat Confederate

General Robert E. Lee. Union General Pope was defeated at the Second Battle of Bull Run in 1862; General Burnside was stopped at Fredericksburg the same year; General Hooker was disastrously defeated by Lee at Chancellorsville in 1863.

The United States Navy's blockade along the southern coast, however, effectively prevented imports of needed Confederate war materials. And in the West, the Union army experienced success. In 1862, Confederate Forts Henry and Donelson in Tennessee were captured by a West Point officer who had served with Robert E. Lee in the Mexican War: General Ulysses S. Grant. Although the Confederates won a bloody battle at Shiloh, Tennessee, they were finally being forced into retreat in the West. Memphis, New Orleans and Vicksburg were captured, and in the words of President Lincoln, the Mississippi River, once controlled by Confederate forces, could now flow "unvexed to the sea."

In spite of this loss to their vital western supply lines, Confederate forces still managed to defeat the Union army at the Battle of Chickamauga in Tennessee, and then almost trapped the Union army at Chattanooga. But Union General Sherman arrived with reinforcements in time to break the siege and recapture Chattanooga. Afterwards, Sherman made his famous, or infamous, march to the sea, cutting a 60-mile swath of destruction through Georgia.

While the Confederate military power in the West was being crushed, General Lee made a second attempt to invade the North—his first attempt in 1862 had been stopped at Antietam, Maryland, in the bloodiest single day of the war. In 1863, at the small town of Gettysburg,

Pennsylvania, the Confederate Army of Northern Virginia was stopped again, this time by Union troops under General Meade. The three-day holocaust resulted in 51,000 casualties.

In March, 1864, General Grant was put in command of the Armies of the United States. The final phase of the war had begun. This time when the Army of the Potomac marched south toward Richmond, the Army of Northern Virginia was forced to give way at the Wilderness, Spottsylvania and Cold Harbor. Losses on both sides were heavy.

In June, 1864, Lee's army dug in at Petersburg, only a few miles from Richmond. Grant settled in for a long siege, and in April, 1865, Lee ran out of men and supplies and his lines were broken. The Confederate capital of Richmond fell. With Grant pressing Lee from the south and east, General Philip Sheridan, who had used a scorched earth policy to win the Shenandoah Valley, blocked Lee's last line of retreat to the west. The Civil War, which had threatened to destroy the Union, ended at a farmhouse at Appomattox, Virginia, on April 9, 1865.

Geographically, the war reached west to Texas and New Mexico and north to Pennsylvania and Ohio. The border states, which sent troops to both the Union and the Confederacy, suffered a particularly virulent guerrilla warfare. Only a few of the war's hundreds of engagements have been mentioned in this account, but most of the major battles were fought in the South. In all, 618,000 Americans died in the tragic conflict, more Americans than died in World War I and World War II combined.

## INDIAN WARS

The cry "Indians!" struck terror in the hearts of European intruders from the time of the earliest Spanish, French and English settlements, through the period of creation of the new American nation, and on until the late 1880s in the American West. The struggle of the Indians against conquest was the longest war in American military history.

For a while, after the colonial battles, the tiny army of the new American nation assumed the role of peacemaker, upholding Congressional treaties with the eastern tribes, persuading Indians like the Iroquois and tribes of the upper Ohio region to peacefully leave their lands. But settlers demanded more and more land, and treaties were broken time and time again.

War with Indians in the Southeast was delayed for a while by a 1790 treaty with the powerful Creeks, a treaty that Spain, then holding Florida and Louisiana, supported to keep up Indian trade. In the old Northwest Territory, however, such Indians as the Shawnee, Miami and Wyandot, encouraged by the French and the English, attacked American settlers pouring into the Ohio Valley. More than 1,500 settlers were killed or captured in Kentucky alone.

Military expeditions against the Indians ended in failure. On November, 1791, 900 American regulars and militia were wounded or killed in a surprise night attack a hundred miles north of Cincinnati, one of the most disastrous defeats the army ever suffered from Indians. It was not until 1793 that Major General Anthony Wayne, with a newly trained army of 3,500, defeated the Miami Indians at the Battle of Fallen Timbers, near Toledo, and the Indians lost their lands in Ohio. The Shawnee Indians, after the Battle of Tippecanoe in 1811, lost their lands in Indiana.

The Creek Indians' land in Alabama was forcibly taken from them after the bloody battle of Horseshoe Bend in 1814. Nine hundred of the thousand Indians in the fight were wounded or killed. Afterward, many Creeks fled to eastern Florida and became part of the Lower Creek "Nation." They settled with the Seminole Indians and with blacks who were fugitives from slavery. Their refuge was short lived.

When Creek Indians in Georgia attacked a keelboat carrying soldiers and their wives, the First Seminole War began. In 1814, General Andrew Jackson marched, without orders, into Spanish-held Florida and destroyed Indian villages and burned the Spanish cities of St. Marks and Pensacola. The war ended in 1819, and Spain ceded Florida to the United States.

The Indian Removal Act passed by the American Congress in 1830 required resettlement of all Indians east of the Mississippi to new lands west of the river. Although some tribes took this blow peacefully, others like the Sauk and Fox in Illinois resisted. The result was the Black Hawk War. Even more fierce resistance came in Florida with the Second Seminole War of 1835. Fighting a guerrilla war from the Everglades, the Seminoles were at first victorious, but starvation tactics, which prevented the Indians from raising crops, ended the fighting in 1842. The Second Seminole War, the last major Indian fight in eastern United States, was waged to ship 3,800 half-starved Indians west and cost the lives of almost 1,600 soldiers.

Forcing Indian tribes into open lands west of the Mississippi only postponed for a short time the inevitable. And, although the treaty ending the Mexican War had added a million square miles of territory to the United States, it had also added 300,000 hostile Indians. Meanwhile, American settlers were crossing the Mississippi, heading west, seeking free land, gold, or simply a new and better life. The violent clash of the two cultures brought about the last tragic stages of the Indian wars.

As Indian resistance increased, the War Department threw up a line of forts across the western frontier. The cordon of forts stretched from the Mississippi River to the coast, from Washington and Minnesota to Texas. By 1869, more than 75 major military forts were scattered throughout the west.

Some of the forts were large and well-established, like the supply forts at Jefferson Barracks, Missouri, and Fort Leavenworth, Kansas. Most of the forts, though, were small and primitive, built of wood or adobe by the soldiers themselves. Only a few of the forts had stockades; and mounted regiments or cavalry were not widely used until after the Civil War.

Duty at the western forts was hard; the pay, poor; the discipline harsh; and aside from an occasional skirmish with the Indians, the life was monotonous and lonely. Surprisingly, the frontier soldier had little training in horsemanship or marksmanship. Many were immigrants, scarcely able to speak English. Some of the best fighting men were black men, called buffalo soldiers by the Indians.

Although the outcome of the Indian Wars in the West was never really in doubt—the nomadic lifestyle of the Indians, the inability of the tribes to unite against a common enemy, made their defeat a certainty—the Plains Indians were formidable opponents. They knew the terrain, could live off the land, and were some of the finest light cavalry in the world. Also, the Indians knew they were fighting for their very survival. Facing such a determined foe, one soldier wrote: "The front is all around and the rear is nowhere."

The Indian Wars in the West were bitter and bloody but consisted of sporadic battles, not one long campaign. Between 1866 and 1891, it is estimated there were over 1,000 engagements between the Indians and the United States Army. To name only a few of the major engagements, there was the Yakima War and the Modoc War in Oregon; the Cheyenne-Arapaho War and the infamous Sand Creek Massacre in Colorado; the Red River War against the Southern Plains Indians; the various Sioux wars beginning in 1854 in Wyoming and going on through the uprisings in Minnesota, ending in the Wounded Knee Massacre in 1890 in the Dakotas; the dozens of campaigns against the Apache, Comanche, Navajo and Ute in the Southwest. Perhaps the most tragic of all the Indian wars was the Nez Perce War of 1877 led by the great Chief Joseph, who led the army on a 1,300 mile chase over the Continental Divide.

By the 1890s, General Sheridan's tactics of attacking the winter camps of the Indians, destroying their supplies and horses, and confining the Indians to reservations, as well as the coming of the railroad, had brought to an end the Indian wars in the United States. The western forts were no longer needed, and one by one, most of them were abandoned, to lie crumbling, forgotten in the sun, the bugle call to arms and Indian war cries still at last.

## THE SPANISH-AMERICAN WAR OF 1898

With the ending of the Indian Wars and the closing of the frontier in the 1890s, the United States began to turn its interest abroad, in particular to Cuba, where revolutionaries were rebelling against a harsh Spanish rule. When the *Maine,* an American warship, was blown up in the harbor of Havana in February, 1898—whether accidentally or deliberately has never been determined—a war fever swept the United States, encouraged by the "jingoistic" newspapers of the time.

The Spanish-American War, for which Spain and the United States were both ill-prepared, lasted only 115 days. The United States navy blockaded Cuba and destroyed the Spanish fleet. The American army, including Theodore Roosevelt's "Rough Riders," captured the heights commanding the city of Santiago, Cuba—San Juan Hill, Kettle Hill and El Caney—forcing the city to surrender. In nearby Puerto Rico, American troops were received enthusiastically by the people. And in the Philippines, Admiral Dewey destroyed the Spanish ships in Manila Bay; and the American Army, with the cooperation of Philippine insurgents, captured Manila. In 1899, however, the Philippine insurgents, seeking independence and led by Aguinaldo, rebelled against American rule. The Philippine Insurrection, an unpopular fight with many Americans, did not end until 1901.

The results of the Spanish-American War were the annexation of Puerto Rico and the Philippines to the United States, while American financial interests controlled most of the island of Cuba. Thus, in defeating Spain, the United States took the first step toward becoming a world military power.

## WORLD WAR I, 1917–1918

American President Woodrow Wilson was reelected in 1915 with the slogan "He kept us out of war." But Germany's unrestricted submarine warfare, its attack on neutral Belgium and reports of German promises to give to Mexico certain southwestern parts of the United States drew this nation into the world conflict on April 6, 1917. This war had new kinds of fighting: in the trenches, under the sea, and in the air.

The war between the Central Powers, led by Germany and Austria-Hungary, and the Allies, led by Great Britain and France, had begun June 28, 1914. The American Expeditionary Force of one and three-quarter million changed the war from near defeat for the Allied powers into victory. Successful fighting by the American First, Second, and Third Divisions in France at Cantigny, Belleau Wood and Chateau-Thierry prevented the Germans from advancing on Paris. A counterattack by eight American divisions and one French division pushed back the German front between Soissons and Chateau-Thierry. By October, 1918, the Allied offensive could not be stopped: the German forces were in retreat from the North Sea to the Argonne forest. The armistice came November 11, 1918.

The cost to the United States was 53,407 dead, 204,002 wounded; the other warring countries suffered a staggering 30,000,000 casualties. American heroes were General John J. Pershing, Admiral William Sims and air aces Frank Luke and Eddie Rickenbacker.

President Woodrow Wilson sought a peace without vengeance and a League of Nations to protect all countries' territorial rights. His peace was not accepted by the Allied powers; his League of Nations was not accepted by the American Congress. The "War to End Wars" led only a little more than twenty years later to another, even bloodier, world-wide holocaust.

## WORLD WAR II, 1941–1945

"Remember Pearl Harbor!" was a popular American battle cry of World War II. The December 7, 1941, Japanese attack on Hawaii was, however, only one of the first manifestations of the war. As early as 1931, Japan had invaded Manchuria and later China, with a master plan for conquering Southeast Asia. In 1935, Italy overran Ethiopia and later Albania. In 1939, the third Axis power, Nazi Germany, invaded Poland, but was forced to share its conquest with Communist Russia, which had recently also taken a part of tiny Finland.

Great Britain and France declared war on Germany and then Italy, but France was quickly defeated. The Nazi "blitzkrieg" had overrun Denmark, Norway, Belgium, Luxemburg, the Netherlands and extended its power into the Balkans. Only Russia prevented German control of the continent of Europe. The Germans invaded Russia on June 22, 1941.

With the Pearl Harbor attack, the United States entered the war against the Axis powers. With such a worldwide sweep of fighting, only turning points of the war can be given here. In 1942, the Philippines were lost in the Pacific, but the Japanese were turned back in the battles of the Coral Sea, Midway and Guadalcanal. In 1943, the Russians broke the German siege of Stalingrad, and British and American forces, having driven the Germans out of Africa, invaded Italy. In 1944, while American forces leap-frogged islands across the Pacific, came the massive Allied D-Day landings of June 6, in Normandy, France. In 1945, along with Allied and Russian advances on Germany came the American retaking of the Philippines and landings at Iwo Jima and Okinawa, at tremendous cost of life.

In April, 1945, President Franklin D. Roosevelt died, succeeded by President Harry Truman. At the end of the same month, Italy's Mussolini was executed by Italian partisans and Germany's Hitler committed suicide. The war in Europe was over. Then, with the dropping of the atomic bombs in August, Japan surrendered on September 2, 1945.

## EXPLORING MILITARY AMERICA

General Dwight D. Eisenhower led the American forces in Europe and Africa; General Douglas MacArthur led the American forces in Asia. A recorded 407,316 Americans were dead; 670,846 were wounded. The peace following this war led to the forming of the United Nations Organization. When Russia declared war on Japan just three weeks before the Japanese surrender, and then occupied North Korea, the seizure eventually brought the United Nations and the United States into the Korean War.

## KOREAN WAR, 1950–1953

Korea, the "Land of the Morning Calm," conquered by Japan in 1910, had been promised independence by the Allies during World War II. When a United Nations Commission was sent to Korea at the end of World War II to organize democratic elections, elections were held in the American-held South but not in the Russian-held North. By 1949, both Russia and the United States reported the departure of almost all of their occupying forces. But the "morning calm" did not last.

On June 25, 1950, in early dawn, 100,000 North Korean Communist troops drove across the 38th parallel and soon forced outnumbered South Korean as well as American troops hurriedly sent from Japan to a desperate beachhead deep in southeast Korea, their backs to the sea. Sixteen United Nations countries sent military help, five sent aid, but the brunt of the fighting was borne by the Republic of Korea and United States forces. In September, General Douglas MacArthur, commanding the United Nations forces, landed at Inchon with an armada of 200 ships. Soon, the North Korean troops retreated to the Yalu River, the North Korean border with China.

The "second" Korean War began as hundreds of thousands of Chinese troops flowed over the border. Wary of a war with China turning into World War III, President Truman refused to allow the bombing of Chinese border bases. The war continued over a narrow strip of central Korea until the armistice was signed July 27, 1953, at Panmunjom.

Korea remained divided as before. United Nations forces had about 400,000 casualties including 260,000 South Korean soldiers and 135,000 Americans. An estimated one million Koreans were dead. The war was not a defeat; it was not a victory. It simply halted the Communist invasion of South Korea. Nevertheless, it was the first time, however inadequately, that countries had freely banded together to declare themselves against military aggression.

## VIETNAM WAR, 1961–1975

With the exception of the American Civil War, no war ever so divided the American people as the Vietnam War. It has left scars still with the nation today. And, like the Korean War, the Vietnam War was essentially two wars.

The first war was from 1946–54, with the American-supported French trying to reestablish control over "French Indo-China," consisting of Vietnam, Cambodia and Laos. The French were defeated by Vietnamese Nationalists and by Communists supported by Russia and China. The Geneva Peace Conference of 1954 divided Vietnam at the 17th parallel, creating a Communist north and a non-Communist south.

The second Vietnam War lasted from 1961 to 1973, with American involvement steadily increasing. After first participating in an advisory capacity, American soldiers soon began fighting the Communist Vietnamese soldiers, and American bombers raided North Vietnam. Eventually, the conflict spread to Cambodia and Laos, with saturation bombings. However, demonstrations against the undeclared war steadily increased in the United States, and with the peace pact of January 27, 1973, the United States withdrew. South Vietnam was given the right to determine its own future. In less than two years, North Vietnam renewed its attacks and South Vietnam fell on April 30, 1975.

At least 2,000,000 Vietnamese were killed in the 30 years of war—and the cost continued as Indo-Chinese refugees fled Communism. The United States lost 51,000 dead, 271,400 wounded and missing. Several thousand soldiers deserted and many thousands more were given less than honorable discharges in this most unpopular war in American history. The Vietnam War, the first war watched on television, had many individual heroes and good American intentions, but left Americans with divided loyalties and wounded national pride.

# PART II

## Military Sites in the United States

EXPLORED BY STATES

# Alabama

While the Spanish explorer Hernando de Soto searched Alabama for gold in 1540, he had to fight Choctaw Indians. But the first military settlements were a line of French forts built along the Gulf Coast in the early 1700s. In 1763, the area encompassing Alabama was ceded to Great Britain at the end of the French and Indian War. Then, while Great Britain was occupied with the American Revolution, Spain seized the Gulf Coast of Alabama. Although Alabama had become a United States possession, Spain retained control of the Mobile area until the War of 1812. Determined Indian resistance to American settlement resulted in the Creek War, which ended at the Battle of Horseshoe Bend in 1814.

The Confederate States of America was first formed in Alabama, and the state and its Gulf forts remained in Confederate hands until 1864 and the Union naval victory at the Battle of Mobile Bay. The Gulf forts were also heavily fortified against possible invasion in the Spanish-American War of 1898.

★ ★ ★

# EXPLORING MILITARY AMERICA

## ANNISTON

FORT MCCLELLAN, one mi. n.e. of Anniston, turn left at SR 31.

EDITH NOURSE ROGERS MUSEUM (WOMEN'S ARMY CORPS MUSEUM), Bldg. 2281, Fort McClellan.
Extensive collection on history of U.S. Women's Army Corps.

U.S. ARMY MILITARY POLICE CORPS MUSEUM, Bldg. 3132, Fort McClellan.
Exhibits on history of U.S. Army Military Police.
Both museums free.

## DADEVILLE

HORSESHOE BEND NATIONAL MILITARY PARK, 12 mi. n. of Dadeville, SR 49.

The Creeks were a people who lived in towns and on farms. After the American Revolution, they signed a treaty defining their land and guaranteeing American friendship. However, the Upper Creeks in Alabama, called Red Sticks, resented white squatters invading their land and in a battle at Fort Mims, north of Mobile, 500 settlers were killed. The Creek War resulted.

Andrew Jackson won an early victory at the Battle of Talladega in November, 1813. (BIG SPRING BATTLE MONUMENT is located in Talladega.) Then on March 27, 1814, Andrew Jackson's 3000 troops and 600 Cherokee Indians bombarded 1000 Red Sticks under Chief Menawa at Horseshoe Bend. The fighting continued until almost all of the Red Sticks were dead. The Creek War opened for settlement much of Alabama and part of Georgia and brought national fame to Jackson.

Tour road, interpretive markers, museum. Free.

## DAUPHIN ISLAND

FORT GAINES, at entrance to Mobile Bay, reached by Dauphin Island toll bridge.

Situated across the bay from Fort Morgan, Fort Gaines was a part of the Battle of Mobile Bay, a battle between ironclad and

# ALABAMA

wooden warships, that made naval history. When both forts fell, the port of Mobile was closed. There was added construction to the fort during the Spanish-American War.

Restored armament, displays, museum. Admission.

## GULF SHORES

FORT MORGAN, 21 mi. w. of Gulf Shores on SR 180 at entrance to Mobile Bay.

Indians, Spanish, French, English, then Spanish again occupied the site of Fort Morgan. In 1813, Americans peacefully captured the fort from the Spanish, and in 1814, successfully defended the fort against British marines and Creek Indians. In the 1820s, Americans constructed the present five-pointed-star fort, designed by a former aide-de-camp to Napoleon. In 1837, 3,000 Indians suffered a deadly imprisonment at the fort before being shipped to Oklahoma. Under the Confederacy in the Civil War, Fort Morgan with Fort Gaines guarded Mobile Bay. In August, 1864, a Federal fleet fought to pass the forts, using torpedoes and smoke screens. Admiral Farragut gave his historic command, "Damn the torpedoes, full speed ahead." Fort Morgan surrendered after 18 days. The fort served as coastal defense in the Spanish-American War, World War I and World War II.

Museum. Free.

## HUNTSVILLE

ALABAMA SPACE AND ROCKET CENTER, accessible from I-65, US 72, 431 and 231.

Center features simulation of trip made by first man to step on moon, U.S. Air Force officer Neal Armstrong. Also, there are scheduled bus tours of NASA's Marshall Space Flight Center. Admission.

## MOBILE

FORT CONDE, Royal and Church Sts.

Three forts and four nations have held this site. In 1711, the

# EXPLORING MILITARY AMERICA

French built a cedar fort and later a brick one; in 1763, the English took possession; in 1780, the Spanish. Under orders from President Madison, American troops captured the fort and Gulf Coast territory during the War of 1812.

Reconstructed 1735 fort, museum. Admission.

U.S.S. ALABAMA BATTLESHIP MEMORIAL, 2½ mi. e. of Mobile on US 90 via Bankhead Tunnel.

This World War II battleship fought in the Atlantic and Pacific oceans. She led the fleet into Tokyo Bay at the end of the war.

Tours: Battleship and submarine *U.S.S. Drum*. Exhibits: Large collection of World War II aircraft. Admission.

## MONTGOMERY

FORT TOULOUSE, 3 mi. s. of Wetupka and 12 mi. n.e. of Montgomery, off US 231 North.

To check growing British influence, the French built this fort in 1717 deep in the heart of the Creek Indian Confederacy. The reconstruction of the fort in 1751 cost the French half of their military budget for the Louisiana colony. Reportedly, one French commander married a Creek princess, and their descendants led the Creeks in the war against American settlers in the early 1800s. The British received the fort after the French and Indian War in 1763, but never garrisoned it. Following Andrew Jackson's Horseshoe Bend victory over the Creeks in April, 1814, his soldiers rebuilt the fort, renaming it Fort Jackson. Here, the Creek treaty was signed, ending Indian threat to settlers in the area.

Partially reconstructed 1751 fort. Admission.

FIRST WHITE HOUSE OF THE CONFEDERACY, 626 Washington Ave.

President Jefferson Davis's home in Montgomery, the first Confederate capital. Free.

U.S. ARMY AVIATION MUSEUM, Andrews Rd., Fort Rucker, 60 mi. s. of Montgomery. From Route 231, take Route 134 west, near Ozark.

Aircraft and history of army aviation. Free.

# ALABAMA

WARRANT OFFICER CANDIDATE HALL OF FAME MUSEUM, Fort Rucker, 60 mi. s. of Montgomery.
Graphic materials and artifacts on Army warrant officer aviators. Hours by appointment. Free.

## SELMA

JOSEPH T. SMITHERMAN HISTORIC BUILDING, 109 Union St.

The ironclad *C.S.S. Tennessee* was built at the important Selma naval ordnance works. In the Battle of Selma, April, 1865, the city was taken and the ordnance works burned. A monument to the fallen stands on Civil War earthworks. The Smitherman Museum, a Civil War hospital, houses rare Civil War items. Free.

# Alaska

The Russians arrived in 1741 in search of furs, and eventually fought the fierce Tlingit Indians. The Russians remained in control in Alaska until 1867, when, through the efforts of William H. Seward, American Secretary of State, Alaska was purchased from the Russians. Though criticized as "Seward's Folly," the sale was at a bargain price of less than two cents an acre.

The few American troops garrisoned in Alaska during the late nineteenth and early twentieth century were there mainly to protect settlers during the violent days of the Alaskan gold rush. Alaska became the only part of continental United States invaded during World War II, when a Japanese attack was repulsed at Dutch Harbor and ten thousand Japanese troops occupied Kiska and two thousand Attu, in 1942. In 1943, American forces drove them out, at a cost of 2,100 American and Japanese lives.

★ ★ ★

# ALASKA

## ANCHORAGE

THE UNITED STATES HISTORICAL AIRCRAFT PRESERVATION MUSEUM, Merrill Field.

A new museum, opened in 1981, houses historical aircraft of the Aleutian Campaign in World War II, among other historical aircraft. Free.

## HAINES

FORT WILLIAM H. SEWARD

Built at the old port of Chilkoot in 1898 to preserve order during the gold rush, Fort Seward was for twenty years the only army post in Alaska.

Renovated fort, renamed Fort Chilkoot; replica of Indian village. Admission for Indian dances in summer.

## KODIAK

FORT ABERCROMBIE STATE PARK, 4½ mi. n.e. on Miller Point.

This World War II fortification defended the coastline of Alaska, although the fort itself was never under attack.

April 15–October 15. Free.

## SITKA

SITKA NATIONAL HISTORICAL PARK, one mi. s. of Sitka.

In 1804, the Tlingit Indians were defeated by Russian colonists in the Battle of Sitka, last major native Alaskan struggle against European domination. The Tlingit tribesmen, who four years earlier had killed or captured some six hundred Russians and Aleuts at Sitka, fiercely resisted for six days.

Tour trail. Visitor Center and museum open April through October. Free.

# Arkansas

In 1686, the French established the first military post in the area: Arkansas Post. In 1762, the territory became Spanish. With the 1803 Louisiana Purchase, the United States took possession. Fort Smith, built in 1817, was used as protection both for and against the Indians and as an outfitting point for Mexican War troops. Although both white and Indian sentiment about the Civil War was divided, Arkansas seceded from the Union in 1861. Important Civil War events in Arkansas were the Battle of Pea Ridge, also known as Elkhorn Tavern, in 1862, and the fall of Little Rock to Union forces in 1863.

★ ★ ★

**FORT SMITH**

FORT SMITH NATIONAL HISTORIC SITE, Rogers Ave. between 2nd and 3d Sts.

From this first United States fort in Arkansas, the army discouraged white squatters and quelled fighting between the Osage Indians, native to the area, and the Indian tribes who had been forced out of the East. In the Mexican War, the fort was garrisoned by Ar-

# ARKANSAS

kansas volunteers, and in the Civil War was a supply depot for both North and South. When Arkansas seceded, federal troops evacuated Fort Smith and all army posts in the Indian territory. The Five Civilized Tribes—Chickasaw, Creek, Cherokee, Choctaw and Seminole—fought for both North and South. Of three Confederate Indian brigades, one commanded by General Watie claimed to be the last Confederate force to surrender. After the war, the tribes attended a Great Council at Fort Smith and lost slaves and land.

Part of old fort. Old Fort Museum, 111 Rogers Ave. Admission.

## GILLETTE

ARKANSAS POST NATIONAL MEMORIAL, SR 69, 7 mi. s. of Gillette, along lower Arkansas River.

This park was the site of a 1686 French fort, first white settlement in the Mississippi Valley. This area was also the site in the Civil War of a three-day land and naval battle that badly damaged the town and ended with the capture of Confederate Fort Hindman. Free.

## JACKSONPORT

OLD JACKSONPORT COURTHOUSE MUSEUM, Jacksonport State Park, e. of town between SR 69 and White River.

Jacksonport was a main mustering point for the Confederate army in Arkansas and was used by five generals, both Confederate and Union, as headquarters.

Closed mornings in winter. Admission.

## PRAIRIE GROVE

PRAIRIE GROVE BATTLEFIELD STATE PARK, adjacent Prairie Grove and 12 mi. s.w. of Fayetteville.

A bitter, inconclusive battle took place here in the winter of 1862. Both armies were forced to withdraw. Also in the town is HINDMAN HALL MUSEUM, containing Civil War relics. Free.

# EXPLORING MILITARY AMERICA

## ROGERS

PEA RIDGE NATIONAL PARK, 10 mi. n.e. of Rogers, via US 62.

In March, 1862, Confederate forces moving toward Missouri were stopped by Union troops dug in on the bluffs of Pea Ridge. One thousand Cherokee Indians and many French-speaking soldiers from Louisiana fought with the Southern forces, while many of the Union soldiers from Missouri spoke German. The two-day battle near ELKHORN TAVERN saved Missouri for the Union.

Restored Elkhorn Tavern. Visitor center, tour. Free.

## SHERIDAN

JENKINS FERRY BATTLEGROUND, Jenkins Ferry State Park, 10 mi. s.w. of Sheridan, on State 46.

On April 30, 1864, Union forces, including the First Kansas Colored Regiment, were attacked at Jenkins Ferry, along the Sabine River. Earlier, at Poison Springs, Arkansas, in the Battle of Marks Mill, Confederates killed captured and wounded black soldiers. In retaliation, at Jenkins Ferry, black troops shouting "Remember Poison Springs" overran a Confederate battery.

Museum on Jenkins Ferry Battle at Sheridan. Battle Marker at Poison Springs State Park, Camden. Free.

# Arizona

The Spanish came to Arizona in 1539 searching in vain for the fabulous golden Seven Cities of Cibola. Spanish settlements were destroyed by the Pueblo Indians until Spain set up a permanent presidio or fortress near present-day Tucson to repress Indian uprisings. In 1821, Arizona became Mexican territory; in 1848, after the Mexican War, American. The territory declared for the Confederacy during the Civil War, but had little Confederate action. A skirmish in Pima County has been called "the fartherest west battle of the Civil War." Seventy military outposts were built across Arizona to protect settlers against fierce Apache warriors led by such famous chiefs as Cochise and Geronimo. The Indian wars in Arizona lasted until the late 1880s.

★ ★ ★

**BISBEE**

CORONADO NATIONAL MEMORIAL. Montezuma Canyon Road, which passes through the memorial, joins SR 92 about 20 mi. w. of Bisbee.

# EXPLORING MILITARY AMERICA

Esteban the Black and Fray Marcos de Niza scouted the area in 1539, followed the next year by Francisco Vasquez de Coronado with Spanish soldiers and Mexican-Indian allies, all searching for the Seven Cities of Cibola. This was the first European military and exploring expedition into the American Southwest.

Interpretive exhibits, viewing platform, spring pageant. Free.

## BOWIE

FORT BOWIE NATIONAL HISTORIC SITE, on secondary road from I-10, about 13 mi. s. of Bowie.

The fort was a center for fighting against the Chiricahua Apache Indians under Cochise. When the Civil War began, Confederate forces arriving in the summer of 1861 found Cochise's men would attack a gray uniform as readily as a blue. Union California Volunteers drove the Confederates from Arizona territory. In July, 1862, an Apache ambush was thrown back by California Union soldiers using the first artillery the Indians had seen. Cochise later said to one of the victors: "You never would have whipped us if you had not shot wagons at us."

Partly restored fort, interpretive program. Free.

## CAMP VERDE

FORT VERDE STATE HISTORIC PARK, 2 mi. e. of I-17.

Fort Verde, built in 1871, served as a base for General Crook's campaign when warfare erupted between settlers and Apache Indians in the Verde Valley. Captured Indians were later moved to San Carlos Indian Reservation in the dead of winter, a ten-day walk that resulted in 200 deaths. The last battle in north central Arizona between Apaches and whites took place in 1881 at "Battle Ground Ridge," 35 miles east of Fort Verde.

Partly restored fort, museum. Admission.

## FREDONIA

WINSOR CASTLE FORT (Pipe Spring National Monument) within Paiute Indian Reservation on SR 389, 14 mi. w. of Fredonia.

# ARIZONA

Built in 1871, fort served Mormons as protection from Indians. Visitor Center. Admission.

## HUACHUCA CITY

FORT HUACHUCA, 70 mi. s.e. of Tucson, I-10 and Fort Huachuca exit at Route 90 to main gate.

The old fort was founded in 1877 and was one of the last important posts established to protect settlers against Apache attacks. The troops from the fort played a major role in the capture of Geronimo, the Apache leader, in 1886, after five months and 3,000 miles of pursuit. The Tenth Cavalry, made up of black troopers, served at the fort for twenty years and joined General Pershing in his punitive expedition into Mexico after Pancho Villa.

Old Fort is just to the west of present day Fort Huachuca, a still-active army post. Museum is in Building 41401, Boyd and Grierson Aves., just w. of Sierra Vista. Statue to black "buffalo" soldiers and visitor passes at main gate. Free.

U.S. ARMY INTELLIGENCE MUSEUM, Jeffords St., Fort Huachuca.

Also at Fort Huachuca is a museum of the history of military intelligence, primarily World War II and later. Free.

## PICACHO

PICACHO PEAK BATTLEGROUND, Picacho Peak State Park, SR 84, about 6 mi. s. of Picacho.

Confederate Texas troops were attacked by Federal California cavalry while returning to their base at Tucson; it was the only Civil War battle in Arizona.

Battle site markers; Confederate monument 2 mi. n. of site. Free.

## TUBAC

TUBAC PRESIDIO STATE HISTORIC PARK.

This first military post in Arizona has flown Spanish, Mexican

# EXPLORING MILITARY AMERICA

and American flags.
> Museum. Admission.

## TUCSON

FORT LOWELL MUSEUM, Fort Lowell and Craycroft Rds.

Fort Lowell was a Civil War supply depot and later was a base for General Miles's final campaign against the Apache Chief Geronimo.

Partly reconstructed fort, 1880 commanding officers qtrs. Free.

## WHITERIVER

FORT APACHE SITE, Fort Apache Indian Reservation, 5 mi. s. of Whiteriver.

The fort had a turbulent history of battles with the Apache and of corrupt Indian agents. Also on the Reservation is CIBECUE CREEK BATTLEFIELD, site of a fight between troopers from the fort and followers of the Indian medicine man Nakaidoklini.

Fort Apache Cultural Center. Donations.

## WILLCOX

COCHISE VISITOR CENTER AND MUSEUM, ½ mi. e. of jct. SR 186 and I-10.

Apache Indian displays and history of U.S. military in area. Free.

## YUMA

FORT YUMA QUECHAN MUSEUM, Fort Yuma Indian Agency.

This fort, first built of brush and willows, was abandoned in 1851 after Indian attacks. Rebuilt in 1854, the post was used in the Civil War to monitor Confederate movements up the Colorado River.

Exhibits on Indians, Spaniards and U.S. military. Admission.

# California

The Spanish came to California as early as 1542; but the first four Spanish forts were built in the eighteenth century, between San Diego and San Francisco. Sixty miles north of San Francisco, the Russians built a trading fort in 1812, but soon withdrew. After winning independence from Spain in 1822, the Mexicans held California. But American settlers rebelled against Mexico in the 1846 Bear Flag Revolt. Within 23 days, the California Bear Flag was lowered for the American flag, as American naval and army forces occupied California during the Mexican War. At the war's end in 1848, Mexico ceded California to the United States.

The next year brought the Gold Rush. In the Civil War, California gold made a vital contribution to the Union. California Volunteers prevented New Mexico and Arizona from being taken by Confederate troops from Texas and protected California routes and later the Mexican border against the threat of invasion by French Imperial Mexican troops. During World War II, California

# EXPLORING MILITARY AMERICA

coastal defenses were strengthened against possible invasion by the Japanese, an attack that never occurred.

★ ★ ★

### FORT BIDWELL

FORT BIDWELL, Modoc County, in n.e. corner of state near Oregon and Nevada lines, e. of US 395.

Garrison fought with General Crook at nearby Battle of Infernal Caverns in September 1867, and in ensuing Snake, Modoc, Nez Perce and Bannack campaigns. Now headquarters of Fort Bidwell Indian Reservation.

Buildings, monument. Free.

### FRESNO

FORT MILLER BLOCKHOUSE MUSEUM, Roeding Park, W. Belmont Ave. and SR 99.

An 1841 fort moved to park after original site was flooded in 1944.

Museum open Saturdays, Sundays and holidays in afternoons. Donations.

### INDEPENDENCE

FORT INDEPENDENCE, Inyo County, US 395, n.e. of Independence on dirt road.

Post helped to quell Indian uprisings of the 1860s.

Fort ruins. Commander's house, moved to 303 N. Edwards, Independence, in 1883. Admission.

### JENNER

FORT ROSS STATE HISTORIC PARK, 19005 Coast Highway 1.

Russian fort, built in 1812 for trade and to expand Russian influence. The Russians left in 1841.

Restored buildings, stockade, museum. Admission.

# CALIFORNIA

## LEBEC

FORT TEJON STATE HISTORIC PARK, 3½ mi. n. on I-5.

This fort, 1854–64, guarded the Tehachapi Mountain pass, served as stage escort garrison, and was terminus of the U.S. Camel Corps, which hauled army supplies from Texas.

Restored fort, museum. Admission.

## LOS ANGELES

AMERICAN SOCIETY OF MILITARY HISTORY, Patriotic Hall, 1816 S. Figueroa St.

American and foreign military history collection. Free.

## MERCED

AIR MUSEUM, Castle Air Force Base, 7 mi. n.w. of Merced at Atwater off Route 90.

World War II bomber collection with theme of history of bombardment and air fueling.

Museum still being prepared. Free.

## MONTEREY

FORT ORD AND THE SEVENTH INFANTRY DIVISION MUSEUM, Ford Ord, 10 mi. n. of Monterey on Route 1.

Artifacts tell the history of Ford Ord and the Seventh Infantry Division. Free.

U.S. ARMY MUSEUM IN THE PRESIDIO OF MONTEREY, off Route 1, north on Pacific Street.

This presidio, built in 1770, was one of the four eighteenth century Spanish forts in California. In 1822, the Mexicans took the forts; in 1846, Americans did. The Presidio of Monterey is still an active Army installation. The Army Museum unfolds the military history of the Monterey Peninsula through Indian, Spanish, Mexican and American occupation of California, as well as through later American wars. Behind the museum is a monument to Commodore Sloat, who raised the American flag over the Monterey Custom House on June 7, 1846. The Custom House, now a museum, stands at Fisherman's Wharf in what is now Monterey State Historic Park. Free.

## PACIFIC GROVE

POINT PINOS LIGHTHOUSE MUSEUM, Ocean View Blvd.
    United States Coast Guard history.
    Open weekend afternoons. Free.

## PORT HUENEME

CEC/SEABEE MUSEUM.

History, models, equipment, work of Seabees and Civil Engineer Corps are offered in this collection. Free.

## RIVERSIDE

MARCH FIELD MUSEUM, March Air Force Base, 12 mi. s.e. of Riverside off I-15.

One of the earliest Air Force bases, built in 1918, the March Field Museum houses exhibits from the early Air Force days, during and after World War I, including historic aircraft.

Museum, self-guided tours of base. Afternoons, closed Saturdays. Free.

## SACRAMENTO

SILVER WINGS AVIATION MUSEUM, Mather Air Force Base, 12 mi. e. of Sacramento on Route 50.

Historic portrayal of Air Force and Mather Air Force Base, including World War II Briefing Room, exhibits, films. Free.

## SAN DIEGO

U.S. NAVAL TRAINING CENTER, Curtis and Rosecrans Sts., Gate 3.
    Museum, self-guided tours. Free.

# CALIFORNIA

## SAN FRANCISCO

FORT MASON HISTORIC DISTRICT. Turn right off Lombard St. onto Franklin St. and into Fort Mason.

Built on the site of an old Spanish fort, Fort Mason was taken over by the United States in 1846 and held by Union forces during the Civil War. After the Spanish-American War, the fort developed into the Army's supply center for the Pacific area.

Historic Buildings, 1855 Ammunition Magazine. Free.

PRESIDIO ARMY MUSEUM, The Presidio of San Francisco, at foot of Golden Gate Bridge.

Built in 1776, the presidio is one of the oldest military posts in the United States. The former Spanish commandant's headquarters is now the Officers' Club. The presidio army museum covers military history of the San Francisco area from the Spanish occupation through the present day. In the presidio is also Fort Point, built during the Civil War as a main defense bastion on the West Coast. Today, the presidio is headquarters of the Sixth Army.

Maps of presidio are available at the Military Police Station, Lincoln Blvd. and Graham Ave. Free.

NAVY/MARINE CORPS MUSEUM, Treasure Island, reached via Oakland-San Francisco Bay Bridge.

Exhibits and murals, weapons, aircraft and armored vehicles depicting the history of the Navy and Marine Corps in the Pacific since 1813. Free.

FORTS BARRY AND CRONKHITE, across Golden Gate Channel from San Francisco. From the north on Route 101, take the fort exit just before the Golden Gate Bridge.

The historical portions of Forts Barry and Cronkhite are part of the Golden Gate National Recreation Area. The batteries at the forts, built for coastal defense, span five eras of military defense and an important age of coastal artillery. The equipment ranges from muzzle loaders to missiles. Free.

# EXPLORING MILITARY AMERICA

## SAN JUAN BAUTISTA

SAN JUAN BAUTISTA STATE HISTORIC PARK, 2nd St., 3 mi. e. of US 101.

The Plaza Hotel was built in 1813 as a Spanish barracks and is one of the historic buildings in the park, centering on the plaza.

Self-guided tours. Admission.

## SAN PASQUAL

SAN PASQUAL BATTLEFIELD STATE HISTORIC PARK, 2½ mi. w. of San Pasqual on SR 78.

General Kearny's American forces, after marching 2,000 miles from Missouri, defeated General Andrew Pico and his Mexican-Californian dragoons here in 1846 in one of the most important battles in California. Free.

## SANTA BARBARA

EL PRESIDIO DE SANTA BARBARA STATE HISTORIC PARK, 122 E. Canon Perido St.

The Presidio has the oldest adobe structure, El Cuatreal, 1782, remaining of the original fort buildings. Admission.

## SONOMA

SONOMA PLAZA, on SR 12.

This was the site of raising of the Bear Flag on June 14, 1846.

Original buildings surround square, monument. Free.

## SUSANVILLE

ROOP FORT AND WILLIAM PRATT MEMORIAL MUSEUM, 75 N. Weatherlow St.

This 1854 fort was called Fort Defiance during the Sagebrush War in 1864, a boundary dispute with Nevada.

May 1–Sept. 30. Free.

# CALIFORNIA

## WILMINGTON

DRUM BARRACKS, 1053 Carey St.

Established in 1862 as U.S. military headquarters for the Southwest, the fort also served as a supply base and terminus for camel pack trains.

Original quarters and powder magazine. Free.

# Colorado

Zebulon Pike explored Colorado in 1806, and was followed by mountain men seeking furs; but it was a trader, Charles Bent, who built the first permanent fort in the area in 1833. The Mexican claim to Colorado was transferred to the United States after the Mexican War. The Colorado Gold Rush of 1858 brought an onslaught of miners and settlers along with troubles with the Cheyenne, Arapaho and Utes. Indian raids increased when the regular Army troops that had protected the Colorado frontier were sent east to fight in the Civil War. The Cheyenne-Arapaho War in the high plains of Colorado, Kansas and Nebraska ended just a few months after the close of the Civil War.

★ ★ ★

**ALAMOSA**

PIKE'S STOCKADE, 14 mi. s. off US 285, just n. of SR 136.

During his exploration of the southwest corner of the Louisiana Purchase, Zebulon Pike erected by mistake a stockade in Spanish territory. The Spanish demanded that he surrender the fort, and he was

# COLORADO

taken to Santa Fe and Chihuahua before being released. He gained for the United States a knowledge of Spanish holdings in the Southwest in 1807.

Reconstructed fort. May 15–Oct. 15. Free.


## ATWOOD

SUMMIT SPRINGS BATTLEGROUND, on Logan-Washington County line, about 10 mi. s.w. of Atwood on unimproved road.

Guided by "Buffalo Bill" Cody, troops from Fort McPherson, Nebraska, and 150 Pawnee scouts, on July 11, 1869, surprised the Cheyenne, killing 50, including Chief Tall Bull, and capturing 117. Only one cavalryman was wounded. Tall Bull and his "Dog Soldiers" had been plundering Kansas and Colorado settlements for months.

Stone monument, springs. Free. Relics from battle at OVERLAND TRAIL MUSEUM, Sterling, Colorado. Free.


## CHIVINGTON

SAND CREEK MASSACRE, about 9 mi. n.e. on SR 96.

Colonel J. M. Chivington and 1,000 Colorado Volunteers in November, 1864, attacked a Cheyenne camp on Sand Creek. The Indians were camped peacefully and believed they were under the protection of Fort Lyon. The unprovoked slaughter of over 200 Indians, many of them women and children, was denounced by the U.S. Congress and brought Plains Indians back into renewed warfare.

Stone marker, descriptive plaque, site overlook. Free.


## COLORADO SPRINGS

U.S. AIR FORCE ACADEMY, Visitor Center, 12 mi. n. on I-25.

Pictorial exhibits of history of U.S. Air Force Academy. Tours. Free.

FORT CARSON MUSEUM OF THE ARMY IN THE WEST, 1 mi. s. of Colorado Springs. I-25, exit 56A, then ½ mi. to Fort Carson.

# EXPLORING MILITARY AMERICA

Although Fort Carson is not one of the western frontier posts, the museum has outstanding displays of the "Army of the West," and the army in Colorado. Realistic views of soldiers' lives in the infantry, engineers, artillery and cavalry are offered. On exhibit are graphics of 180 active forts of the early West and of 1880 army vehicles. In addition, the museum shows military artifacts from the Revolutionary War through the Vietnam War. Free.

## CRAIG

THORNBURGH BATTLEFIELD SITE, 17 mi. s. of Craig, on SR 13, then left 11 mi. on side road and right .6 mi. to site.

Major Thornburgh and 160 troopers were pinned down by a Ute war party. Black soldiers from the Ninth Cavalry Regiment slipped in at night, holding off the Indians until reinforcements arrived. Sergeant Henry Johnson of the Ninth won the Medal of Honor in this 1879 engagement. In the 30 years the buffalo soldiers, as the Indians called the black troopers, served on the frontier, fourteen noncommissioned officers won the Congressional Medal of Honor.

Granite shaft and battlefield site. Free.

## FORT COLLINS

FORT COLLINS MUSEUM, 200 Mathews St.

Guns and exhibits of old fort; first settler's cabin. Free.

## FORT GARLAND

OLD FORT GARLAND MUSEUM, US 160 and SR 159, s. edge of town.

An adobe post established 1858 to protect settlers and travelers on the road to Taos, New Mexico. The post was the famous frontier scout Colonel Kit Carson's last command, 1866–67. After the Meeker Massacre of 1879 by Ute Indians, 1,500 troopers were stationed at the post.

Restored fort, museum. Summers only. Admission.

# COLORADO

## FORT MORGAN

FORT MORGAN LIBRARY AND MUSEUM COMPLEX, 8 blocks s. of I-76 in City Park at 400 Main St.

Named Camp Tyler, Camp Wardwell and finally Fort Morgan in 1866, the fort protected the Overland Trail.

Museum. Free.

## JULESBURG

FORT SEDGWICK-JULESBURG MUSEUM.

This fort was attacked by southern Plains Indians reacting to the Sand Creek Massacre. About 1,000 Cheyennes, Arapahos and Sioux attacked the post and sacked and later burned the town.

Museum interprets the fort's history. Admission.

## LA JUNTA

BENT'S OLD FORT NATIONAL HISTORIC SITE, 8 mi. e. on SR 194.

Built in 1833, this adobe stronghold was an important base in the Mexican War in 1846. Colonel Doniphan's Missouri Volunteers marched from Fort Leavenworth, Kansas, via Fort Bent to Santa Fe, and then to Monterey, Mexico, fighting battles along the 3,600 miles.

Reconstructed fort. Free.

## LOS ANIMAS

FORT LYON, US 50 e. from Los Animas to County Road 183, turn right and proceed one mi. to site, on U.S. Naval Hospital grounds.

From Fort Lyon, Colonel Chivington and his volunteers rode out to commit the massacre of peaceful Indians at Sand Creek. To Fort Lyon officers who protested, the former minister Chivington cried, "I have come to kill all Indians and I believe it is right to use any means under God's heaven!" The KIT CARSON MUSEUM, 125 9th St., Los Animas, has a Fort Lyon Room with artifacts.

# EXPLORING MILITARY AMERICA

Some original fort structures on hospital grounds.
Museum open summer afternoons. Free.

## MEEKER

WHITE RIVER MUSEUM, 565 Park St.

When Indian Agent Meeker summoned the army to put down a Ute uprising in 1879, the Indians ambushed the military relief column. They killed Meeker and nine employees and took the women and children as hostages.

Museum is housed in an 1880s officers' quarters near site of massacre. Free.

## PUEBLO

EL PUEBLO MUSEUM, 905 S. Prairie Ave.

Historical replica of the 1842 Spanish adobe fort, recalling Indian and Spanish occupation.

Open summers only. Admission.

## WRAY

BEECHER ISLAND BATTLE SITE, on Route 53 near Wray.

Colonel Forsyth and fifty soldiers were trapped at Beecher Island and held for eight days under siege by several hundred Indians, led by the fierce warrior Roman Nose. Without medical supplies, forced to eat rancid horse flesh, the command was rescued by the Tenth Cavalry, black soldiers from Fort Wallace, Kansas, who covered 100 miles in two days.

Site is marked by monument and five gravestones. Free.

# Connecticut

The first English settlers in Connecticut had to face hostile Pequot Indians. Later, settlers became involved in border disputes with Rhode Island and Pennsylvania, which led to open skirmishes before the American Revolution. Connecticut contributed the second largest number of troops to the Continental Army and her privateers raided English ships, but few significant battles were fought on her shores. As with most New England states, Connecticut was not a strong supporter of the War of 1812. But troops from Connecticut were among the first to volunteer during the Civil War, and the state produced much of the small arms used by the Union.

★ ★ ★

**EAST GRANBY**

OLD NEW-GATE PRISON AND COPPER MINE, ¾ mi. w. on SR 20, 1 mi. n. on Newgate Road.
Prison for British in the Revolutionary War, 1775–1782.
Museum. Open May 15–Oct. 31. Admission.

# EXPLORING MILITARY AMERICA

## GREENWICH

PUTNAM COTTAGE, 243 E. Putnam Ave.

General Israel Putnam was reportedly surprised here by the British in 1779. It was then Knapp's Tavern. Putnam escaped.

Museum includes Putnam memorabilia. Admission.

## GROTON

U.S.S. CROAKER SUBMARINE MEMORIAL, 395 Thames St.

World War II submarine, available for tours. Also, during summer, commercial tours are offered, by bus and by boat, of the Submarine Base at Groton, including a visit to the SUBMARINE FORCES LIBRARY AND MUSEUM, 440 Washington St., Middletown.

Submarine open year round. Admission.

FORT GRISWOLD STATE PARK, Monument and Park Aves.

On September 8, 1781, British troops under the command of turncoat Benedict Arnold attacked and partly destroyed New London, home port for American privateers. The British also attacked Fort Griswold, garrisoned with 150 militia commanded by Colonel William Ledyard. British Colonel Eyre threatened no quarter, but Colonel Ledyard refused to surrender. After an artillery barrage and bayonet charge, the British marched in. Colonel Ledyard surrendered but was immediately killed with his own sword and more than 80 Americans were massacred. West of the fort on park grounds is the EBENEZER AVERY HOUSE, where American wounded were taken after the battle. Also on the grounds is the GROTON BATTLE MONUMENT, dedicated to victims of the massacre, and MONUMENT HOUSE with relics.

Monument and Avery Houses open Memorial Day to Oct. 12, Free.

Park and battle monument open year round. Free.

## NEW HAVEN

THE WINCHESTER GUN MUSEUM, 275 Winchester Ave.

The model 1873 Winchester has been called "the gun that won the West." Buffalo Bill Cody wrote to the Winchester Gun Company

# CONNECTICUT

in 1875, "An Indian will give more for one of your guns than any other gun he can get." The Army repeating rifle manufactured by Winchester often made up for the western soldier's indifferent marksmanship and was a deciding factor in many a skirmish with the Indians. Free.

FORT NATHAN HALE, off Townsend Ave., I-95, Exit 50.

Used during the Revolution and the Civil War, the fort commands the eastern shore of New Haven Harbor and was a part of the 1779 defense of New Haven during the British attack.

Park open year round, guides Memorial Day to Labor Day. Free.

## NEW LONDON

FORT TRUMBULL at Fort Neck.

The original fort was an important defense during the Revolution and continued in service until 1838. Present fort was completed in 1850. Free.

SHAW MANSION, 11 Blinman St.

Mansion, visited by Washington and Lafayette, was a naval office during the Revolution.

Tuesday through Saturday afternoons. Admission.

THE U.S. COAST GUARD ACADEMY, off I-95 on SR 32, Mohegan Ave.

Founded 1876, the Academy suffered its first official war casualties in World War I.

Visitor's pavilion, museum of historical exhibits. Free.

## REDDING

PUTNAM MEMORIAL STATE PARK, Jct. Rtes. 58, 107.

Winter encampment of 1778–79 for General Israel Putnam's army. Putnam's Revolutionary War forces prevented British advance on inland Connecticut, despite British ship raids on Norfolk and New Haven.

Restored blockhouses, palisades. Museum open summers. Free.

# EXPLORING MILITARY AMERICA

## RIDGEFIELD

KEELER TAVERN, 132 Main St.

This tavern was headquarters for Revolutionary War patriots. It was embedded with a cannon ball in the 1777 Battle of Ridgefield.

Open Wednesdays, weekends, Monday holidays, all in afternoons only. Admission.

## STONINGTON

OLD LIGHTHOUSE MUSEUM, end of Water St.

Collection contains War of 1812 Battle of Stonington relics.

Open July 4 to Labor Day. Admission.

## WASHINGTON

HISTORICAL MUSEUM OF THE GUNN MEMORIAL LIBRARY, Wykeham Rd.

The museum includes Revolutionary, Civil War and World War I items as well as an Oglala Sioux Dakota Indian collection.

Tuesday, Thursday, Saturday, afternoons only. Free.

## WETHERSFIELD

JOSEPH WEBB HOUSE, 211 Main St.

General George Washington and Count de Rochambeau of France prepared the French-American plans here on May 22, 1781 that led to Yorktown and victory in the Revolution. Admission.

## WINDSOR LOCKS

BRADLEY AIR MUSEUM, Bradley International Airport, SR 75.

Air Force, Navy and Army aircraft are in the collection. Admission.

# Delaware

The first permanent military settlement in Delaware was erected by Swedes at Fort Christina in 1638. Earlier Dutch settlers had been massacred by Indians. The Dutch, however, returned and conquered all of what is now Delaware in 1655, and the English, in turn, captured the Dutch strongholds in 1664. The British army invaded Delaware during the American Revolution, seizing the capital city of Wilmington and all of the American forts on the Delaware River. The British fleet also raided freely along the Delaware coast. Opposed to the War of 1812, many Delaware seamen, nevertheless, fought in the young American Navy in that war. Delaware sided with the Union during the Civil War, although there were strong Southern sympathies in the state. The du Pont powder mills made a substantial contribution to the Union war effort.

★ ★ ★

# EXPLORING MILITARY AMERICA

## DELAWARE CITY

FORT DELAWARE STATE PARK, Pea Patch Island in the Delaware River.

An 1813 earthwork fort, followed by an 1821 masonry structure, were supplanted in 1859 by pentagonal granite fortification covering almost six acres. The fort held Confederate prisoners in the Civil War and was garrisoned during the Spanish-American War and World War I.

Museum of Civil War memorabilia. Park is open Saturdays, Sundays, holidays, April 15–Oct. 15. Free. Boats for island leave frequently from dock at foot of Clinton St. Admission.

## LEWES

ZWAANENDAEL MUSEUM, Savannah Rd. and King's Highway.

The Dutch town of Lewes, founded 1631, survived Indian attacks, pirates, and bombardment by the British during the War of 1812.

Museum collection includes Indian and military relics. Free.

## NEWARK

BATTLE OF COOCH'S BRIDGE, one mi. e. of SR 896.

In September 1777, about 700 American troops under General William Maxwell tried to ambush a section of the British army that was crossing Christiana Creek and advancing on Philadelphia. The Americans were repulsed and forced into disorganized retreat.

Bridge, monument on site. The nearby Cooch House, once occupied by British General Cornwallis, is privately owned.

## NEW CASTLE

THE GREEN, Delaware St. between Market and 3rd Sts.

Peter Stuyvesant in 1655 planned the Green as Governor of New Netherlands as public grounds. An 1809 arsenal stands on the Green. Free.

# DELAWARE

## WILMINGTON

HAGLEY MUSEUM, 3 mi. n. of Wilmington on SR 52, then ½ mi. e. on SR 141.

Original site of du Pont black powder mills established 1802 on Brandywine River. In the Civil War Henry du Pont, a West Pointer, furnished the Union with 4 million pounds of powder.

Museum complex of 200 acres. Jitneys available to indoor and outdoor exhibits. Admission.

FORT CHRISTINA SITE, at foot of E. 7th St.

"The Rocks" mark landing place of the Dutch-Swedish settlers of 1638 and site of Fort Christina. The park also has an eighteenth century log cabin.

Monument. Free.

# District of Columbia
## (Washington, D.C.)

Washington, D.C., was established as the capital of the United States in 1790. The city was invaded by the British during the War of 1812 and many public buildings, including the White House, were burned before the British withdrew. In the hasty evacuation of the capital, Dolley Madison, President Madison's wife, managed to save the White House portrait of George Washington.

During the Civil War, the city lived under the constant threat of a Confederate invasion; Fort Stevens, on the outskirts of Washington, did come under Confederate attack in July 1864. President Lincoln visited the fort while it was being bombarded by General Jubal Early's troops, thus becoming the only American president to come under enemy fire while in office.

★ ★ ★

# DISTRICT OF COLUMBIA

## WASHINGTON, D.C.

ANDERSON HOUSE, 2118 Massachusetts Ave., NW.

Headquarters and museum of The Society of the Cincinnati founded by George Washington and a group of Revolutionary War officers in 1783.

Museum has displays on Revolution. Afternoons. Free.

ARMED FORCES MEDICAL MUSEUM, 6825 16th St. NW

During America's early wars, as many men died from disease and lack of medical knowledge of how to treat wounds as were killed in battle. Amputation was the chief treatment for severe wounds in the arms and legs during the Civil War. It was not unusual, after a battle, for stacks of limbs to lay like cordwood outside of whatever church or farmhouse was serving as a hospital. During the Mexican War, many of the volunteers died of the dread "vomito" or yellow fever in Mexico. The Medical Museum, through its collection of historic medical equipment, instruments and memorabilia, presents a fascinating chronology of military medical history. Free.

DAUGHTERS OF THE AMERICAN REVOLUTION MUSEUM, Memorial Continental Hall, 1776 D St., NW

Collection contains 50,000 Revolutionary War objects, including a portrayal of the everyday life of the citizen-soldier.

Closed weekends, holidays and one week in April. Free.

FORT DE RUSSY, Rock Creek Park, near Oregon Ave. and Military Rd.

One of the circle of forts defending Washington, D.C. during the Civil War. Ruins remain, which can be reached on foot. Free.

FORT LESLEY J. MCNAIR, 4th and P Sts. SW

This many-times-renovated fort houses the National War College and the Inter-American Defense College. Established as the "Fort at Turkey Buzzard" in 1794, it then became, in order, an arsenal, a barracks, the penitentiary where the Lincoln conspirators were tried and executed, and the hospital forerunner of Walter Reed Army Medical Center. Little remains of original buildings. Free.

# EXPLORING MILITARY AMERICA

FORT STEVENS, Piney Branch Rd. and Quackenbos St., NW

Renamed Fort Stevens in 1863, from Fort Massachusetts, this post commanded the northern approach to the capital during the Civil War. When Confederate General Early made a last desperate attack on Washington in July, 1864, the garrison at Fort Stevens repulsed the attack, suffering almost 900 casualties. President Lincoln stood on the fort parapet, the only president to watch a battle under fire.

Western magazine reconstructed; a chapel now stands on eastern magazine site. Free.

THE HERITAGE GALLERY, National Guard Memorial, 1 Massachusetts Ave., N W.

Life-size models, artifacts, weaponry, relics of the Revolution. Set of wood carvings of the militia of every state. Exhibit of model aircraft tracing history of military aviation from 1909 to the present. Closed weekends and holidays. Free.

MARINE CORPS MUSEUM, 9th and M Sts., SE, in Washington Navy Yard.

The collection offers more than two centuries of Marine Corps history, including associations with Navy and amphibious operations. Free.

MUSEUM OF HISTORY AND TECHNOLOGY OF THE SMITHSONIAN, Constitution Ave. between 12th and 14th Sts. NW.

The divisions of Military History and Naval History of the Smithsonian present extensive exhibits, including the gondola *Philadelphia,* only surviving American Revolution gunboat. Free.

NATIONAL AIR AND SPACE MUSEUM OF THE SMITHSONIAN, 6th St. and Independence Ave., SW.

The developments of air and space technology and of military aviation are exhibited. Free.

TRUXTON-DECATUR NAVAL MUSEUM, 1610 H St., NW.

The collection of artifacts, models, prints and paintings relate to United States Navy history. Free.

# DISTRICT OF COLUMBIA

U.S. NAVY MEMORIAL MUSEUM, Building 76, Washington Navy Yard, Main Gate at 9th and M Sts., SE.

Indoor and outdoor exhibits of U.S. naval history, including operable submarine periscope, movable guns on gundeck, rigged foremast of *U.S.S. Constitution*. Free.

# Florida

The Spanish first explored Florida in 1513. Although the French built a fort in 1564, the Spanish established the first permanent European settlement in the United States, in 1565, at St. Augustine. In ensuing centuries, Indians, Spanish, French and British fought for control of the area. The British relinquished it to the Spanish after the American Revolution. In 1817, however, American troops invaded the Spanish-held territory in the First Seminole War. Spain ceded Florida to the United States in 1821. American attempts to force the Indians out of Florida resulted in the Second Seminole War, which ended in 1841. Some Seminoles remained in the Everglades, their descendants to this day not recognizing the United States government.

In the Civil War, Tallahassee was the only Confederate state capital east of the Mississippi River not captured by the Union. During the Spanish-American War of 1898, Tampa was the embarkation point for troops destined for Cuba.

★ ★ ★

# FLORIDA

## BRADENTON

DE SOTO NATIONAL MEMORIAL, 5 mi. w. of Bradenton on SR 64, then 2 mi. n. on 75th St. W.

Hernando de Soto and his 600 Spanish conquistadors landed in 1539 at some point between St. Petersburg and Fort Myers. The expedition, which lasted four years and traveled 4,000 miles in southeastern United States, engaged in frequent battles with Indians.

Visitor center, exhibits. Free.

## BUSHNELL

DADE BATTLEFIELD STATE HISTORIC SITE, 1 mi. s. of Bushnell, ¼ mi. w. of US 301.

Major Francis Dade's command of 110 men was ambushed here in 1835—there were only three survivors—touching off the Second Seminole War. Alligator, the Seminole leader, claimed only three of his warriors were killed in the attack. The Seminoles fought for seven years against being placed on an Oklahoma reservation.

Museum, marked battlefield and military road. Admission.

## CAPE CANAVERAL

AIR FORCE SPACE MUSEUM, CAPE CANAVERAL AIR FORCE STATION, n. on SR A-1-A to South Gate of Air Force Station, Complex 5/6, Complex 26.

Development of aerospace power—missiles, rockets and related space equipment—is the theme.

Exhibits of the space age. Free.

KENNEDY SPACE CENTER, on US 1 south of Titusville and north of Cocoa, turn east on tour signs, on SR 405 causeway.

Sprawling spaceport.

Visitor center, starting point of NASA tours. Free.

# EXPLORING MILITARY AMERICA

## FERNANDINA BEACH

FORT CLINCH STATE PARK, 2601 Atlantic Ave.

This 1847 fort was occupied by Confederate and then by Union forces in the Civil War. In 1898, the fort was reactivated for the Spanish-American War.

Preserved fort, exhibits. Admission.

## FORT WALTON BEACH

AIR FORCE ARMAMENT MUSEUM, Eglin Air Force Base, East Gate.

Historical aircraft and memorabilia in outdoors and indoors displays. Free.

## GARDEN KEY

FORT JEFFERSON, 68 mi. w. of Key West on Garden Key of the Dry Tortugas Islands. Fort can be reached by seaplane or boat chartered at Key West, Grassy Key or Marathon.

Masonry fort built to be the "Gibraltar of the Gulf" was used only briefly by the Union in the Civil War and as a naval base in the Spanish-American War. The fort is famous as the prison of Dr. Samuel Mudd, who set the leg of John Wilkes Booth, after Booth assassinated President Lincoln.

Museum, tours. Free.

## JACKSONVILLE

FORT CAROLINE NATIONAL MEMORIAL, 10 mi. e. off SR 10, 12713 Fort Caroline Rd.

This 1564 fort was built by French Huguenots attempting to capture Spanish treasure fleets. Mutiny and hunger led the French to seize Timucua Chief Outine, hoping to force the Indians to give them food; but instead the French force was ambushed. Relief came with the arrival of the French fleet under Jean Ribault. Ribault then tried to attack the Spanish under Menedez at St. Augustine, but a hurricane

# FLORIDA

struck. The shipwrecked French, who had escaped both storm and Indian arrows, returned to be massacred by the Spanish, who captured Fort Caroline. In 1568, the fort was attacked and burned by the French in revenge; the Spanish survivors were massacred by Indians.

Reconstructed fort, visitor center, Ribault column. Free.

THOMAS CREEK BATTLEFIELD, at jct. of I-95 and Nassau River, n. of Jacksonville.

Aided by Spanish informants, troops from Georgia made three attempts to capture British-held St. Augustine between 1776 and 1778. The second attempt was at Thomas Creek in May, 1777; 200 British and their Indian allies defeated 200 Americans, leaving St. Augustine in British control.

State battlefield park, markers. Free.

## KEY WEST

LIGHTHOUSE MILITARY MUSEUM, US 1 to Truman Ave. and Whitehead St.

Military exhibits include items from Civil War to Vietnam, as well as a two-man Japanese submarine from Pearl Harbor. Admission.

## OLUSTEE

OLUSTEE BATTLEFIELD STATE HISTORIC SITE, 2 mi. e. of Olustee on US 90.

This major engagement of the Civil War in Florida resulted in a Union loss of 1,861 men, a Confederate loss of 46. The battle, which took place in a pine forest in February, 1864, was a Union defeat. It stopped an attempt to cut off food supplies to the South from eastern Florida.

Museum, markers. Free.

## PENSACOLA

FORT PICKENS STATE PARK, on Santa Rosa Island, near Pensacola.

In the winter of 1861, Union troops landing to reinforce Fort

# EXPLORING MILITARY AMERICA

Pickens were attacked by Confederates, who were finally driven back by the fort guns. In 1888, the famous Indian chief Geronimo was imprisoned at the fort. During the Spanish-American War, the fort served as coastal defense.

Museum in old fort headquarters, descriptive markers. Free.

NAVAL AVIATION MUSEUM, Naval Air Station, Pensacola.

Exhibits on naval aviation and aircraft from the beginning in 1919, including the famous World War II F6F Hellcat fighter. Also on the base are the SEA AND LAND SURVIVAL EXHIBIT and the *U.S.S. Lexington* aircraft carrier. Both receive visitors.

Inquire at Main Gate for self-conducted tour. Free.

## ST. AUGUSTINE

CASTILLO DE SAN MARCOS NATIONAL MONUMENT, 1 Castillo Dr., St. Augustine, reached by US 1 and Fla. A1A.

After an unsuccessful attempt to capture French ships at Fort Caroline (see Jacksonville), the Spanish under Menendez established St. Augustine in 1565. In the succeeding century, English attacks destroyed the settlement twice, but the Spanish rebuilt a stone fort in 1672–1695. Further English attacks were repulsed, as was a Spanish attack from St. Augustine on English Fort Frederica in Georgia. During the Revolution, the English held Florida, but in 1783 it was turned over to the Spanish, and in 1821 to the United States. Indians were held prisoners in the Castillo. During the Civil War, Confederate forces held it; in the Spanish-American War, it was a military prison.

Fort, exhibits. Admission.

FORT MATANZAS NATIONAL MONUMENT, on Hwy A1A, 14 mi. s. of St. Augustine.

After the killing of 250 shipwrecked French by the Spanish leader Menendez at Matanzas (Slaughter) Inlet, the Spanish built a watch station to warn St. Augustine of attack. Pirates in 1683 overran the watch garrison, but the St. Augustine garrison replied with a successful ambush. In 1686, the Matanzas garrison repulsed another

# FLORIDA

pirate attack. In 1742, a stone Fort Matanzas was built on Rattlesnake Island by the Spanish.

Visitor center on Anastasia Island. Free ferry service. Free.

FLORIDA NATIONAL GUARD AND MILITIA MUSEUM, 82 Marine St.

Collection of artifacts, pictures, flags.

Monday through Friday, by appointment only. Free.

## ST. MARKS

SAN MARCOS DE APALACHE STATE MUSEUM, off SR 363, 1 mi. s.w. on Canal St., St. Marks, just s. of Tallahassee.

Site of Spanish fort built in 1679. Indian and Spanish military artifacts and military cemetery.

Museum. Admission.

## ST. PETERSBURG

FORT DE SOTO, southern end of Mullet Key, Fort De Soto State Park.

Fort was begun in Spanish-American War but not completed. Guns were never fired in battle. Free.

## SUMATRA

FORT GADSDEN HISTORIC SITE, SR 65, 6 mi. s.w. of Sumatra.

When the British abandoned this fort in Spanish-held Florida in 1814, it was taken over by Indians and escaped slaves and called Fort Negro. American troops from Fort Scott attacked with gunboats. On July 27, 1816, a gunboat shell hit the fort magazine. Of the 300 persons manning the fort, only 30 survived the explosion. In the first Seminole War, Andrew Jackson used the fort as a provision base. In the Civil War, it was occupied by Confederate troops.

Earthworks and trenches remain. Free.

# EXPLORING MILITARY AMERICA

## TALLAHASSEE

NATURAL BRIDGE BATTLEFIELD STATE HISTORIC SITE, 12 mi. s.e. of Tallahassee, off US 319.

Old men and young seminary cadets swelled the ranks of Confederate regulars to fight, in March, 1865, against Union troops trying to capture Tallahassee, last Confederate capital east of the Mississippi River. The Union attack failed.

Markers, breastworks, monument. Natural Bridge. Free.

## TAMPA

U.S.S. REQUIN, moored on Hillsborough River behind Curtis Nixon Hall at Kennedy Blvd. Bridge.

Restored World War II submarine.

Tours. Admission.

## ZEPHYRHILLS

FORT FOSTER HISTORIC SITE, Hillsborough River State Park, Route 4.

This post was built in March, 1836, as Fort Alabama, to protect the river crossing against Seminoles. The fort was repeatedly attacked, then abandoned and reestablished as Fort Foster. Because of unhealthy living conditions, the fort was abandoned during the Second Seminole War and reactivated briefly in 1849 when it appeared the Seminoles would again go to war.

Reconstructed fort and bridge, authentic equipment. Free.

# Georgia

During the sixteenth century, the Spanish built military posts on the coast of Georgia as a defense against Indians and against the French, who also claimed the region. Great Britain, too, claimed areas of Georgia and built forts at Savannah and along the coast. In 1742, at the Battle of Bloody Marsh, the British drove the Spanish from Georgia. During the American Revolution, Georgia patriots managed to hold onto their colony despite a British invasion and the loss of Savannah to the British fleet. After the Revolution, conflict with the Creeks and Cherokee Indians intensified until the Indians were finally removed to Arkansas and Oklahoma. During the Civil War, Georgia joined the Confederacy, and Union General Sherman's famous "march to the sea" from Chattanooga to Savannah cut a destructive path 60 miles wide through the state.

★ ★ ★

# EXPLORING MILITARY AMERICA

## AMERICUS

ANDERSONVILLE NATIONAL HISTORIC SITE, 9 mi. n. of Americus on US 49.

This infamous Confederate Civil War prison consisted of a log stockade built to house 10,000. At one time it held over 32,000. Nearly 13,000 died in the camp. The South, unable to provide food and medicine for its own men, had none to spare for its prisoners. One prisoner wrote, "I never saw such misery . . . the men look sickening with sunken eyes . . ."

Prison remains, museum, interpretive walks, cemetery. Free.

## ATHENS

NAVY SUPPLY CORPS MUSEUM, Navy Supply Corps School, 73 mi. e. of Atlanta.

Exhibits of naval equipment. Free.

## ATLANTA

ATLANTA BATTLE CYCLORAMA, Grant Park, Boulevard at Atlanta.

Atlanta, vital Confederate arsenal in the Civil War, fell to Union General Sherman after a fierce battle and siege in September 1864. Grant Park contains Old Fort Walker and Civil War breastworks. The locomotive *Texas*—which engaged in the "Great Locomotive Chase" after the *General,* a well-known Civil War incident—is also housed in the Cyclorama. MCELREATH HALL, 3099 Andrews Dr., NW, also has exhibits of the Battle of Atlanta.

Cyclorama gives three dimensional panorama of battle. Admission. McElreath Hall is free.

THE WAR IN GEORGIA AND HERITAGE MUSEUM at Confederate Hall, Stone Mountain Park, e. from I-285 via US 78 from Atlanta.

Sound and light effects with three-dimensional map used to show decisive Civil War battles in Georgia. Admission.

# GEORGIA

## AUGUSTA

MACKAY HOUSE, 1822 Broad St.

1760 British Indian trading post and scene of attacks by Georgia patriots in the Revolutionary War. Thirteen patriots were hanged on the grounds during the war.

Harris-Pearson-Walker Revolutionary War Museum. Free.

U.S. ARMY SIGNAL MUSEUM, Fort Gordon, 5 mi. s.w. of Augusta. From I-20 near Augusta, turn onto Bobby Jones Expressway east, 3 mi. to Fort Gordon Turnoff, Route 78.

Collection offers history of Signal Corps and exhibits from major United States conflicts since 1775.

Museum, Commandant Road and 38th St., 5 mi. from main gate. Free.

## BRUNSWICK

FORT FREDERICA NATIONAL MONUMENT, 12 mi. from Brunswick on St. Simons Island. Take Brunswick-St. Simons toll causeway which connects with US 17 at Brunswick.

Built in 1736, the fort was said to be the "largest, most regular and perhaps most costly" British fortification in North America. General James Oglethorpe used the fort as headquarters for operations against the Spanish in Florida, from 1739 to 1748. The great fire of 1758 destroyed much of the fort, and the few remaining soldiers withdrew in 1763.

Visitors center, museum, tours, ruins of fort and town. Free.

BLOODY MARSH BATTLE SITE, 6 mi. s. of Fort Frederica.

On July 7, 1742, outnumbered British troops ambushed a Spanish column and halted a Spanish attack on Fort Frederica and an attempt to regain Georgia and South Carolina. Bloody Marsh is considered the first great decisive battle fought in the New World.

Recordings at site describe battle. Free.

# EXPLORING MILITARY AMERICA

## COLUMBUS

CONFEDERATE NAVAL MUSEUM, 202 4th St.

The South lost their shipyards in the first year of Civil War. Columbus, on the Chattahoochee River, then became a naval arsenal, where ironclads were built to try to break the Union blockade. The Confederates improvised a navy that used some weapons now a part of modern naval warfare: rams, torpedoes, submarines and mines.

Exhibits include salvaged Confederate ironclad *Muscogee,* wooden gunboats, dioramas of Confederate navy in action. Free.

NATIONAL INFANTRY MUSEUM, Fort Benning, 5 mi. s. of Columbus. Museum is 3 mi. from gate on Dixie Rd., Bldg. 1234.

Outstanding exhibits display the history of Infantry from 1775 to present, including sutler's store and German and Japanese weapons. Free.

## CORDELE

GEORGIA VETERANS MEMORIAL MUSEUM.

Equipment used by Georgia veterans in various wars. Free.

## CRAWFORDVILLE

CONFEDERATE MUSEUM, Alexander H. Stephens State Park.

Arms and memorabilia of Civil War; Confederate Vice President's home. Free.

## DALLAS

PICKETT'S MILL BATTLEFIELD SITE, n.e. off SR 92.

One of several engagements during Sherman's campaign in Georgia. Confederate forces defeated the Union forces here; more than 1,500 troops were killed.

Site shows troop lines, trenches, embankments and large trees, potmarked with grapeshot, lying across lines. Free.

# GEORGIA

## DARIEN

FORT KING GEORGE HISTORIC SITE, 1½ mi. e. of US 17 on Fort King George Dr.

In 1721, English planter John Barnwell returned from England with soldiers to construct a typical European field fort on the site of a former Indian village and Spanish mission. The Spanish had been forced into Florida by English-Indian raids. When the Fort King George garrison was withdrawn to Fort Royal, lookouts remained to warn of Spanish raiders until 1733.

Reconstructed fort. Museum of Indian, Spanish, English occupation. Free.

## FITZGERALD

BLUE-GRAY MUSEUM, Municipal Bldg. (Old Depot).

Town originated as a Union soldiers' colony. Museum has relics and mementoes of the Civil War.

Apr. through Sept., Monday through Friday afternoons; Oct. through Mar. by appointment only. Free.

## FORT GAINES

FORT GAINES OUTPOST REPLICA, S. SR 39, right on Commerce St., 3 blocks on left.

Reconstructed fort, one-third size of original of the 1816–1830 period, used to protect settlers from Creek-Seminole Indian attacks.

Admission.

## FORT OGLETHORPE

CHICKAMAUGA-CHATTANOOGA NATIONAL MILITARY PARK.

Fort Oglethorpe has a military museum of Civil War relics and guns in the park. The largest section of the CHICKAMAUGA-CHATTANOOGA NATIONAL MILITARY PARK is in Georgia but the visitors center is in Tennessee. (See Tennessee listings) This oldest and largest of

# EXPLORING MILITARY AMERICA

national military parks has more than 1,800 monuments and markers of battles. Free.

## HINESVILLE

INFANTRY MUSEUM, Fort Stewart, Hinesville, 10 mi. w. of Savannah.

Mementoes and equipment of Infantry from Civil War to present, including primitive weapons used in the Philippines Insurrection.

Afternoons only. Free.

## KENNESAW

BIG SHANTY MUSEUM, 2829 Cherokee St.

James Andrews, Union secret service agent, with 21 men, stole *The General* locomotive at Kennesaw in April 1862, and headed northward, intending to burn Southern bridges. The "Great Locomotive Chase" followed, with the locomotive *Texas* in pursuit. Andrews and his men were finally captured.

*The General* locomotive, films, exhibits. Admission.

## LINCOLNTON

ELIJAH CLARK STATE PARK MUSEUM, Rte. 4.

Exhibits of uniforms, archives, history artifacts of 1770s.

Memorial Day through Labor Day. Other times by appointment. Free.

## MACON

FORT BENJAMIN HAWKINS, US 80 E.

Reconstructed blockhouse of first modern settlement in Macon in 1806.

Apr.–Oct., Sunday afternoons. Other times, by appointment. Free.

OLD CANNONBALL HOUSE AND CONFEDERATE MUSEUM, 856 Mulberry St.

House, now museum, was struck by cannonball in Union attack. Admission.

# GEORGIA

## MARIETTA

KENNESAW MOUNTAIN NATIONAL BATTLEFIELD PARK, 2½ mi. n.w. of Marietta on US 41.

In June, 1864, the Confederate army, retreating before the Union march on Atlanta, held this strong position until driven back by Union flanking movements.

Visitor center, on old US 41, at foot of the mountain, offers exhibits. Battlefield, earthworks, maps. Free.

## MIDWAY

SUNBURY HISTORIC SITE, Rte. 1, Midway, 8 mi. e. of I-95.

Once Georgia's second largest colonial seaport and important site during the Revolutionary War and War of 1812.

Visitor center, with history of earthen Fort Morris, and "lost" town of Sunbury. Free.

## RICHMOND HILL

FORT MCALLISTER, 10 mi. e. of I-95, SR 144.

The key to Savannah's fortifications during the Civil War, this earthen fort held under 9 naval assaults, but fell to Sherman's troops in hand to hand fighting in December, 1864.

Restored fort, military exhibits and mementoes from Confederate cruiser *Nashville*. Free.

## SAVANNAH

FORT JACKSON, 3 mi. e. of Savannah on Islands Expressway, on the Savannah River.

Oldest remaining brickwork fort in the city, the fort was built in 1808 and remained in use until 1876.

Museum contains military artifacts. Admission.

FORT PULASKI NATIONAL MONUMENT, 17 mi. e. of Savannah on US 80 East, at the mouth of the Savannah River.

# EXPLORING MILITARY AMERICA

The present fortification was preceded by Fort George in 1761 and Fort Greene in 1794. The new fort, built between 1829 and 1847, was made of masonry in an irregular pentagon shape and was considered impregnable. But in the Civil War, in 1862, a 30-hour bombardment by Union rifled guns forced the Confederate garrison to surrender. The fort walls still contain projectiles from that bombardment.

Visitor center, fort. Admission during summer. Free during rest of year.

NATIONAL GUARD TROPHY ROOM, 1248 Eisenhower Dr.
Sabres, trophies, uniforms dating back to 1800s.
Weekdays only. Free.

SAVANNAH VOLUNTEER GUARD MUSEUM, 340 Bull St.
Military relics dating back to the early 1800s. Free.

## TYBEE ISLAND

FORT SCREVEN AND TYBEE MUSEUM.
Fort, built in 1875, was manned during the Spanish-American War, World War I and World War II. Tybee Museum, housed in Spanish-American coastal defense battery, contains historical material dating back to pre-colonial Georgia.
Admission.

## WASHINGTON

BATTLE OF KETTLE CREEK, 8 mi. s.w. via SR 44.
On February 14, 1779, a Georgia and South Carolina patriot militia under Colonel Andrew Pickens attacked a Tory force under Colonel John Boyd and drove them back when Boyd fell mortally wounded. This victory broke the hold of the British in Georgia and checked the Loyalist cause.
Battle site preserved. Free.

WASHINGTON-WILKES HISTORICAL MUSEUM, 308 E. Robert Toombs Ave. on US 78 near intersection with SR 17.

# GEORGIA

Collection of Confederate relics, including valuable file of old newspapers. The Confederacy's government was dissolved in Washington. Donations.

## WINDER

FORT YARGO, 1 mi. s. on SR 81.

Restored blockhouse, built 1793, with pine logs bearing marks of heavy caliber bullets from Creek Indian wars. Free.

# Hawaii

Although visited by British explorer Captain James Cook in the eighteenth century, the Hawaiian islands were not annexed by a European power and were united into the kingdom of Hawaii in 1810 by Kamehameha I, a native Hawaiian. A strong American influence came to the islands with Yankee whalers and missionaries, despite an attempt by the British in 1843 to take over the islands. The kingdom of Hawaii continued until 1898, when Queen Liliuokalani was deposed and the islands annexed to the United States. The Japanese attack on Pearl Harbor on December 7, 1941, brought the United States into World War II, and the Islands' defenses were of strategic importance all during the war.

★ ★ ★

## ISLAND OF HAWAII

**KAILUA-KONA**

CITY OF REFUGE (Puuhonua o Honaunau) off SR 16, 20 mi. s. of Kailua-Kona.

# HAWAII

Before European or American settlers arrived in Hawaii, the City of Refuge, now reconstructed, was used by Hawaiians in time of war as a place of safety for escaping warriors, as well as for noncombatants.

Relics, tours. Free.

## ISLAND OF OAHU

### HONOLULU

NUUANU PALI LOOKOUT, Pali Highway, SR 61.

The spectacular view from the Nuuanu Pali Lookout is associated with the rise to power of Kamehameha I. In this area the last great battle that unified the Hawaiian Islands was fought. The Battle of Nuuanu, fought in this valley in 1795, established the Kamehameha dynasty. The invading conqueror, Kamehamaha I, drove the warriors of Kalanikupule, King of Oahu, to the pali and forced them over the precipice. Notches in the pali line above the lookout are believed to be fortifications either for the cannons of Kamehameha I or locations from which defenders rolled boulders down upon the enemy. The area is a state park. Free.

U.S. ARMY MUSEUM, BATTERY RANDOLPH, Fort De Russy, Kalia Rd.

Battery Randolph, a pre-World War I coast artillery defense bastion, is located in historic Fort De Russy, one of the earliest military posts established by the United States in the Hawaiian Islands. Museum offers Hawaiian and Pacific military history.

Museum is housed in the Battery. Free.

NATIONAL MEMORIAL CEMETERY OF THE PACIFIC (Punchbowl Hill) via Puowaina Dr.

For military killed in World War II and Korea. Also, GARDENS OF THE MISSING MONUMENT, a landscaped memorial with names of those missing in action is inscribed on a court of honor. Free.

### PEARL HARBOR

U.S.S. ARIZONA NATIONAL MEMORIAL, U.S. Naval Base, off SR 90, via Halawa Gate, in vicinity of Pearl City.

# EXPLORING MILITARY AMERICA

On Sunday morning, December 7, 1941, some 350 Japanese aircraft attacked Pearl Harbor, Hawaii. The planes bombed and strafed army, navy/marine and air force installations, destroying about 170 aircraft. All battleships at anchor in Pearl Harbor at the time were sunk or badly damaged, as were many other vessels. The casualties in all came to about 3,400 military and civilians, and the attack has been called "the greatest military and naval disaster in our nation's history."

The battleship *U.S.S. Arizona* was one of the ships sunk, with 1,102 men entombed aboard. A memorial and visitors' center has been built on the superstructure of the battleship, dedicated to the sailors who gave their lives at Pearl Harbor.

The navy operates a shuttle boat to the memorial several times a day from the memorial landing near Halawa Gate, Pearl Harbor Naval Base, just off the Kamehameha Highway. Free.

PACIFIC SUBMARINE MUSEUM, Naval Submarine Base at Pearl Harbor.

Original equipment from submarines, working and static models, flags, photos and personal mementoes of submarines. Collection contains exhibit on first U.S. submarine constructed by David Bushnell in Revolutionary War period. Exhibits include manned suicide submarine-torpedo of Japanese in World War II. Free.

## WAHIAWA

TROPIC LIGHTNING HISTORICAL CENTER, Schofield Barracks.

Schofield Barracks, home of the Twenty-fifth Infantry Division, came under air attack during the Japanese attack at Pearl Harbor. A pre-World War I military post, the museum contains material on the history of the post as well as exhibits on the military history of the Twenty-fifth Infantry Division. Free.

# Idaho

The Lewis and Clark expedition explored Idaho in 1805 and built the first fort there. Missionaries and fur traders soon followed. Troubles with the peaceful Nez Perce Indians developed in the 1870s when treaties were ignored and gold-seekers and settlers overran the Indian land. Although he defeated American troops in the two battles in Idaho, the great Nez Perce chief Joseph was finally defeated in the last battle of the Nez Perce War in 1877.

★ ★ ★

**GRANGEVILLE**

WHITE BIRD BATTLEFIELD AND HILL, 20 mi. s. on US 95.

This first battle of the Nez Perce War was a victory for the native Americans. This battlefield is included in the Nez Perce National Historical Park, which includes twenty-four separate areas scattered throughout northern Idaho. A brochure for a self-guiding tour is provided at the Spalding Visitor Center of the park, near Lewiston. Free.

# EXPLORING MILITARY AMERICA

## HARPSTER

CLEARWATER BATTLEFIELD, SR 13, about 7½ mi. n.

Although outnumbered, the Nez Perce fought off pursuing troops here. The battlefield is included in the Nez Perce National Historical Park.

Interpretive marker. Free.

## LAPWAI

FORT LAPWAI.

Some of the old fort's buildings are still used. The area is Indian Agency headquarters for the Nez Perce, Coeur d'Alene and Kootenai Indians of Idaho and is a part of the Nez Perce National Historical Park. Free.

## LEWISTON

NEZ PERCE NATIONAL HISTORICAL PARK, Spalding Visitor Center and headquarters for the park, 12 mi. e. of Lewiston, jct. of US 12 and old US 95.

Although Chief Joseph of the Nez Perce tried to peacefully resist encroachment of settlers and miners into Nez Perce territory in the 1870s, he failed. When several whites were killed by angry young warriors, the Nez Perce War of 1877 resulted. After fighting off troops at White Bird Canyon and at Clearwater, the Indians retreated toward Canada but had to battle again at Big Hole, Montana, and in the final battle at Bear Paw Mountains, Montana, Chief Joseph was the only chief left alive. After a flight of more than a thousand miles, the Nez Perce were forced to surrender. The Indian trail, called the Lolo Trail, used by the Nez Perce and also by the Lewis and Clark expedition in 1805 and 1806, runs through the Nez Perce Park.

Visitor Center, museum, interpretive markers, Indian exhibits in summer. Free.

# IDAHO

## POCATELLO

FORT HALL REPLICA.

This fur trading post was built in 1834 by the Hudson Bay Company. It served as a military post from 1849 to about 1860. At the nearby town of Fort Hall, Indian sun dances are held.

Dances in late June or early July. Fort Hall, Apr. 1–Sept. 15. Free.

# Illinois

Spain, England and France all claimed the fur-rich Illinois region, but French influence declined after the defeat of Indian chief Pontiac, an ally of France, in 1765. The Revolutionary War came to Illinois in 1778 when George Rogers Clark and his troops captured the British fort at Kaskaskia. Indian dissatisfaction with treaties caused them to join with the British in the War of 1812 and brought on the massacre of settlers and soldiers near Fort Dearborn (now Chicago). The last revolt of the Indians in Illinois was the Black Hawk War of 1832. With the defeat of the Sauk and Fox warriors in that war, the Indian threat ended.

Illinois was the home of President Abraham Lincoln, and although Civil War sentiment in the state was split between the North and the South, Illinois stayed with the Union. There were no Civil War battles in Illinois, but one of the largest prisoner of war camps for Confederate soldiers was located on Rock Island.

★ ★ ★

# ILLINOIS

## BYRON

BATTLE OF STILLMAN'S RUN, 5 mi. e. of Byron, SR 2.
   First battle of Black Hawk War.
   Interpretive marker. Free.

## CAHOKIA

CAHOKIA COURTHOUSE HISTORIC SITE, 1st and Elm Sts., s. of East St. Louis, off SR 3.
   Cahokia, along with Kaskaskia and Fort Chartres, was a French settlement in the seventeenth century, surrounded in all directions by Indian country. In 1763, France ceded her Illinois land to England, but warfare with Pontiac, Chief of the Ottawas, kept the British from taking over the land for two years. Pontiac was killed in April 1769, at Cahokia, assassinated by an Indian assailant. During the American Revolution, Cahokia was seized, without resistance, by George Rogers Clark's American forces on July 4, 1778. Clark held council with the Cahokia Indians and persuaded them to remain neutral in the war.
   Exhibits, tours at Cahokia Courthouse. Free.

## CHESTER

FORT KASKASKIA STATE HISTORIC SITE, 10 mi. n. off SR 3 on Mississippi River.
   The first town of Kaskaskia, washed away by the Mississippi River in the early nineteenth century, was founded by the French in 1703. The original wooden stockade fort was rebuilt in 1761 but destroyed six years later to prevent British occupation. During the American Revolution, George Rogers Clark's force reached Kaskaskia July 4, 1778, and surprised the British garrison at the rebuilt fort, called Fort Gage. Clark took the fort without firing a shot. The parish bell was rung in celebration of the victory and was afterwards known as the "Liberty Bell of the West." In 1784, John Dodge, leader of a group of desperadoes, seized and fortified Fort Kaskaskia and terrorized villagers for several years.
   The "Liberty Bell of the West" now hangs in a shelter on Kaskas-

# EXPLORING MILITARY AMERICA

kia Island and may be reached via bridge from town of Saint Mary's on US 61. A nearby reconstructed 1675 church houses colonial memorabilia.

At Fort Kaskaskia State Park on SR 3 are earthwork remains of a French 1733 fort. Free.

## CHICAGO

CANTIGNY WAR MEMORIAL, on Cantigny Estate, on Winfield Rd. off Roosevelt Rd., 31 mi. w. of Chicago Loop, 2 mi. w. of Wheaton.

World War I and II battles are dramatically reenacted in sound and scene as visitors hear the roar of artillery and skies flash with bursting of shells. The museum also presents the history of the First Division (The Big Red One) which has fought in every American war since 1776. Free.

FORT SHERIDAN MUSEUM, Fort Sheridan, 25 mi. n. of Chicago on SR 42. Museum is ½ mi. from main gate on Lister Rd.

Fort Sheridan was established in 1887 to maintain order after the railroad riots of 1877 and the Haymarket riot in 1886. Museum has military exhibits dating back to the Civil War and foreign military equipment from World War I. Free.

GRAND ARMY OF THE REPUBLIC MEMORIAL HALL, Chicago Public Library, 78 E. Washington.

Notable Civil War collection. Free.

U.S.S. SILVERSIDES, Naval Armory at foot of Lake St.

Commissioned eight days after the attack on Pearl Harbor, the *Silversides* had officially sunk 23 ships in the Pacific theater by the end of World War II. This is the third highest number of ships sunk by a submarine during World War II. Tour. Free.

## GALENA

THE STOCKADE, 208 Perry St.

Stockade of roughhewn logs with solid rock underground room was used as refuge by pioneers during the Black Hawk War.

# ILLINOIS

May 1–Nov. 1. Admission.
ULYSSES S. GRANT HOME, Bouthillier and 4th Sts.
Free.

## METROPOLIS

FORT MASSAC MUSEUM, Fort Massac State Park, west off I-24 via US 45.

Fort Massac (1757) was the last fort erected by the French in the Ohio territory, which included the state of Illinois. The fort stood off a Cherokee Indian attack but was abandoned in 1764 and burned by the Chippewas. The ruined fort belonged to the British at the end of the French and Indian War, but was not occupied by them. In late June, 1778, George Rogers Clark and 150 buckskinned irregulars, called "Long Knives," spent a night in the ruined fort before their march overland to capture Kaskaskia. Fort Massac remained empty until spring, 1794, when President Washington ordered General Anthony Wayne to rebuild it. As late as 1812, the fort was occupied by a Tennessee regiment, but in 1814, the fort was abandoned.

Partially reconstructed fort, museum. Free.

## PRAIRIE DU ROCHER

FORT CHARTRES HISTORIC SITE, 4 mi. w.

The French used the fort, built in 1719, as a center of military and civil government in the Illinois country in the eighteenth century. The fort was not attacked during the French and Indian War and was the last place in North America to lower the French flag, on Oct. 10, 1765. The British garrisoned the fort from 1765–1772.

Restored fort, interpretive centers, tours. Free.

## ROCK ISLAND

BLACK HAWK STATE PARK, s. of town of Rock Island on SR 5.

Black Hawk and his Sauk Indians fought with the British in the War of 1812, and in 1832 fought against the removal of their tribe to

## EXPLORING MILITARY AMERICA

land west of the Mississippi. Although the Indians won a bloody skirmish in Illinois on May 14, 1832, Chief Black Hawk's band was practically annihilated at the Bad Axe River, Wisconsin, in August, 1832. Before his exile, Chief Black Hawk's departing words to his conqueror's were: "I loved my towns, my cornfields and the home of my people. I fought for it. It is now yours. Keep it as we did."

HAUBERG INDIAN MUSEUM on Watch Tower Hill overlooking Rock River displays relics of the Black Hawk War. Free.

ROCK ISLAND ARSENAL, on Arsenal Island, between Rock Island, Illinois, and Davenport, Iowa. From Rock Island, take 24th St. n. to Arsenal.

Built in 1816 and garrisoned for twenty years, Fort Armstrong on Arsenal Island was a hub of military activity during the Black Hawk War. The present blockhouse is a replica of the 1816 original. Since 1863, Rock Island has been the government's largest arsenal. Rock Island was also a Union prison during the Civil War, guarded by black troops. A smallpox epidemic killed many prisoners and guards. The National Cemetery at east entrance has remains of soldiers from frontier Indian Wars to Vietnam.

Tours. Free.

JOHN M. BROWNING MEMORIAL MUSEUM at Rock Island Arsenal.

Military history of Arsenal and weapons and equipment, antique and modern, from all American wars. Free.

# Indiana

The French in the 1700s built several military forts along the Wabash and Maumee Rivers. After the French and Indian War, Indiana became an English possession, but the Indians, who had sided with the French during the war, continued to raid the English forts and settlements. During the American Revolution, George Rogers Clark captured Vincennes and other outposts in Indiana from the British. Indian attacks continued after the war until the Indian defeats at the Battle of Fallen Timbers, near Toledo, Ohio, and the Battle of Tippecanoe, near Lafayette. Indiana, a Union state, had only one military engagement during the Civil War, when Confederate General Morgan made a brief, daring raid into the state in July, 1863.

★ ★ ★

**CORYDON**

BATTLE OF CORYDON, US 460, SR 62, 1 mi. s. of Corydon.
   Confederate raiders of General John Hunt Morgan struck north into Indiana in July, 1863, and engaged the Corydon Home Guard in

# EXPLORING MILITARY AMERICA

the only Indiana battle of the war. The Guard was overpowered and held captive during the raiders' brief occupation of town.

Descriptive marker.

## FORT WAYNE

FORT WAYNE (FORT MIAMI) 107 South Clinton St. or 7 blocks n. on Barr St.

The French established the first Fort Miami before 1720. In 1750, the then-current fort was surrendered to the British. In 1794, American General Anthony Wayne constructed Fort Wayne, naming it after himself. This fort, rebuilt in 1800 and again in 1815, was abandoned in 1819.

Reconstructed fort, museum. Mid-Apr. to Oct. 31. Admission.

## INDIANAPOLIS

THIRTY-EIGHTH INFANTRY (CYCLONE) DIVISION MEMORIAL MUSEUM, Stout Field.

Chronological arrangement of exhibits tracing Indiana's military history through the activities of the Thirty-eighth Infantry Division.

STOUT FIELD MILITARY EQUIPMENT MUSEUM is an annex to the above museum and consists of aircraft, tanks, artillery and armored personnel carriers. Both museums free.

U.S. ARMY FINANCE CORPS MUSEUM, U.S. Army Finance and Accounting Center.

Military mementos relating to Army finance matters dating back to the Revolutionary War, as well as currency and liberation notes from foreign countries. Closed weekends. Free.

FORT BENJAMIN HARRISON MUSEUM, Fort Benjamin Harrison, E. 56th St. at Post Rd. Museum is on Hawkins Ave. at Maine St., one mi. from gate.

# INDIANA

Museum contains history of Fort Harrison, as well as U.S. Army and foreign military artifacts from Revolutionary War to present. Free.

INDIANA WAR MEMORIAL MONUMENT AND MUSEUM, 431 North Meridian St.

The Military Museum, in the lower concourse, offers displays of the Hoosier contributions to American military history from the Battle of Tippecanoe through Vietnam. Free.


## LAFAYETTE

FORT OUIATENON, 4 mi. s.

Alarmed by English expansion into Indiana territory, the French built this fort in 1717. The British took over the fort in 1756. During Pontiac's uprising, Chief Pontiac captured seven British forts but spared Fort Ouiatenon when the French settlers intervened for the British garrison. Later in the same year, 1763, a preliminary treaty with Pontiac was negotiated at the fort, ending Pontiac's War. In 1778 George Rogers Clark captured Vincennes and sent a detachment to take Fort Ouiatenon, but its inhabitants surrendered willingly. American control of the area, however, was not firmly established until 1795 after the Battle of Fallen Timbers.

Partially reconstructed fort, museum. Mid-Apr.–mid-Nov. Admission.

TIPPECANOE BATTLEFIELD, Tippecanoe and Railroad Sts., 7 mi. n.e. of Lafayette on SR 225 (off the SR 43 exit of I-65.)

Chief Tecumseh and his brother, the Prophet, planned a confederation of northern and southern tribes to block westward expansion of settlers into their lands. William Henry Harrison led 400 regular soldiers of the Fourth Regiment and 800 militiamen to the junction of Tippecanoe and Wabash Rivers. The Indians attacked before dawn November 7, 1811, and the battle raged over a 16-acre triangle before the Indians were decisively defeated. Although the British did not participate in the battle, the settlers believed they

# EXPLORING MILITARY AMERICA

encouraged it in the hope that the Indians would destroy American settlements. In June of 1812, war was declared against England.

Battlefield, museum, Prophet's Rock, monument, guided tours. Admission.

## SCOTTSBURG

PIGEON ROOST STATE MEMORIAL, 7 mi. s.w. off US 31.

Monument marks site of massacre between sunset and dusk on September 8, 1812. An Indian war party surprised settlers, killing 16 children, 5 women and 3 men in this last Indian raid in Indiana during the War of 1812.

Monument, interpretive marker. Free.

## VALLONIA

FORT VALLONIA MUSEUM, s. of SR 135.

Fort was built in 1811 as protection against hostile tribes of Shawnee, Delaware and Miami. At one time the fort housed up to four companies of frontier soldiers.

Partially reconstructed fort, museum. May 1–Oct. 30. Rest of year by appointment. Free.

## VINCENNES

GEORGE ROGERS CLARK MEMORIAL NATIONAL HISTORICAL PARK, 401 S. Second St. Off Vigo St. near Lincoln Memorial Bridge or w. end of Barnett St., sw of US 50 and Lincoln Memorial Bridge.

Memorial stands at site of French Fort Vincennes (1732), which was taken over by the British and renamed Fort Sackville. Clark's capture of Vincennes in 1779 with 175 American volunteers and his military dominance of the Northwest Territory were deciding factors in the region being ceded to the United States after the Revolution. It was also at Fork Sackville that Clark captured the British officer Hamilton, called "the hairbuyer" because he paid Indians for scalps of Americans.

Visitors center, exhibits. Free.

# INDIANA

GROUSELAND, 3 West Scott St.

It was at his spacious home, Grouseland, that William Henry Harrison, first governor of the Indiana Territory, met with the Shawnee Indian leader, Tecumseh. Grouseland was also used as sanctuary for settlers during Indian scares, and it was from here that Harrison launched the campaign that ended in the bloody battle of Tippecanoe. Admission.

# Iowa

The French explorers, Marquette and Joliet, came into Iowa in 1673, and later La Salle claimed the region for France, setting up fur trading forts. The land passed to Spain, then back to France, and finally under the Louisiana Purchase of 1803, Iowa became United States territory. As a result of the Black Hawk war of 1832, some of the Indian land in Iowa was opened to settlement despite Indian resistance. The Sioux uprising in 1857 ended Indian resistance, and by the end of the 1850s, almost all the Indian land had passed out of their hands. Iowa was a staunch supporter of the Union during the Civil War, sending 75,000 volunteers to the Union Army.

★ ★ ★

**ESTHERVILLE**

SPIRIT LAKE MASSACRE LOG CABIN (GARDNER LOG CABIN) in Arnold Parks, w. of Estherville on US 71.

In a five-day siege in 1857 a band of renegade Indians from the Sioux nation laid waste an entire settlement. It was the bloodiest Indian massacre in Iowa history. Today, there is a monument with a

# IOWA

tablet listing the forty victims of the massacre, placed near their burial site.

The only building left standing after the Indian attack was the Gardner cabin. The whole Gardner family was killed, except for a daughter, Abigail, who was taken captive by the Indians. The cabin has been restored with mementoes from the period of the attack. Historic markers are placed at location of other cabins and deaths. Summers only. Free.

## FORT ATKINSON

FORT ATKINSON MONUMENT STATE PARK, ½ mi. n. on SR 24.

This fort was built in 1840 to protect peaceful Winnebago Indians from the hostile Sioux. The fort was abandoned in 1849 and only a few buildings survive today.

Museum. Summers only. Free.

## FORT DODGE

FORT DODGE HISTORICAL MUSEUM FORT AND STOCKADE, 1¾ mi. s.w. of Fort Dodge on US 20.

Replica of fort built in 1850 to protect settlers.

Museum. Summers only. Admission.

## FORT MADISON

OLD FORT MADISON SITE, 313–335 Ave. H.

The fort was built to promote Indian trade and divert the Indians from dealing with the British traders. In 1813, unable to defend itself against constant Indian attacks, the fort was burned by the military and deserted. The site has been partially excavated. Free.

**The Navy/Marine Corps Museum,** Building 1, Treasure Island, San Francisco, California, has a collection that deals with the history of the Navy and Marine Corps in the Pacific since 1813. The collection includes uniforms, weapons, ship models, aircraft and armored vehicles, and is the largest museum of its kind in the United States. OFFICIAL U.S. NAVY PHOTOGRAPH, NAVY/MARINE CORPS MUSEUM, SAN FRANCISCO

**The Naval Aviation Museum,** Naval Air Station, Pensacola, Florida, offers more than 60 aircraft on exhibit portraying the development, heritage and history of United States Naval Aviation, together with models, paintings and memorabilia. The historical period covered is from 1911 to the SKYLAB Command Module. UNITED STATES NAVAL AVIATION MUSEUM

**Castillo de San Marcos,** St. Augustine, Florida, was completed by Indians under Spanish control in 1696. The fort repulsed several English attacks, but came under English control in 1763 and was a force against the American cause in the Revolution. From 1783 to 1821, the Castillo was Spanish. Later, it served in American wars, mostly as a prison. FLORIDA DIVISION OF TOURISM

**The Confederate Naval Museum,** Columbus, Georgia, has as primary exhibits the hull of the iron-clad Confederate *C.S.S. Muscogee,* salvaged in the 1960s from the Chattahoochee River, and the wooden gunboat *Chattahoochee.* Other relics and exhibits from the Confederate navy are also featured.
TOURIST DIVISION, GEORGIA DEPARTMENT OF COMMUNITY DEVELOPMENT

**Fort Massac,** Metropolis, Illinois, was built in 1794 under order of President Washington to keep American control during trouble between France and Spain in nearby area. Earlier French fortifications on the site were subjected to Indian attacks. METROPOLIS PLANET, METROPOLIS, ILLINOIS, and COURTESY OF FORT MASSAC STATE PARK

**Historic Fort Wayne,** Fort Wayne, Indiana, is on the site of earlier French and English forts. In 1794, General Anthony Wayne built the first American post, rebuilt in 1800 and 1815. Today's reconstructed fort offers original artifacts and a living history program. HISTORIC FORT WAYNE, FORT WAYNE, IND.

**British General William Howe** preparing for the battle in "Whites of Their Eyes," life-size figures in a multi-media presentation at Raytheon's Bunker Hill Pavilion, Charlestown, Massachusetts. In this 1775 battle, Americans proved they could stand up to British regulars. RAYTHEON HISTORICAL FOUNDATION, 141 SPRING ST., LEXINGTON, MASS. 02173

**Fort Michilimackinac,** Mackinaw City, Michigan, was built by the French in 1715, then fortified by the British in 1761. In the Pontiac's uprising that soon followed, the fort's entire garrison was captured or killed. From here, in the American Revolution, the British sent Indians to raid Ohio and Pennsylvania settlements. MACKINAC ISLAND STATE PARK COMMISSION, LANSING, MICHIGAN

**Custer Battlefield National Monument,** southeastern Montana, commemorates the defeat of Lt. Colonel George Armstrong Custer's force of 225 men by several thousand Sioux and Cheyenne. The June 25 and 26, 1876, battle cost the lives of Custer's entire command in the valley of the Little Bighorn River. CUSTER BATTLEFIELD NATIONAL MONUMENT, NATIONAL PARK SERVICE

**The submarine U.S.S. Ling 297,** docked in Borg Park, Hackensack, New Jersey, provides a vivid experience of life on 93-crew submariners of World War II. Nearby is a small museum of World War II and a memorial to the 52 submarines "still on patrol" lost during that war. SUBMARINE MEMORIAL ASSOCIATION, HACKENSACK, NEW JERSEY

**Fort Ticonderoga** (Fort Carillon), Ticonderoga, New York, was built in 1755 by the French. In the French and Indian War and the American Revolution, the fort was attacked six times, three times successfully. Here, Ethan Allen and his Green Mountain Boys captured, without a shot, the cannon essential for Washington's forces against the British in Boston. NEW YORK STATE DEPARTMENT OF COMMERCE

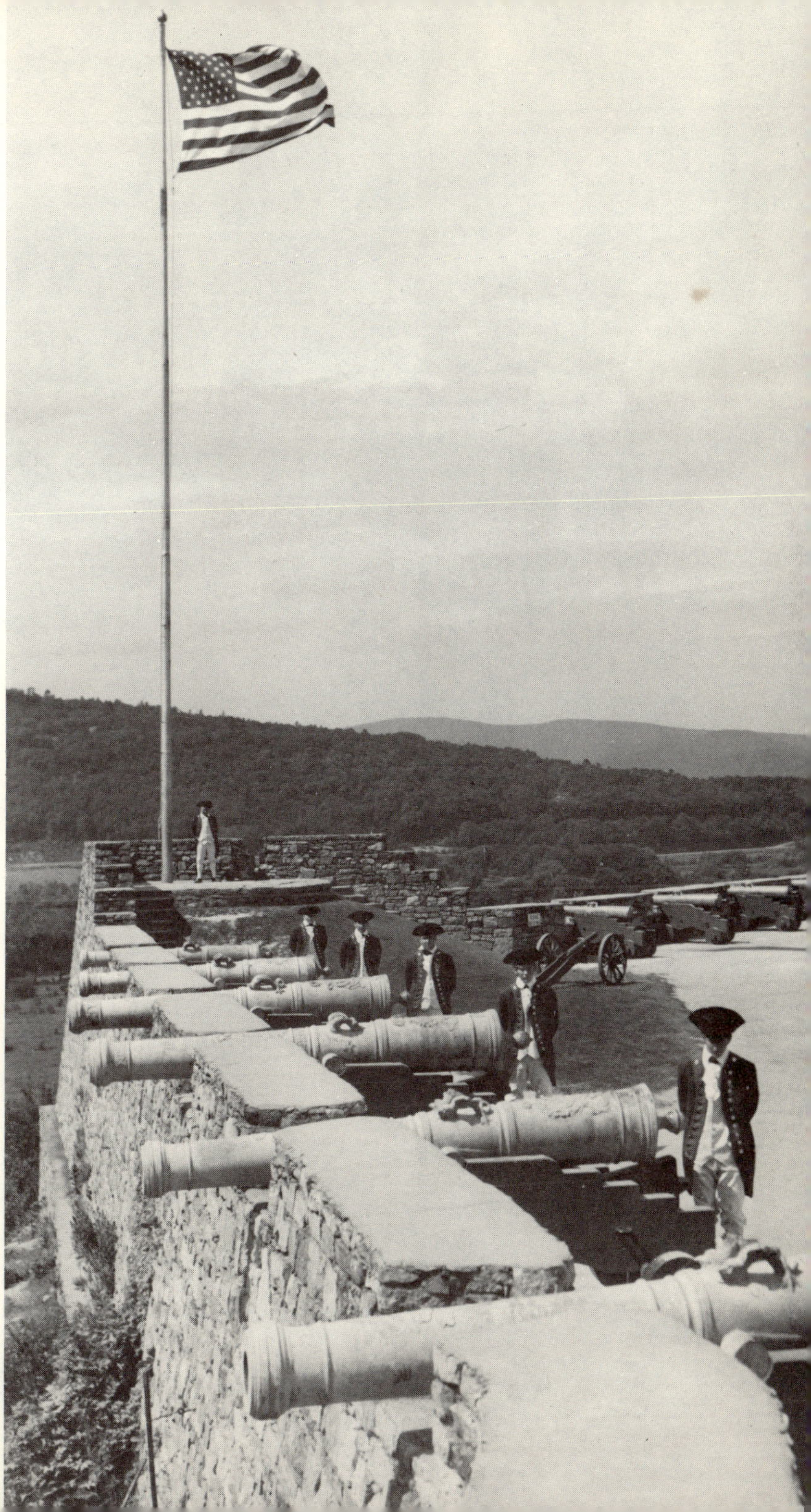

**Old Fort Niagara,** near Youngstown, New York, was built in castle style by the French in 1726, though Iroquois Indians were told it was only a fur storage area. After capturing the fort in the 1750s, the British sent out Indian raids from here during the American Revolution and also held this fort in the War of 1812. OLD FORT NIAGARA ASSOCIATION, YOUNGSTOWN, NEW YORK

Diorama at the visitor center, **Moores Creek National Military Park,** 20 miles northwest of Wilmington, North Carolina, showing the February 27, 1776, Patriot victory over a larger Loyalist force marching to join a British squadron. The battle at the bridge ended royal authority in North Carolina and helped prevent a full-scale invasion of the South.
MOORES CREEK NATIONAL MILITARY PARK, NATIONAL PARK SERVICE, U.S. DEPARTMENT OF THE INTERIOR

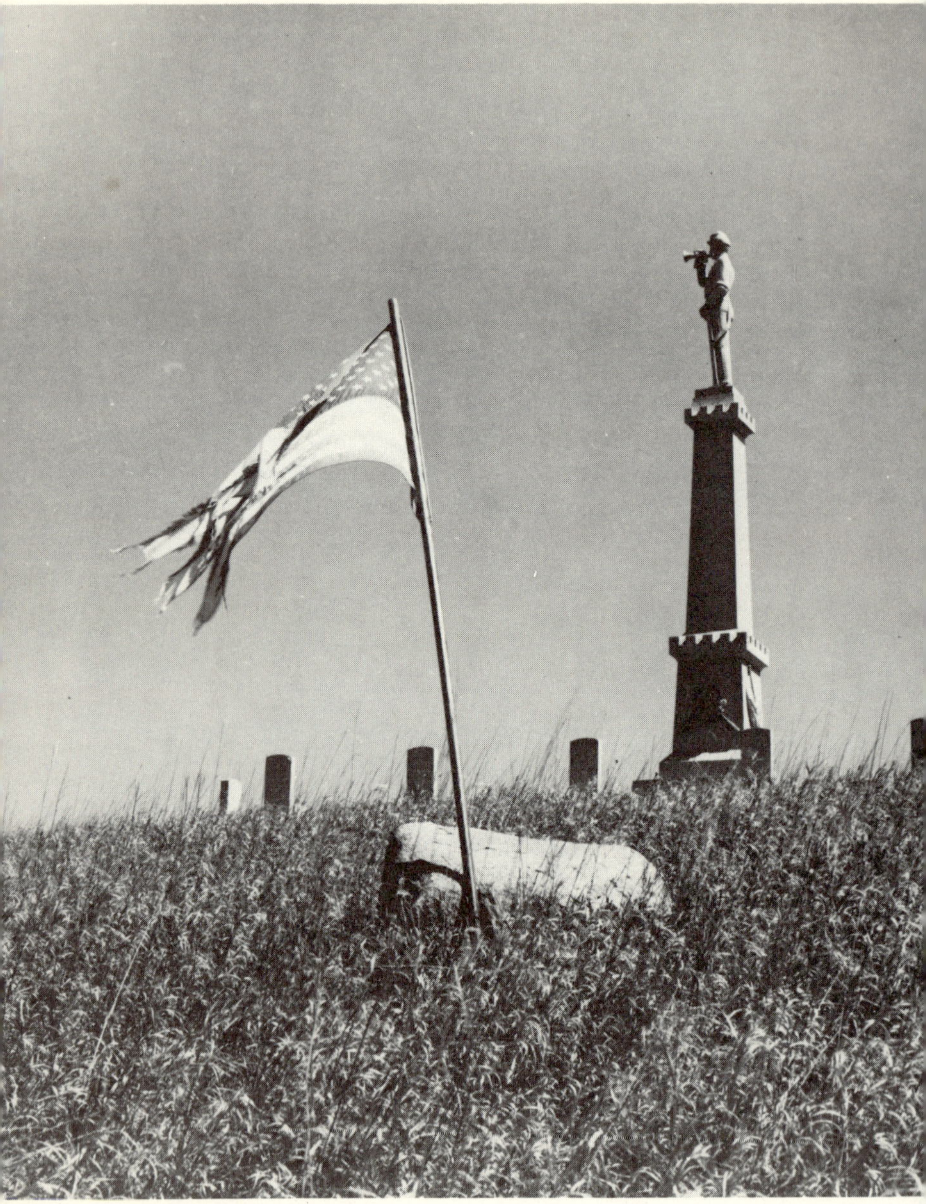

A reconstructed blockhouse at **Fort Lincoln State Park,** near Mandan, North Dakota, serves as a backdrop to a modern version of the Seventh Cavalry interested in preserving the history of Custer's Seventh Cavalry. Fort Lincoln was their last post prior to the Battle of the Little Bighorn.
KEN JORGENSEN, NORTH DAKOTA TRAVEL DIVISION

**Whitestone Hill Historic Site,** near Ellendale, North Dakota, is where 350 Sioux warriors, women and children were killed in a cavalry attack in September 1863. The attack was in reprisal for the 1862 Great Sioux Uprising in Minnesota. However, the Sioux at Whitestone had not been involved in the Minnestoa uprising. The unprovoked attack angered the Sioux tribes throughout Dakota territory. RUSS HANSON, NORTH DAKOTA TRAVEL DIVISION

# Kansas

Spanish and French explorers crossed Kansas in the seventeenth century, followed by the inevitable trappers in search of furs. After Kansas became American territory in 1803, three separate military expeditions explored the Kansas region. By the Indian Removal Act of 1830, eastern tribes of Indians were settled in Kansas, causing conflicts with the Osage, Pawnee, Cheyenne and other plains tribes who were already in the territory. Opening of the Indian lands to white settlement finally forced the tribes even farther west.

Slavery and anti-slavery forces warred for control of "Bleeding Kansas" before the Civil War, but in 1861 Kansas came into the Union as a free state, sending two-thirds of its eligible males to the Union Army. Kansas anti-slavery Jayhawkers and Confederate raiders like Quantrill continued their own private guerrilla warfare in Kansas during the Civil War.

★ ★ ★

# KANSAS

## FORT SCOTT

FORT SCOTT NATIONAL HISTORIC PARK, edge of business district of Fort Scott.

The fort was built in 1842 to protect settlers against Indians as well as to preserve peace among the various Indian tribes. Abandoned in 1853, the fort was reactivated in 1861 to be a Union supply depot and to help quell the fighting between pro-slavery and free-soil forces. It was during this virulent warfare that guerrillas like William Quantrill and his Confederate raiders rode into Lawrence, Kansas, in August 1863, killing 150 men and women and burning a portion of the city. (Oak Hill Cemetery at Lawrence has a monument marking the gravesite of the victims of the Lawrence Massacre.)

Restored fort, museum, tours. Free.

## HAYS

FORT HAYS FRONTIER HISTORICAL PARK, on US 183 alt. at s. edge of Hays, 4 mi. s. of I-70.

An important frontier fort, both the Seventh U.S. Cavalry and the black Tenth U.S. Cavalry were stationed at Fort Hays. General Sheridan made Fort Hays his headquarters during his Indian Campaign. At that time, Hays was a wild frontier town, and the army was often called to keep the peace, in addition to fighting hostile Indians. As the Indian menace declined, so did the need for the post, and Fort Hays was abandoned in 1889.

Ruins of fort, museum. Free.

## KANOPOLIS

FORT HARKER GUARD HOUSE MUSEUM, n.w. corner of Wyoming and Ohio Sts.

Fort Harker (1867) was one of three forts built to guard the route to Denver. Abandoned in 1873, the only surviving original building that has not been greatly altered is the two-story guardhouse. Originally, cells were on the second floor and officers' quarters on the first.

# EXPLORING MILITARY AMERICA

Museum. Open summers, weekend afternoons only in winter. Free.

### LARNED

FORT LARNED NATIONAL HISTORIC SITE, 5 mi. w. on US 156.

One of the best preserved mid-nineteenth century western forts, Fort Larned guarded the Santa Fe trail. In 1864, travel was not permitted beyond the fort without an armed escort. Although peaceful means were sought to solve the conflict between Indians and settlers, Fort Larned became the center of military operations against the Indians of the central plains, who raided from Kansas to Texas. Black Kettle's defeat at the Battle of the Washita in 1868 ended Indian resistance around Fort Larned.

Restored fort, visitor center, exhibits, tours in summer. Free.

### LEAVENWORTH

FORT LEAVENWORTH, adjacent to Leavenworth, on US 73 and 92, 35 mi. n.w. of Kansas City. Museum at Gibbon and Reynolds Ave. within fort.

Fort Leavenworth was built in 1827, the first fort west of the Missouri River. It protected caravans on the Santa Fe and Oregon Trails. During the Mexican War, the fort was an important staging area for General Kearny's and Colonel Doniphan's regiments, who then marched south to battle in Mexico. Union Civil War troops were also mustered and trained here.

Post museum has one of the largest collections of historic army transport wagons in the world. Tours. Free.

### MEDICINE LODGE

MEDICINE LODGE STOCKADE, US 160.

In October, 1867, five tribes of Plains Indians, with such leaders as Little Bear and Satana, met with a U.S. Peace Commission at

# KANSAS

"Medicine Lodge" and signed a treaty that opened west Kansas to settlement. The treaty, however, did not end the Plains Wars.

Replica of stockade, museum. Apr. 1–Sept. 30. Admission.

## PHILLIPSBURG

FORT BISSELL, ½ mi. w. on US 36.

Replica of Fort Bissell built of cottonwood logs in 1872 for protection against Apache Indian raids. Fort was kept stocked with provisions so that when riders warned of Indians, all settlers had to do was ride for the fort.

Museum. Free.

## PLEASANTON

BATTLE OF MINE CREEK, 2 mi. s. of town.

A Civil War border skirmish took place here on October 25, 1864 between John Brown's men and pro-slavery forces.

Interpretive markers. Museum at City Park in Pleasanton has mementos of battle. Free.

## TOPEKA

FORT RILEY, 75 mi. n. of Topeka, I-70 west 75 miles, Fort Riley exit n. 1 mi to post. Museum is 1½ mi. from entrance.

Fort Riley, a still-active army post, was established in 1853 to protect the Santa Fe trail. Since the fort was headquarters of the famous Seventh Cavalry, Fort Riley has been called "the cradle of the cavalry." The U.S. Cavalry Museum in Bldg. No. 30 tells the history of the U.S. Cavalry in the American West. Custer's headquarters with historical military relics is adjacent to the Cavalry Museum.

Museum, tours. Free.

# EXPLORING MILITARY AMERICA

## WALLACE

FORT WALLACE MEMORIAL MUSEUM, ½ mi. e. on US 40.

Once an Indian Wars outpost, today the only evidence of this fort's existence is a monument erected by Custer's Seventh Cavalry to their lost men and a museum of cavalry mementos.

Monument, museum. Summers only. Free.

# Kentucky

England and France competed for control of Kentucky in the eighteenth century, but the French and Indian War interfered with settlement of the territory by both. After Daniel Boone brought his party of settlers through the Cumberland Gap, other settlers soon followed, arousing Indian hostility. Encouraged by the British, the Indians destroyed almost all settlements in Kentucky during the American Revolution. Despite George Rogers Clark's capture of British forts in Illinois and Indiana, Indian raids continued in Kentucky during and after the war. The Battle of Blue Licks, although it was a victory for the Indians, finally ended the Indian threat. Kentucky supported the War of 1812 and the Mexican War, but as a border state tried to stay neutral in the Civil War. The state sent troops to the North and the South and was invaded by both the Union and Confederate forces.

★ ★ ★

# EXPLORING MILITARY AMERICA

## BLUE LICKS SPRINGS

BLUE LICKS BATTLEFIELD STATE PARK (n.e. of Lexington.)

On August 19, 1783, Indians and British ambushed and defeated a pursuing force of Kentuckians under Daniel Boone. Against Boone's advice, the Kentuckians had crossed Licking River into a ravine, which turned out to be a natural trap. Of the Kentuckians, seven were taken prisoner and sixty killed, including one of Boone's sons. The conflict is often called the last battle of the Revolutionary War.

Battle site, monuments, cemetery, museum, Apr. 1–Oct. 31. Admission.

## CLARKSVILLE

FORT CAMPBELL MUSEUM, Fort Campbell, 5 mi. n. of Clarksville.
Museum in Wickam Hall, 1 mi. from main gate.

Located on still-active army post, the Fort Campbell Museum centers around the history of the famous 101st Airborne Division, as well as the history of the Kentucky-Tennessee area surrounding the fort.

Free.

## COLUMBUS

COLUMBUS-BELMONT BATTLEFIELD STATE PARK, on SR 58.

The Battle of Belmont was a major skirmish at the beginning of Grant's western campaign, which ended in the fall of Vicksburg. During the winter of 1861, Confederate troops fortified the bluffs overlooking the Mississippi River with 140 guns, as well as floating batteries and a chain stretched across the river. The Confederates hoped to stop Union gunboats, but instead General Grant attacked Belmont, then turned his guns on Columbus. Unable to take the town by direct assault, Grant captured weaker positions on the Tennessee and Cumberland Rivers.

Battlefield, museum. Summers only. Admission.

# KENTUCKY

## FAIRVIEW

CONFEDERATE MUSEUM, Jefferson Davis Monument State Park, e. on US 68.

Civil War museum and artifacts from Confederate President Jefferson Davis are housed in the monument, a 351-foot-high obelisk. Summers and weekends only during winter months. Admission.

## FRANKFORT

KENTUCKY MILITARY HISTORY MUSEUM, East Main St.

Housed in Old State Arsenal (1850), the museum has material relating to the military history of Kentucky. The Arsenal, itself, was used to repulse an attack on Frankfort during the Civil War. Free.

## HARRODSBURG

FORT HARROD, Pioneer Memorial State Park, Lexington and Warwick Sts.

This fort, site of the oldest permanent English settlement west of the Allegheny Mountains, was built in 1777. Indians repeatedly attacked Fort Harrod and Fort Boonsborough during the Revolution, but the forts survived to become centers of large communities. At Fort Harrod, George Rogers Clark planned his 1778 campaign of the conquest of the British-held Northwest Territory.

Restored fort, cabins, museums, tours. Admission.

## LEXINGTON

BRYAN STATION MEMORIAL, Bryan Station Rd.

Memorial honors pioneer women who risked their lives to bring water to the besieged stockade that stood here. Some 500 Indians and 50 white British soldiers and renegades failed in their attack, but when pursued, successfully ambushed pursuers at Blue Licks Battlefield. (See Blue Licks Springs Battlefield Museum).

# EXPLORING MILITARY AMERICA

## LOUISVILLE

PATTON MUSEUM OF CAVALRY AND ARMOR. Fort Knox. From Louisville take SR 31W 36 mi. s. to Chaffee Ave. turnoff to main gate.

Exhibits are on the history of the U.S. Cavalry and Armored Forces, as well as the personal effects of World War II General George S. Patton. Fort Knox is an active military post and, of course, also the home of the U.S. Gold Depository, which is not open to the public!

Patton museum free.

## MIDDLESBORO

CUMBERLAND GAP NATIONAL HISTORICAL PARK. Visitor center near Middlesboro entrance, on US 25E and 58.

Historic pass, long used by Indians, was discovered in 1750 by Dr. Thomas Walker and later used by Daniel Boone, who led a party through the Gap in 1775 to found Boonesborough. The pass was a strategic point during the Civil War. Union forces captured the gap in 1862, had to retreat, then recaptured it, despite "Long Tom," the largest Confederate gun then in action, which guarded the pass entrance.

Museum. Free.

## PERRYVILLE

PERRYVILLE BATTLEFIELD STATE SHRINE, 2 mi. n. of Perryville, off US 68, or take US 68 s. from Lexington to Perryville.

On October 8, 1862, Confederates, under General Bragg, attacked Union forces, under General Buell. After one afternoon's fighting, which saw 6,000 soldiers from both the Blue and Gray killed or wounded, Bragg withdrew. Neither side could claim victory, but the battle marked the end of any serious attempt by the South to gain possession of Kentucky.

Near the park are two shrines: the Crawford house, which served as General Bragg's headquarters; and the Squire H. P. Bottom

# KENTUCKY

house, which was the scene of heaviest fighting. After the battle, with his "yard full of wounded men, shrieking with pain," Squire Bottom searched the woods for Confederate dead, placing them in piles and burying them in a small cemetery marked with a monument.

Battlefield, museum. Apr. 1–Oct. 31. Admission.

## WINCHESTER

FORT BOONESBOROUGH STATE PARK, Fort and museum about 9 mi. s. of Winchester, off SR 627, or ¼ mi. s.e. of jct. SR 627 on SR 388.

Site of Daniel Boone's famous settlement on the Kentucky River, besieged by Indians during the Revolutionary War in 1777 and 1778.

Replica of fort, museum. Apr. 1–Oct. 31. Admission.

# Louisiana

La Salle claimed Louisiana for France in 1682, and the first French fortification was built in 1699. Louisiana came under Spanish rule in 1762, but the colony remained French in customs and culture and was sympathetic to the American colonies during the American Revolution. After the Louisiana Purchase of 1803, the territory became American, and the last battle of the War of 1812 occurred outside of New Orleans. Andrew Jackson's mixed American forces of Kentucky backwoodsmen, Creoles, Indians, free blacks and even pirates defeated British veteran soldiers. Ironically, the battle took place after the war had already ended. Southern in sympathy, the cities of New Orleans and Baton Rouge were captured by the Union early in the Civil War and the capture of Port Hudson in 1863 gave the Union vital control of the Mississippi River.

★ ★ ★

# LOUISIANA

## BATON ROUGE

OLD ARSENAL MUSEUM, State Capitol grounds, Lafayette St. and North Blvd.

Built in 1835, the arsenal contains artifacts from Louisiana's military history. Some of the original graffiti of the earliest military men who served here remain on interior walls. Free.

OLD PENTAGON BARRACKS, corner of River Rd. and State Capitol Ave.

Built in 1822 to house troops, the barracks is headquarters now for the Louisiana National Guard. The Old Powder Magazine, staging point for Creek War of 1813, contains a "please touch" museum of military history. Admission.

BATTLE OF BATON ROUGE STATE MONUMENT, 330 S. 19th St.

Monument occupies site of two-hour conflict in August, 1862, in Civil War battle for Baton Rouge. Descriptive markers. Free.

## BOSSIER

EIGHTH AIR FORCE MUSEUM, Barksdale Air Force Base, e. of Shreveport.

Mementos of Eighth Air Force and Second Bomb Wing, primarily World War II materials with some World War II aircraft on display. Closed weekends. Free.

## BURAS

FORT JACKSON, s. of Buras on SR 23.

One of the forts near New Orleans that Union Admiral Farragut needed to pass in the spring of 1862. A massive, star-shaped fort, it sustained a week of shelling before Union gunboats were able to pass and take New Orleans.

Fort, museum. Free.

## GRAND TERRE ISLAND

FORT LIVINGSTON, a 5-minute boat ride from Grand Isle.

A large masonry fort occupied by Confederate forces until 1862

# EXPLORING MILITARY AMERICA

and then by Union forces for rest of war. The fort has been abandoned since 1893. Exploration is permitted in daylight hours. Free.

## LEESVILLE

FORT POLK MILITARY MUSEUM, Fort Polk is 1 mi. s. of Leesville. Museum is ¾ mi. from gate.

A still-active military post, the museum at Fort Polk has examples of U.S. and foreign weapons from the Civil War to the present, also material on the history of the Seventh and Eleventh Armored divisions. Free.

## MANSFIELD

MANSFIELD STATE COMMEMORATIVE AREA, about 4 mi. s.e. on SR 175, 3 mi. s.e. of jct. US 84.

The battle fought here in April, 1864 was the climax of the Red River campaign. Confederate forces stopped a Union advance on Texas, and the Union troops retreated back down the Red River. No further major Federal effort was made west of the Mississippi.

Museum. Admission.

## MANY

FORT JESUP STATE COMMEMORATIVE AREA, 7 mi. n.e. on SR 6.

Built in 1822, the fort became known as the "Cradle of the Mexican War" when its troops were sent to aid Texas, after Texas voted for annexation to the United States over Mexican protests. General Taylor's troops from Fort Jesup were also involved in the storming of Chapultapec during the Mexican War. During the Civil War, the fort served as a supply base for the Confederacy.

Partially reconstructed fort, visitor center, exhibits. Admission.

## NEW ORLEANS

CONFEDERATE MUSEUM, 929 Camp St.

Military museum, primarily on early Louisiana military history and the Civil War. Admission.

# LOUISIANA

BATTLE ABBEY BEHIND THE CABILDO, facing Jackson Square.

War relics are housed in the Battle Abbey, while the Cabildo also has exhibits about the Civil War. After the Union Navy captured New Orleans, the city was run with an iron hand by much-hated Union General Butler. Admission.

LOUISIANA MILITARY HISTORY AND STATE WEAPONS COLLECTION MUSEUM, Jefferson Barracks.

Located in Old Powder Magazine, museum contains small arms, flags and relics of military service of Louisiana National Guard units. Free.

FORT PIKE STATE COMMEMORATIVE AREA, 30 mi. e. via US 90.

This fort was built in 1819 to guard the entrance to Lake Pontchartrain and was captured by Confederates in 1861. Today, the fort is a state monument surrounded by a park. Admission.

CHALMETTE NATIONAL HISTORICAL PARK, on SR 46 (River Rd. East Bank) Arabi, 6 mi. from New Orleans. From Canal Street, follow main thoroughfare that begins at Rampart St. and merges into St. Claude Ave. then into St. Bernard Highway to park.

In early December, 1814, a British force of 7,500 veteran soldiers under General Sir Edward Pakenham marched overland to attack New Orleans. The two previous British offensives, at Lake Champlain and in Chesapeake Bay, had failed, leaving the capture of New Orleans as England's main hope for securing a favorable peace settlement in the War of 1812. By controlling the mouth of the Mississippi River, England would control the economy of the Mississippi Valley. But on December 23, Andrew Jackson's militia, consisting of white, black, red and Creole Americans, halted the British advance in a fierce night attack; Jackson's army then fell back to the Chalmette plantation and formed a mile-long defensive line. Withering fire from Jackson's artillery and infantry tore into the British ranks. In less than 30 minutes, the British suffered 2,000 casualties; the American loss was 13. The British withdrew to their ships. Though the battle occurred after the 1812 peace treaty had been signed, it established American occupation of Louisiana territory.

Battlefield, interpretive markers, museums. Free.

# EXPLORING MILITARY AMERICA

**SHREVEPORT**

FORT HUMBUG MEMORIAL PARK, foot of Stoner Ave. on grounds of the VA hospital.

Fort Humbug guarded Shreveport from Union gunboats approaching from the south on the Red River during the Civil War. Charred logs were placed so as to appear to be cannon, thus "humbugging" enemy scouts into believing the fort was well-armed. Old log ramparts and breastworks have been replaced. Free.

# Maine

The first fortification in Maine was built by the English in 1607. In a number of Indian wars from 1675 to 1763, the Indians, aided by the French, tried to drive out the English settlements. Later, Maine settlers resisted Great Britain early in the American Revolution, holding their own tea party at York, Maine, against British taxes. The first naval battle of the Revolution took place off the coast of Maine, and several Maine coastal towns were attacked. During the Civil War, Maine, an abolitionist stronghold, fought on the side of the Union with 6,000 Maine men fighting at the Battle of Gettysburg.

★ ★ ★

**AUGUSTA**

FORT WESTERN, Bowman and Cony Sts.

This fort was built by the Plymouth Company in 1754, during the French and Indian War, as part of the defense of the Kennebec River. In the American Revolution, Colonel Benedict Arnold began his march to Quebec at Fort Western on September 24, 1775. He arrived at Quebec in early November with 600 of his original 1,100 men.

Fort, original barracks, reconstructed blockhouses and palisade, museum. May 15–Labor Day. Admission.

## BUCKSPORT

FORT KNOX STATE MEMORIAL, SR 174.

Started in 1846, at a time of controversy between the United States and Great Britain over boundaries between the U.S. and Canada, this fort was never completed. The controversy is known as the bloodless "Aroostook War."

Fort, interpretive program. May 1–Nov. 1. Admission.

## CAPE ELIZABETH

TWO LIGHTS STATE PARK.

During World War II, this area was an army coastal fortification. Bunkers are closed for public safety, but the cement tower, on north ridge, used for observation, range finding and triangular plotting, is open. Free.

## CASTINE

FORT GEORGE, Battle Ave.

The French, the Dutch and the English struggled for control of the area in the seventeenth and early eighteenth centuries. In 1779, 600 British troops completed the construction of Fort George, aided willingly by Tories and unwillingly by American patriots of the Revolution. Between July 29 and August 13, the fort was unsuccessfully besieged by the patriot Penobscot Expedition of 40 vessels sent from Massachusetts, and all of the American patriot fleet was destroyed. In September, 1814, the British reoccupied Fort George with 60 cannon, evacuating in 1815.

Partly restored fort. Open Memorial Day to Labor Day. Free.

# MAINE

FORT MADISON, Perkins St.

In 1811, Americans, in preparation for war, also built, in Castine, Fort Porter, later Fort Madison. The British captured the fort during the War of 1812. It was rebuilt during the Civil War. Also among the many batteries in the Castine area is

FORT GRIFFITH, Wadsworth St.

Fort remains, earthworks, moats. Free.

STATE OF MAINE, Maine Maritime Academy dock.

The ship is the former *USNS Upshur,* which served in the Vietnam War and is now an academy training ship.

Guided tours when in port, usually July–Apr. Free.

## FORT KENT

FORT KENT STATE MEMORIAL, off Maine St.

The 1839 fort was constructed at the time of the bloodless Aroostook War boundary dispute with Canada.

Blockhouse. Memorial Day–Labor Day. Free.

## KITTERY

FORT MCCLARY MEMORIAL, 2 mi. e. on SR 103.

The first fort to protect this shipping center was built in 1809 and reconstructed in 1846.

Blockhouse, interpretive signs. Daily mid-June to mid-Sept.; weekends only May 30 to mid-June and mid-Sept. to Oct. 10. Admission.

THE KITTERY HISTORICAL AND NAVAL MUSEUM, jct. US 1 and SR 236.

At Kittery was built and launched the *USS Ranger,* first ship to receive foreign salute to the Stars and Stripes. The *Ranger* was commanded by John Paul Jones. JOHN PAUL JONES MEMORIAL nearby.

Museum. Tues. through Sat. afternoons. Free.

# EXPLORING MILITARY AMERICA

## MACHIAS

FORT O'BRIEN OR FORT MACHIAS, 5 mi. from Machias on Route 92.

The breastworks of the fort overlook Machias Bay, site of the first naval engagement of the Revolution. The British armed schooner *Margaretta* came to Machias for lumber for British barracks in Boston, following the Battle of Lexington and Concord. But the townspeople put up a liberty pole, and the British ship was captured by the American sloop *Unity* under Jeremiah O'Brien. The British captain died of wounds the next day. BURNHAM TAVERN, where they took the battle wounded, still stands. The fort, constructed in 1775, had a large garrison until late 1777. It was held by the British in the War of 1812 and rebuilt in 1863 during the Civil War.

Fort breastworks, in state park, open May 31 to Labor Day. Free. Battle Marker on Court House lawn. Burnham Tavern Museum, Main and Free Sts., Mid-June to Labor Day. Admission.

## PEMAQUID POINT

FORT WILLIAM HENRY MEMORIAL, at end of a long peninsula. From Damariscotta on Rt. 129, 4 miles, then take Rt. 130 for 9 mi., bear right 1 mi.

The first fort in Maine, Fort Pemaquid was built for use against pirates in 1630. On the same site in 1692, Fort William Henry was constructed by the British. In 1696, the French destroyed it. In 1729, Fort Frederick was erected by the British on the site, but it was leveled by the Americans during the Revolution.

Reproduced fort, exhibits. Memorial Day–Labor Day. Admission.

## POPHAM BEACH

THE ARNOLD TRAIL, see sites indicated.

The Arnold Trail stretches 194 miles, from Fort Popham at the Kennebec River, north and west to the Canadian border at Coburn Gore, Maine. The trail traces the route followed by Benedict Arnold and his American troops in autumn 1775, on the Maine portion of their historic but unsuccessful march on Quebec. There are 33 inter-

## MAINE

pretive panels at 9 different sites, including Popham, Hollowell, Skowhegan, Solon, Moscow, Stratton, Sarampus, Chain of Ponds and Coburn Gore. Some buildings passed by Arnold's men are still standing, including Fort Western in Augusta, Fort Halifax in Winslow, and old Pownalborough Court House in Dresden.

Panels are available for viewing May 30 to Labor Day. Admission for memorials and historic sites is set by the Maine Bureau of Parks and Recreation. Brief histories may be purchased on sites.

FORT POPHAM MEMORIAL, Popham Beach.

This granite and brick fortification was started in 1861 but never completed.

Fort, circular staircases to towers, interpretive signs. Memorial Day to Labor Day only. Admission.

## PORTLAND

FORT GORGES, Diamond Island, Portland Harbor.

Started in 1858, this granite fort was built to protect Portland harbor.

Fort can be viewed by boat or from Eastern Promenade, Portland. Free.

FORT ALLEN PARK, Fore St. off Eastern Promenade.

This historic park contains a gun from the Battleship *Maine* blown up in Havanna, Cuba, an event that began the Spanish-American War. Also in park, overlooking Portland harbor, is the main mast and navigational bridge shield of World War II cruiser *U.S.S. Portland*. Free.

## ROCKLAND

FIRST COAST GUARD DISTRICT MARINE EXHIBIT, G.A.R. Hall, 104 Limerock St.

Coast Guard exhibits with audio-visual displays that visitors may operate. Civil War uniforms and weapons.

June 1–Oct. 31. Free.

# EXPLORING MILITARY AMERICA

## STOCKTON SPRINGS

FORT POWNALL, leave US 1 at Stockton Springs, then 3½ mi.

The wooden fort was built here by Massachusetts Royal Governor Thomas Pownall. To prevent its being taken by American patriots, the British twice fired the wooden fort, in 1775 and 1779.

Earthworks, archeological restoration in process. Free.

## WINSLOW

FORT HALIFAX, on US 201, 1 mi. s. of Winslow-Waterville Bridge.

Erected in 1754 during the French and Indian War, this oldest surviving log blockhouse in the United States was part of a larger fortification used at time of Benedict Arnold's expedition. Free.

## WISCASSET

FORT EDGECOMB MEMORIAL, south off US 1 at Edgecomb and Wiscasset Bridge, then next right. South end of Davis Island.

This 1808 octagonal wooden blockhouse was built to protect Wiscasset, then the most important shipping center north of Boston. The fort overlooks the Sheepscot River.

Blockhouse, earthworks, interpretive program. Memorial Day to Labor Day. Admission.

# Maryland

Colonized by the British in the early seventeenth century as a haven of religious freedom, the Maryland settlements faced little hostility from the peaceful, agricultural Indians. Although there was no military action in Maryland during the American Revolution, Maryland troops fought in almost every major engagement of that war. In the War of 1812, Maryland was a main theater of action. It was during the British bombardment of Fort McHenry that Francis Scott Key wrote the American National Anthem while he watched "the rocket's red glare" over the fort. In the Civil War, Maryland was occupied early by Federal troops to keep the "border state" loyal to the Union. Several important battles were fought within the borders of Maryland, including the bloodiest day of the Civil War at the Battle of Antietam.

★ ★ ★

**ANNAPOLIS**

THE NAVAL ACADEMY MUSEUM, U.S. Naval Academy, bordered by King George St. and the Severn River.

# EXPLORING MILITARY AMERICA

The museum at Preble Hall contains naval memorabilia ranging from ordnance to ship models to swords of John Paul Jones, Stephen Decatur, Lafayette, and others.

Free. Also free guided walking tours depart from Visitor Information Center, Ricketts Hall. Free.

## BALTIMORE

BALTIMORE SEAPORT and THE BALTIMORE MARITIME MUSEUM, Pier 4, Pratt St.

Collection of historic ships, including the *U.S.S. Torsk,* the Galloping Ghost of the Japanese Coast, last American submarine to sink Japanese warships in World War II.

Sound and light presentations on the *U.S.S. Torsk* simulating battle conditions of World War II. Admission.

U.S.S. CONSTELLATION, Constellation Dock, Pier I, Pratt and Light Sts.

This is the first commissioned ship of the United States navy and the oldest American ship continuously afloat. This 1797 ship has served in every war since the Revolution except the Vietnamese War and served as flagship of the Atlantic fleet during World War II. Admission.

FORT MCHENRY, drive. s. from Baltimore on Light St. to Key Highway, turn right at Lawrence to E. Fort Ave., then left to end of Fort Ave.

Although a temporary fortification was built here in 1776, the star-shaped Fort McHenry was not completed until the 1790s and saw action in 1814. The British attacked, but the fort was invincible. Francis Scott Key on a boat near the mouth of the Patapsco River saw "In the dawn's early light" on September 14, 1814, that "our flag was still there," and composed the "Star Spangled Banner." The first War Memorial erected in the United States was the Battle Monument dedicated to those slain at Fort McHenry and North Point in the battle, and nearby is a modern statue dedicated to "The Negro Heroes

## MARYLAND

of the United States." Fort McHenry served in every war through World War II. Monuments in park, Calvert and Fayette Sts.

Restored fort, visitor center, exhibits. Free.

U.S. ARMY ORDNANCE MUSEUM, Aberdeen Proving Ground, 25 mi. n. of Baltimore, off I-95 n. Museum on Maryland Blvd. and Aberdeen Rd., 1 mi. from main gate.

Historical and modern ordnance, American and foreign tanks, Chemical Corps collection. Free.


## BOONESBORO

SCOPER HOUSE MUSEUM, 113 N. Main St.

Civil War relics from the Battle of South Mountain are included in this private collection, along with historical weapons and Indian artifacts.

Sunday afternoons, May through Sept. Donations.


## BURKITTSVILLE

GATHLAND STATE PARK, 1 mi. w. of Burkittsville.

George Townsend, noted Civil War journalist, left a monument to war correspondents and exhibits of the Civil War.

Visitor center, exhibits. Weekdays and holidays, or by appointment. Admission.


## CLEAR SPRING

FORT FREDERICK STATE PARK, 1 mi. s.w. of Big Pool exit of I-70.

This French and Indian War fort, built of stone in 1756, provided protection on the frontier. In 1763, during Ottawa Chief Pontiac's rebellion, 700 settlers flocked to the fort. In the American Revolution, thousands of British and Germans were imprisoned within the walls. In the Civil War, Union soldiers held the fort against Confederate attempts to dislodge them.

Memorial Day to Labor Day. Weekends off season. Free.

# EXPLORING MILITARY AMERICA

## CUMBERLAND

FORT CUMBERLAND TRAIL AND GEORGE WASHINGTON'S HEADQUARTERS, c/o Alleghany County Tourism, Baltimore at Greene Sts.

A walking trail covers several city blocks in downtown Cumberland, with sites related to Fort Cumberland, built in 1754 and 1755, where young Colonel George Washington had his headquarters in the French and Indian War. The trail includes 27 narrative plaques, markers of the old fort, reconstructed fort palisades and the 1755 log cabin headquarters.

Cabin has window viewing and taped history. Free.

## FORT MEADE

FORT GEORGE G. MEADE ARMY MUSEUM, 4674 Griffin Ave.

Historical war weapons and equipment from the Revolution to the present, both American and foreign. Free.

## FREDERICK

MONOCACY BATTLEFIELD, Rt. 355, 3 mi. s. of Frederick.

In summer of 1864, General Early's Confederates marched toward Washington and were delayed here, but not defeated, by General Lew Wallace's forces, which consisted mainly of clerks, convalescent soldiers and armed police hastily recruited in Washington.

General Early levied a ransom of $200,000 on the city of Frederick. The city had to borrow funds, and the last repayment of the loan was made October 1, 1951! Free.

## GREENBELT

GODDARD SPACE FLIGHT CENTER, National Space Science Data Center.

The National Aeronautics and Space Administration maintains here a collection of scientific data on magnetic tape, photographic film, microform or punched card form, data covering all NASA space missions and lunar experiments except samples handled in Houston. All data are highly technical but are available to the public. Free.

# MARYLAND

## OXON HILL

FORT WASHINGTON, about 7 mi. s. off SR 210.

A military installation was built here in 1797 but was destroyed by the British during the War of 1812. The present fort, completed in 1824, is an excellent example of nineteenth century coastal defense with ramparts, bastions, gun ports, towers and drawbridge. Civil War vintage small arms and cannon are fired every Sunday. Free.

## PAX RIVER

NAVAL AIR AND TEST EVALUATION MUSEUM, Naval Air Test Center.
Naval air and test operations exhibits. Free.

## SCOTLAND

POINT LOOKOUT STATE PARK at confluence of Chesapeake Bay and Potomac River, on SR 5.

Several times during the Revolutionary War and the War of 1812, British troops occupied the Point. During the Civil War, a prisoner of war camp was established. Exposure, disease and starvation took their toll of the Confederate prisoners. One prisoner wrote: "Two of our men were so hungry today that they caught a rat and cooked him and ate it." The prison site is now under Bay waters, but the earthwork remnants of Fort Lincoln may be seen.

Park headquarters has walking tour maps and slide lectures.

## SHARPSBURG

ANTIETAM NATIONAL BATTLEFIELD, Rt. 65.

This battle, also called the Battle of Sharpsburg, took place on September 17, 1862, and produced the bloodiest day of the Civil War, with more than 23,000 Confederate and Union soldiers killed or wounded. Antietam was the first of General Lee's two attempts to carry the war into the North. The battle had three phases: The Union morning attack at the cornfield, with the fighting sweeping back and forth a dozen times; the Union midday attack at the sunken road or

# EXPLORING MILITARY AMERICA

Bloody Lane, which caused 4,000 casualties, and the Union afternoon attack at Burnside Bridge, where a few hundred Georgia riflemen held off four Union divisions. Three Federal and three Confederate generals lost their lives at Antietam. Lee was finally turned back to Virginia.

Visitor center, exhibits, well-marked battlefield, tours. Free.

# Massachusetts

The Pilgrims were not the first European visitors to Massachusetts, but they built the first permanent fortified settlement at Plymouth in 1620. Although the Pilgrims had come to America seeking religious freedom and not military conquest, conflict with the Indians erupted into the King Philip's War in 1675 and into the French and Indian War in the mid-1700s. Many of the Indians allied themselves with the French and against the British colonists.

By the time of the American Revolution, Massachusetts colonists had turned against England and were in the forefront of the drive for independence. Some of the first military engagements of the Revolution took place in Massachusetts, which also sent the largest number of colonial troops to the war. The War of 1812 was not popular in Massachusetts because it interfered with the shipping industry, but the Mexican War and the Civil War were widely supported. Massachusetts volunteers were among the first to report for duty in the Civil War, and the

# EXPLORING MILITARY AMERICA

Springfield Armory turned out 1,000 rifles a day to support the Union cause.

★ ★ ★

**BOSTON**

The city of Boston was called a "hotbed of rebellion" by the British because it was in Boston that Samuel Adams and his Sons of Liberty plotted resistance against British rule. There is a well-marked Freedom Trail Walking Tour to historic sites in Boston, departing from the Boston City Hall. Free.

BOSTON MASSACRE SITE, State St., east front of Old State House.

A ring of cobblestones marks the site where jeering Bostonians clashed with a British guard unit in 1770, resulting in the "massacre" of six Americans.

OLD STATE HOUSE (1713) Washington and State Sts.

From the State Street balcony of the Old State House, the Declaration of Independence was proclaimed. The Boston Massacre occurred to the east of this building.

Museum of Revolutionary War artifacts. Admission.

ANCIENT AND HONORABLE ARTILLERY COMPANY OF MASSACHUSETTS, Faneuil Hall, Faneuil Hall Square at Merchants Row.

This artillery company began in 1638, and the museum collection started about 1865. The museum is housed in historic Faneuil Hall, which has been called the "Cradle of Liberty" because it was a meeting place for the American rebels before the Revolution. The hall now contains military artifacts from all of America's wars. Free.

OLD SOUTH MEETING HOUSE, Milk and Washington Sts.

On the night of December 16, 1773, Americans congregated at the meeting house and learned that Governor Thomas Hutchinson had refused to place a ban on shiploads of tea waiting in Boston harbor. A crowd of men then left the church dressed as Indians. They boarded

## MASSACHUSETTS

the ships and threw the tea into the harbor in protest against paying British taxes. Admission.

BOSTON TEA PARTY SHIP AND MUSEUM, downtown waterfront, Congress State Bridge.
A full-scale replica of one of the Tea Party ships.
Museum adjacent to ship. Admission.

OLD NORTH CHURCH, 193 Salem St. at foot of Hull St.
It was from this church that signal lanterns were hung, warning of the British Redcoats' advance on Lexington and Concord. Upon seeing the signal lights, Paul Revere and William Dawes rode out to spread the alarm. Major John Pitcairn, British second in command in the march to Lexington, was later killed at Bunker Hill and lies buried in a crypt in the church. Free.

BOSTON COMMON, bounded by Beacon, Charles, Boylston, Tremont and Park Sts.
At the time of the American Revolution, the Common, now a public park, was a military training field. The British assembled their troops here before the Battle of Bunker Hill and started their march to Lexington and Concord from the Common.

SOLDIERS' MONUMENT, Dorchester Heights, Thomas Park, South Boston.
By fortifying the Dorchester Heights, General Washington was able to drive the British from Boston in March, 1776, one of the first military successes of the Continental Army. Free.

ROXBURY HIGH FORT, Beach Glen St. at Fort Ave. (Highland Park)
Earthwork fort was erected here during Revolutionary War to prevent British from receiving supplies during the siege of Boston. Partially restored. Free.

CASTLE ISLAND, Gardner Way, South Boston.
Built in 1801, Fort Independence on Castle Island was one of the forts built to protect Boston during the War of 1812 and Civil War. Only the yard of the fort is now open. Free.

# EXPLORING MILITARY AMERICA

STATE HOUSE MUSEUM, Beacon Hill, Beacon St. at head of Park St.

The museum contains priceless Revolutionary War relics. Guided Tours. Free.

SHAW MONUMENT, facing the State House on Beacon St.

One of the most famous black regiments in the Civil War was the Fifty-fourth Regiment of Massachusetts led by Colonel Robert Gould Shaw. At Fort Wagner, South Carolina, the regiment engaged in hand-to-hand combat, clawing their way to the parapet of the fort; Colonel Shaw was killed and 245 men from the Fifty-fourth were killed or wounded. Twenty years after the battle, the famous artist, Augustus Saint-Gaudens completed this impressive bronze memorial in memory of the Massachusetts Volunteers. Free.

## BREWSTER

DRUMMER BOY MUSEUM, SR 6A, w. of Brewster Center (Cape Cod)

Guided tour of twenty-one life-size scenes of American Revolution.

May 15–Oct. 15. Admission.

## CAMBRIDGE

FORT WASHINGTON, 95 Waverly St.

This was the only Revolutionary War fortification in Cambridge, and one of a series of half-moon batteries ordered built by General Washington in 1775. During his stay in Cambridge, after he was appointed Commander in Chief of the Continental Army, General Washington lived at 105 Brattle Street, now the Longfellow home.

No admission to Fort Washington. Admission to Longfellow Home.

## CHARLESTOWN

BUNKER HILL MONUMENT, High St. and Monument Ave., across the Charles River and Charles Bridge from Boston.

The Battle of Bunker Hill on June 17, 1775, could more accu-

## MASSACHUSETTS

rately have been called the Battle of Breed's Hill. The British HMS *Lively* began firing broadsides on American redoubts built on Breed's pasture, the lower portion of Bunker Hill. Although the battle ended in American defeat, it was a gallant defense, which let the British know that they were in for a difficult struggle. Small museum at base of monument has relics of battle and honors General Joseph Warren and Peter Salem, a black soldier, both heroes of the battle. Admission.

WHITES OF THEIR EYES, Bunker Hill Pavilion adjacent to *U.S.S. Constitution*. Multi-media presentation of the Battle of Bunker Hill. Admission.

U.S.S. CONSTITUTION, Charlestown Navy Shipyard, Wapping and Chelsea Sts.
Launched in 1797, this historic 44-gun frigate fought French privateers and the British fleet during the War of 1812, bringing her the affectionate name of *Old Ironsides*. Free.
Adjacent to the ship is the U.S.S. CONSTITUTION MUSEUM, which offers exhibits on the history of *Old Ironsides*. Admission.

## CHELMSFORD

OLD CHELMSFORD GARRISON HOUSE, 105 Garrison Rd., off SR 110 at Westford town line.
Built in 1690 to defend settlers against Indians, the house and barn are now a museum, displaying colonial domestic and military artifacts.
June 15–Oct. 15, Sunday afternoons. Guided tours. Admission.

## CONCORD

OLD NORTH BRIDGE and MINUTEMAN STATUE, W. of Monument St.
After the Battle of Lexington, the British troops marched on to Concord, April 19, 1775, to confiscate military supplies stored there. A group of colonists met at WRIGHT'S TAVERN in Concord to consider action against the oncoming British. At the North Bridge, 400 Minute-

men and militia fought and defeated British in a battle that lasted about three minutes, with only a few casualties. However, the 16-mile march of the British back to Boston was more deadly. By nightfall, the British had lost 19 officers and 250 men had been killed or wounded; the Americans had about 90 killed and wounded. The famous MINUTEMAN STATUE beside the OLD NORTH CHURCH commemorates these early battles of the Revolutionary War.

>THE CONCORD ANTIQUARIAN MUSEUM, ½ mi. s.e. on SR 2A contains exhibits on the Battle of Concord. Mid-Mar.–Oct. 31. Admission.

## DEERFIELD

MEMORIAL HALL MUSEUM, Memorial Street.

Deerfield, settled in the 1660s, survived several brutal Indian raids, including the Bloody Brook Massacre of 1675, and the Great Deerfield Raid of 1704, when the town was overwhelmed and burned and captives were carried off by the French and Indian raiders. At the Memorial Hall Museum, which contains colonial, Indian and military relics, may be seen a door with a hole hacked in it by tomahawk. Many historic homes in Deerfield may be visited. Guide service at Information Center in the Hall Tavern. Admission to homes and museum.

## FAIRHAVEN

FORT PHOENIX, s. of US 6 in Fort Phoenix Park.

During the Revolutionary War, this fort was built to protect the harbor from the enemy. In September 1778, British troops marched overland and destroyed the fort. Immediately, local militia rebuilt the horseshoe shaped fort, walls of which are still standing today. Free.

## FALL RIVER

BATTLESHIP COVE, off I-195, at Exit 5.

One of the most complete collections of twentieth-century vessels of the U.S. Navy is berthed here. Visitors may tour the battleship,

# MASSACHUSETTS

*U.S.S. Massachusetts,* which survived 35 battles in the Atlantic and Pacific, a destroyer, a submarine, a gunboat and a PT boat. Admission.

## FORT DEVENS

FORT DEVENS MUSEUM, 30 mi. w. of Boston off SR 2.

An active military post, with a museum that depicts the history of Fort Devens and the units that have been stationed there. Free.

## HAVERHILL

HAVERHILL HISTORICAL SOCIETY MUSEUM, 240 Water St.

Haverhill suffered frequent Indian attacks. In one raid in 1697, Hannah Duston was kidnapped; she killed and scalped ten of her captors to escape and reach her home again. Hannah Duston relics and other colonial military artifacts may be seen at the museum, which is housed in an early nineteenth-century home. Afternoons, June 1– Aug. 31. Admission.

## LEXINGTON

LEXINGTON GREEN. Massachusetts Ave. and Bedford St.

The first skirmish of the American Revolution occurred here on April 19, 1775, between 60 to 70 Minutemen and British troops heading toward Concord. The words of the American commander, Captain John Parker, are inscribed on the site: "Stand your ground. Don't fire unless fired upon. But if they mean to have a war, let it begin here." Which side fired first is not known, but "the shot heard round the world" rang out and 8 Americans lay dead and 10 wounded. The MINUTEMAN STATUE, representing Captain Parker, faces the line of the British approach.

BUCKMAN TAVERN, opposite Battlegreen, on Bedford Street, is where
the Minute Men met before facing the oncoming British. July 1–
Aug. 31. Guided tours. Admission.

# EXPLORING MILITARY AMERICA

MUNROE TAVERN, 1332 Massachusetts Ave., is where British Earl Percy made his headquarters and hospital in April, 1775. Restored tavern with historical relics. July 1–Aug. 31. Admission.

MINUTE MAN NATIONAL HISTORICAL PARK includes historic military sites in Lexington, Lincoln and Concord and encompasses the four-mile stretch of Battle Road along which the British and pursuing colonials fought.

Visitors may obtain information at the BATTLE ROAD VISITOR CENTER, next to Buckman Tavern, on SR 2A in Lexington, and see exhibits and movie of battle. Free. The NORTH BRIDGE VISITOR CENTER in Concord also has interpretive exhibits, open May–Sept. Free.

There is also a Fiske Hill information station on SR 2A, w. of SR 128. One mile west on SR 2A is Park Headquarters.

JASON RUSSELL HOUSE, s. of Lexington at 7 Jason St., Arlington.

The Russell house was a refuge for Minutemen during retreat of British after Lexington-Concord fight. Bullet holes in house were made by British. Relics of battle. Apr. 1–Nov. 1, or by appt. Admission.

## MARBLEHEAD

FORT SEWALL, n.e. end of Front St.

The fort, overlooking the harbor, was built in 1742 and manned through the Spanish-American War. It was improved during the Revolutionary War with barracks and underground quarters, still to be seen. The frigate *Constitution,* fleeing from British men-of-war, sought shelter here. Free. At 37 Green Street is the OLD POWDER HOUSE (1755) where muskets and powder were stored from the French and Indian War through the War of 1812. The original of the famous painting, "The Spirit of '76," is on display in the Selectmen's Room, Abbot Hall. Free.

## NEW BEDFORD

FORT TABER, E. Rodney French Blvd.

Fort Taber (1846) is one of the finest examples of American seacoast defensive fortifications. It was designed by Captain Robert E. Lee

## MASSACHUSETTS

and Major Richard Delafield and was garrisoned through World War I. During the Civil War, the fort was armed with the famous Rodman and Parrott cannons and protected one of the Union's most important harbors.

Visitor center, exhibits, guided tours. Summers only. Free.

## PLYMOUTH

There are many historic sites at Plymouth, the first permanent white settlement north of Virginia. The area contains PLYMOUTH ROCK, on Water St., PILGRIM HALL, Court and Chilton Sts. (includes military relics), PLIMOTH PLANTATION, 3 mi. s. on SR 3A, a living history museum of Pilgrim life, and the *Mayflower II,* reproduction of the ship that brought the Pilgrims to Plymouth.

Actual military sites within Plymouth are more limited and include:

BURIAL HILL, head of Town Square.

Site of old fort built in 1622 and watchtower, 1643. A replica of the powder house used by the early Puritans has been built on the site, which was also a place of worship. Free.

COLE'S HILL, Carver St.

Only 50 colonists survived that first winter at Plymouth. The rest are buried here. Also at this site is statue of the Indian Chief Massasoit. One of the first Indian treaties in America was ratified by Massasoit in 1621. Free.

Plymouth Information Center, North Park, e. of US 44 and SR 3A. Apr. 15–Nov. 30. Free.

## SALEM

SALEM MARITIME NATIONAL HISTORIC SITE, Derby St. Information at Custom House.

Salem, during the American Revolution, was one of few significant ports not to fall into British hands. More than 200 Salem vessels were commissioned by the Continental Congress to harass the British merchant fleet and capture British supply ships. Derby Wharf, built 1762, served as base for outfitting American privateers and for auctioning captured British vessels. Guided tours in summers. Free.

FORT PICKERING, Winter Island, Salem.

Original forts at this site were earth and wood structures, but a 1794 fort was built of masonry with powder house and bomb shelter. One of the oldest forts in the state, it was garrisoned as late as the Spanish–American War. Free.

## SOMERVILLE

THE OLDE POWDER HOUSE, Powderhouse Blvd., Powderhouse Park.

It was at Prospect Hill at Somerville, one of America's strongest strategic positions during the Revolutionary War, that the Grand Union Flag was first raised. According to Massachusetts legend, the revolution started here with the seizure of 250 half barrels of colonial gunpowder by British General Gage in September, 1774. The magazine was also used by the Revolutionary Army during its siege of Boston. Free.

## SPRINGFIELD

SPRINGFIELD ARMORY NATIONAL HISTORIC SITE, Federal St.

In 1777, George Washington personally selected this site for the first U.S. Arsenal. For 190 years the country's most important weapons were developed and produced here. The museum in the Armory has the largest collection of military small arms in the world. Free.

# Michigan

The French came into Michigan from Canada in the seventeenth century, at the time they began setting up a line of forts from Quebec to New Orleans. After the French and Indian War the territory was ceded to England, but Pontiac and other Ottawa Indian chiefs still remained loyal to France. They attacked the British forts and settlements in what has become known as Pontiac's War of 1763. These same forts were used during the American Revolution as supply bases for British and Indian raids into the frontier settlements around Michigan. Following the Revolution, Michigan became American territory, although the forts in Michigan were captured again by the British during the War of 1812. Michigan remained loyal to the Union during the Civil War, and the military forts became training grounds for Michigan soldiers, 15,000 of whom lost their lives in the Union cause.

★ ★ ★

# EXPLORING MILITARY AMERICA

## COPPER HARBOR

FORT WILKINS STATE PARK, 3 mi. e. on US 41.

Established in 1844, Fort Wilkins was abandoned in 1870, after its troops had seen service in the Civil War.

Partially restored fort, exhibits. June 1–Oct. 15. Free.

## CROSS VILLAGE

GREAT LAKES INDIAN MUSEUM, 1 block n. on SR 131.

Of particular interest in this collection are the war regalia and weapons of various Great Lakes Indian tribes.

June 15–Labor Day. Admission.

## DEARBORN

DEARBORN HISTORICAL MUSEUM, 21950 Michigan Ave.

The museum is housed in two buildings of the original United States Government Arsenal built in the 1830s, at the time of the Black Hawk War in Illinois and Wisconsin. The arsenal repaired rather than manufactured weapons. The commandant's quarters contains exhibits of Dearborn's and Michigan's military history. Free.

## DETROIT

HISTORIC FORT WAYNE, 6053 West Jefferson at Livernois.

The city of Detroit, founded 1701, endured a five-month siege during Pontiac's War and was captured by the British in the War of 1812. After Michigan became an American territory again, Fort Wayne was built on the border between United States and Canada and is an outstanding example of middle-nineteenth-century military architecture. Although equipped with a dry moat, casemates, sally ports, powder magazine and stone barracks, the fort was never actually armed because a treaty of friendship was signed between England and the United States in 1848. Instead the fort saw service as a troop training center during the Civil War, Spanish–American War and later American wars.

Restored fort, museum. May 1–Oct. 31. Admission.

# MICHIGAN

## MACKINAW CITY

FORT MICHILIMACKINAC NATIONAL HISTORIC LANDMARK.
The French were primarily interested in fur trading when they built this fort in 1715, but the British fortified it after the French and Indian War. During Pontiac's uprising, all the soldiers at the fort were either killed or taken prisoner. It was from this fort that the British, during the American Revolution, sent out parties of Indians to raid American outposts in Ohio and western Pennsylvania. In 1781 the fort was abandoned when a new fort was built on Mackinac Island. Old Fort Michilimackinac is today an authentic restoration of an American Revolutionary War fortified town.

Restored fort, museum, tours. May 15–Oct. 20. Admission.

## MACKINAC ISLAND

OLD FORT MACKINAC, I-75, accessible by boat from St. Ignace or Mackinaw City.

The fort (1781) was occupied by the British until after the Revolutionary War when American troops garrisoned the fort. The British continued to stir up trouble with the Indians against American settlers, however, and at the outbreak of the War of 1812, the British, with their Indian allies, recaptured both Detroit and Fort Mackinac. The fort was returned to the United States in 1815 and remained an active American army post until 1895.

Original fort buildings, exhibits, Indian museum, tours. May 15–Oct. 20. Admission.

## NILES

FORT ST. JOSEPH MUSEUM, 5th and Main Sts.

Flags of four nations, France, England, Spain and the United States, have flown over the city of Niles. The Fort St. Joseph museum contains relics of every period of the city's history as well as relics from the site of Fort St. Joseph, itself. There is also Civil War memorabilia and a rare collection of drawings by Sitting Bull. Free.

# Minnesota

The French came to Minnesota and built forts there as early as 1686; they were primarily fur-trading posts, but also offered protection against the Chippewa and Sioux Indians. England took over the Minnesota territory in 1763, and the United States gained possession after the Revolutionary War, although the British flag flew over the trading posts until after the War of 1812. It wasn't until 1819 that Fort Snelling was built, the northwesternmost military post in the United States. During the Civil War, Minnesota supported the Union but was also busy fighting an Indian war within her own borders. In the summer of 1862, the fierce Sioux uprising had begun. The Indian raids did not cease until military expeditions in 1863 and 1864 drove the Sioux west, beyond the Missouri River.

★ ★ ★

**CAMP RIPLEY**

OLD FORT RIPLEY.

Only ruins of the powder magazine remain on this second most important military site in Minnesota. Built to keep peace among the

# MINNESOTA

Indian tribes and between settlers and Indians, the fort was manned during the Sioux uprising by volunteers. Free.

## FOREST CITY

FOREST CITY STOCKADE.

During the Sioux War, in which hundreds of settlers were killed, many Meeker County families fled to Forest City for safety. A stockade was hastily built by the home guard, and it furnished protection while the Minnesota Valley was ravaged by war.

Restored stockade. Summers only. Admission.

## JACKSON

FORT BELMONT, 2 mi. s. of jct US 71 and I-90.

Replica of fort built by settlers for protection during the Sioux uprising. With the regular army sent off to fight in the Civil War, the forts in Minnesota were garrisoned by the home guard and volunteers during the Sioux War. Additional forts for protection were built by the settlers themselves.

Fort, pioneer buildings. Summers only. Admission.

## LITCHFIELD

G.A.R. HALL AND MUSEUM, across from Central Park, 308 N. Marshall.

Civil War mementos of the men from Minnesota who served in the Union Army, the Grand Army of the Republic. Free.

## MORTON

BIRCH COULEE BATTLEGROUND PARK, 1½ mi. n., off US 71 on Renville County Rd. 2.

A decisive battle occurred here in September, 1862, between the Sioux and 150 soldiers under Colonel Sibley. The camp was surrounded by Indians; but using overturned wagons, dead horses and hastily dug breastworks, the soldiers fought back for 31 hours until

# EXPLORING MILITARY AMERICA

reinforcements arrived from Fort Ridgely and drove the Indians away. May–Sept. Free.

Also 2 mi. s.e. of Morton at REDWOOD FERRY, along the Minnesota River, one of the first disastrous battles of the Sioux War occurred, when Captain John Marsh and 45 men from Fort Ridgely attempted to repel an Indian attack on the Lower Sioux Agency. Half of the command, including Captain Marsh, were killed.

## REDWOOD FALLS

LOWER SIOUX AGENCY, 6 mi. e. on US 71 and SR 19, then 3 mi. s.e. on CR 2.

Loss of their lands, corrupt Indian agents and starvation brought on the greatest Indian uprising ever to take place in the United States, the Sioux War of 1862. With the Civil War pulling regular troops east, leaving the forts dangerously undermanned, 1500 Sioux Indians made ready for war under Little Crow. The Lower Sioux Agency was the scene of the first organized Indian attack. A heroic ferryman carried surviving refugees from the agency across the river until he, himself, was killed.

Interpretive center of the background and history of the Sioux War. Open all year, closed Monday and Tuesday, Nov. 1–Mar. 31. Free.

## ST. PAUL

HISTORIC FORT SNELLING, from US 949 and SR 5 and 55.

This 1820 limestone fort was one of the earliest military forts west of the Mississippi; after the Sioux uprising, it served for a time as an Indian prison camp. After the uprising, 400 Sioux were brought to military trial and 306 were condemned to death. President Lincoln commuted all but 39. Little Crow, leader in the outbreak, was killed near Hutchinson.

Restored fort, tours. June 1–Oct. 31. Hours vary. Admission.

# MINNESOTA

## ST. PETER

TRAVERSE DES SIOUX STATE PARK, 1 mi. n.w.

On this site in July, 1851, a treaty was signed with Sioux Indians, granting to white settlers 24 million acres, most of southern Minnesota, the largest single area involved in an Indian treaty in U.S. history. It was this treaty that helped bring about the Sioux War of 1862.

Log cabin at site, descriptive marker. Free.

## SLEEPY EYE

FORT RIDGELY, Fort Ridgely State Park, 10 mi. n.w. of Sleepy Eye, SR 4, or from SR 4, 7 mi. s. of Fairfax.

After almost completely destroying the town of New Elm (bronze monument next to courthouse square honors the defenders of the town against the Sioux Indian attack), Little Crow attacked Fort Ridgely. The siege continued for two days. Although garrisoned by volunteers, the fort was successfully defended, and the Sioux withdrew to attack Fort Abercrombie, further north. The outcome of the war was that the Sioux were expelled from Minnesota. In 1867 Fort Ridgely was abandoned.

Partially restored fort, battlefield around fort, tours, museum. May–Oct. 15. Admission.

# Mississippi

Mississippi was explored in the early sixteenth century by the Spanish, led by Hernando de Soto, although it wasn't until the French arrived that the first permanent fort was built in 1702 on Mobile Bay. The British were ceded the Mississippi territory in 1763, but the Spanish occupied the Gulf Coast while England was busy with the American Revolution. After America took possession of Mississippi, settlements increased, as did troubles with the Indians, especially during the War of 1812.

Mississippi was the second state to secede from the Union; the most important battle of the Civil War fought in Mississippi was the battle for Vicksburg.

★ ★ ★

**BALDWYN**

BRICE'S CROSS ROADS BATTLEFIELD, 6 mi. w. on US 45.

Confederate General Nathan B. Forrest forced the retreat of Union troops, who had been sent into Mississippi to defend General Sherman's vulnerable supply line. Muddy roads, torrential rains and a Federal wagon overturned on a bridge turned the Union retreat to

# MISSISSIPPI

Memphis into a rout and a brilliant tactical victory for Forrest in June, 1864.

Battlefield, interpretive markers. Free.

BRICE'S CROSS ROADS MUSEUM is located on US 45 in Baldwyn and contains artifacts from the battlefield. Free.

## BILOXI

THE OLD SOUTH MUSEUM, in the old Confederate Soldiers' Hospital building, 5½ mi. w. on US 90.

A Civil War museum is located near Beauvoir, the last home of Jefferson Davis, President of the Confederacy. The museum and home are maintained as a Confederate shrine. Admission.

SHIP ISLAND, 12 mi. s. of Biloxi, part of Gulf Islands National Seashore.

Fort Massachusetts still stands on Ship Island, guarding the entrance to Biloxi Bay as it did during the Civil War. The fort was captured early in the war by Federal forces, lost, then recaptured, and finally served as part of the important Union naval blockade of the Confederate states. The still visible dungeons of Fort Massachusetts housed Confederate prisoners of war.

Boat trips to Fort Massachusetts are available from Biloxi Small Craft Harbor and from Gulfport during the summer. Admission.

## CORINTH

BATTERY ROBINETT, HISTORIC BATTLEFIELD PARK.

After the battle of Shiloh, Tennessee, Confederate troops retreated to Corinth. General Grant followed and captured the town, using it as his base as he pushed towards Vicksburg. Battery Robinett is all that remains of the battle of Corinth, but plans are underway to have the historic battlefield reconstructed, complete with fortifications and descriptive markers.

# EXPLORING MILITARY AMERICA

## JACKSON

HISTORIC BATTLEFIELD PARK, Porter St.

General Sherman and Union troops attacked and occupied the city of Jackson in May, 1863. After the fall of Vicksburg, the city was again besieged for a week and so completely destroyed it was known as Chimneyville. In Battlefield Park may be seen earthwork trenches and cannon. MUSEUM of the battle located at Old Capitol, North State and Capitol Sts. Free.

## PASCAGOULA

OLD SPANISH FORT, Krebs Lake off US 90.

Built by the French in 1718 to withstand Indian attacks, the walls of the fort were made of oyster shells, mud and moss. A tunnel under one of the fireplaces led to a nearby bluff for escape by water if all else failed. In the late eighteenth century the building was used by a Spanish Army officer as a fortified residence, giving the fort its present name.

Original fortified outpost, museum. Admission.

## PORT GIBSON

GRAND GULF MILITARY STATE PARK, 6 mi. w.

Civil War forts of Fort Coburn and Wade, located along bluffs of Grand Gulf on Mississippi River, harassed Federal fleet. Earthworks, rifle pits and gun embrasures are still visible although the river altered its course in 1929 and is now ½ mile from defensive position. Free.

## TUPELO

TUPELO NATIONAL BATTLEFIELD SITE, within city limit on SR 6, about 1 mi. w. of intersection with US 45.

After the Union defeat at the Battle of Brice's Cross Roads, General Sherman ordered his commander in Memphis "to go out to

## MISSISSIPPI

follow Forrest to the death, if it cost 10,000 lives and breaks the Treasury." Although the battle at Tupelo in July, 1864, was not a defeat for Forrest, neither was it a victory. The Confederates forces were repulsed but in the blistering hot weather, soldiers on both sides dropped from heat exhaustion. The battles at both Brice's and Tupelo introduced a new kind of warfare, what the twentieth century would call "total war," which would eventually defeat the Confederacy.

Battlefield, visitor center, exhibits. Free.

NATCHEZ TRACE PARKWAY, Visitor Center located at entrance of Parkway on US 45 at Tupelo.

The Old Natchez Trace was a nineteenth-century frontier road that ran across Mississippi, Alabama and Tennessee and was used by Indians, "Kaintuck" boatmen, post riders and the military. General Andrew Jackson's Tennessee militia marched down the Trace to protect New Orleans from a threatened Spanish invasion in 1812. Earlier, in 1736, Chickasaw warriors and British troops defeated French forces at the battle of Ackia, 3 miles northwest of Tupelo on the Natchez Trace. The French defeat helped end French influence in the area. A monument marks the site of this significant battle. The important Civil War Battles of Raymond (part of the Vicksburg campaign), Tupelo and Brice's Cross Roads were also fought near the Trace.

Visitor center, exhibits. Free.

## VICKSBURG

VICKSBURG NATIONAL MILITARY PARK, adjoins city of Vicksburg on two sides. Entrance to park at eastern edge of US 80.

The impregnable fortifications built at Vicksburg by the Confederacy gave it the name of the "Gibraltar of the Confederacy." General Sherman's attack by land was thrown back in 1862. Then in 1863, General Grant started siege operations. In the course of 47 days of bombardment from land and the river, food, ammunition and supplies ran low and the citizens of Vicksburg had to move into caves

# EXPLORING MILITARY AMERICA

to escape the constant bombardment. The city finally surrendered on July 3, 1863. The surrender of Vicksburg, coupled with Lee's defeat at Gettysburg, was the beginning of the end for the Confederacy.

Battlefield, monuments, interpretive markers, visitor center, exhibits, tours. Also of interest are the remains of the *U.S.S. Cairo,* sunk during the Civil War and being restored. Free.

# Missouri

French explorers Marquette and Joliet, as well as La Salle, claimed the Missouri area for France in the seventeenth century and set up outposts in the region for trade with and protection from the Fox, Sauk and Osage Indians. In the eighteenth century, Missouri became a Spanish possession, then French again, and finally American in 1803. Jefferson Barracks, the first permanent military installation west of the Mississippi River, trained and supplied the military for duty in the Indians Wars in the West, as well as later wars.

Since the Santa Fe Trail ran from Missouri to New Mexico, the state had a strong economic interest in the outcome of the Mexican War, and Missourians were among the first to enlist in that war. At the time of the Civil War, Missouri was split between slavery and anti-slavery factions, which brought guerrilla warfare to the state before and during the war. One county in Missouri, Calloway, refused to join either the Union or the Confed-

# EXPLORING MILITARY AMERICA

eracy and briefly became the independent Kingdom of Calloway.

★ ★ ★

## HANNIBAL

SOUTH RIVER FORT, 4805 McMasters.

The only fort in northeast Missouri protected by garrisoned troops during the Civil War. Museum. Admission.

## INDEPENDENCE

FORT OSAGE, near Old Sibley on the Missouri River, 14 mi. n.e. of Independence, via US 24 and County BB.

General William Clark of the Lewis and Clark expedition built Fort Osage in 1808, two years after his return from the Pacific Coast, as a "factory" or fur trading post for the U.S. Government. The fort's existence also served notice upon the British and Spanish that the United States would resist encroachments upon its new territory, secured through the Louisiana Purchase. The fort was too isolated to protect during the War of 1812 and the troops withdrew, returning in 1816. The fort was abandoned in 1827.

Restored fort, exhibits. Free.

## KANSAS CITY

LIBERTY MEMORIAL, 100 W. 26th St.

World War I relics, as well as mementos from other wars, are displayed in this memorial to Kansas City war dead. Free.

## LEXINGTON

ANDERSON HOUSE AND LEXINGTON BATTLEFIELD STATE HISTORIC SITE, off US 24, near Lexington.

The Battle of Lexington is popularly known as the "Battle of the Hemp Bales" because the Confederate soldiers used movable, water-

# MISSOURI

soaked hemp bales as breastworks during the battle. The Union forces, after running short of water and ammunition, were forced to surrender on September 20, 1861. This is one of the few Civil War battlefields never cultivated as farmland, and original trenches and earthworks are still visible.

THE ANDERSON HOUSE, n. on SR 13, between 10th, Utah and 15th Sts., overlooks the battlefield. A field hospital during the battle, it changed hands three times during the fighting and bullet holes may still be seen in the house.

Battlefield, museum. Admission to Anderson House.

## LONE JACK

LONE JACK CIVIL WAR MUSEUM AND BATTLEFIELD, off SR 50, 1 mi. from Lone Jack.

On August 11, 1862, the Confederates launched their major attack in Missouri, captured Independence and then attacked the town of Lone Jack. Five hours of fierce hand-to-hand combat ensued before the Federal forces withdrew. The Confederates were supported by the notorious Quantrill's guerrillas, including such later outlaws as the Younger brothers.

Battlefield, museum, with included information on the Battle of Westport (Kansas City), the largest Civil War battle fought west of the Mississippi River. Free.

## NEVADA

BUSHWHACKER MUSEUM, 231 N. Main St.

Guerrilla warfare during the Civil War in Missouri was a war of raids, ambushes and arson, with such well-known bushwhackers as William C. Quantrill and the Cole and Younger brothers taking part on the Confederate side. On the Union side, the unofficial participants in the war were known as Jayhawkers.

Museum housed in century-old jail. Summers only. Admission.

# EXPLORING MILITARY AMERICA

## NEW MADRID

NEW MADRID MUSEUM, Main St.

In 1862 the Confederates strongly fortified an outpost on Island No. 10 at New Madrid, where the Mississippi River swings a lazy S at the Tennessee-Kentucky-Missouri border. Unable to get close enough to destroy the outpost, Union forces dug a canal through the neck of the S to New Madrid. One daring ironclad then slipped by the outpost on a dark, stormy night and destroyed the enemy batteries. Island No. 10 was forced to surrender its 7,000 men and three generals. HUNTER DAWSON HOME in New Madrid served as hospital during the battle.

Museum. Free.

## PILOT KNOB

FORT DAVIDSON HISTORIC SITE, SR 21.

In September, 1864, the clash of Union and Confederate troops at the Battle of Pilot Knob left 1,000 men killed or wounded within 20 minutes and ended in defeat for the Confederates. The area has remained almost untouched since the battle.

Earthworks, descriptive marker. Free.

## ST. LOUIS

JEFFERSON BARRACKS POWDER MAGAZINE, Jefferson Barracks, Grant Rd. at Kingston, off Broadway. Museum about 100 yards within gate.

Many famous military men—such as Generals Lee, Grant and Sherman—saw service at the barracks. Built in 1826, Jefferson Barracks was a main supply center during the Indian wars in the West and the Mexican War. During the Civil War, the barracks enabled the Federal government to retain control of both banks of the Mississippi River.

Museum in restored powder magazine, historical buildings. Free.

A second military museum in the park is KIEFNER-KANE MUSEUM, Sherman Rd., open by appointment. Admission.

# MISSOURI

SOLDIERS MEMORIAL, 1315 Chestnut St.

War memorabilia from Civil War to Vietnam is displayed in this memorial to St. Louis area war dead. Free guided tours.

U.S.S. INAUGURAL #242, 400 N. Wharf St.

Veteran U.S. Navy minesweeper from Battle of Okinawa, World War II.

Summers, or by appointment. Admission.

## SPRINGFIELD

WILSON'S CREEK NATIONAL BATTLEFIELD, 2 mi. s. of US 60 on SR M and ZZ about 10 mi. s.w. of Springfield.

The Confederates attempted to gain control of Missouri at the Battle of Wilson's Creek on August 10, 1861. Untrained troops on both sides fought for Bloody Hill overlooking the creek. The ground was so covered with dead and wounded that "one could have stepped from one man to another." It was a Southern victory, but the crippled Confederate force was later defeated at Pea Ridge, Ark.

Battlefield, museum, tours. Free.

## WARSAW

BENTON COUNTY MUSEUM, on Van Buren St.

A Confederate town, Warsaw was burned twice during the Civil War and several skirmishes took place within the town. A walking and riding tour map is available showing where Civil War incidents took place. The museum has exhibits of the Civil War in Missouri.

June 1–Oct. 15. Admission.

## WAYNESVILLE

FORT LEONARD WOOD MUSEUM. Fort Leonard Wood is off I-44 (90 mi. east of Springfield). Museum is 1½ mi. from main gate.

Museum contains weapons and uniforms from World War II, Korea and Vietnam, including the General Leonard Wood military collection. Outdoor displays of military equipment.

Closed weekends. Free.

# Montana

French fur traders reached Montana before 1800 but the territory was relatively unexplored until the Lewis and Clark Expedition arrived in 1805. It was in Montana, near Two Medicine Lake, that the expedition met the hostile Blackfoot Indians, resulting in the only Indian casualty of the expedition. With the arrival of fur traders, gold miners and ranchers came problems with the Indians in the 1860s and 70s, particularly the Sioux, Cheyenne and the Nez Perce. Fort Benton had been built in 1846 as a fur-trading/military post on the Missouri River, but now more forts were built for protection against Indian uprisings. An all-out campaign by the Army to crush the Plains Indians led to the most famous Indian victory in American military history: General Custer's defeat at the Little Bighorn River. Ironically, the victory spelled the final defeat of the Plains Indians.

★ ★ ★

# MONTANA

## BILLINGS

CUSTER BATTLEFIELD NATIONAL MONUMENT, 65 mi. s.e. of Billings. The battlefield lies within the Crow Indian Reservation, entrance 1¼ mi. e. of I-90, s. of Hardin.

Little Bighorn, in June 1876, was one of the last major battles in the war with the Plains Indians. It resulted in the death of General George Custer and 225 men of the Seventh Cavalry. Custer had underestimated the fighting power of the Indians and split his regiment; he was ambushed by several thousand Sioux and northern Cheyenne. One of the Indians described the battle: . . . "the smoke was like a great cloud . . . we circled, swirling like water round a stone. We shoot, we ride, we shoot again. Soldiers drop and horses fall on them . . ."

Museum, tours, markers. Free.

## BROWNING

MUSEUM OF THE PLAINS INDIANS, ½ mi. w. of Browning at jct. US 2 and 89, 13 mi. from Glacier National Park.

The Plains Indians fought more than fifty years against the U.S. Army. Free.

## BUTTE

BIG HOLE NATIONAL BATTLEFIELD, s.e. of Butte on SR 43, 12 mi. w. of Wisdom. Or s. of Missoula, 17 mi. e. of US 93.

The traditional homeland of the Nez Perce Indians in Idaho was overrun by settlers and gold miners, forcing the Indians onto ever smaller reservations until Chief Joseph revolted, bringing about the tragic Nez Perce War of 1877. The Nez Perce were victorious in their first battles with the U.S. Army and headed east to join the Crow tribe in Montana. The Army pursued them, and at Big Hole Valley, the Nez Perce suffered heavy losses in a before-dawn battle. Chief Joseph escaped with some of his people and sought sanctuary by retreating toward Canada. Visitor center, exhibits, tours. Free.

# EXPLORING MILITARY AMERICA

## FORT BENTON

FORT BENTON HISTORIC DISTRICT, US 87, e. of Great Falls.

A fur-trading post and an important river port on the Missouri River when gold fields in Montana were supplied by riverboat, Fort Benton was also a military post. Fort ruins, museum, exhibits. May 15–Sept. 15. Free.

## HAVRE

CHIEF JOSEPH BATTLEFIELD OF THE BEAR PAW STATE MONUMENT, 22 mi. e. of Havre on US 2, 16 mi. s. of Chinook.

On September 30, 1877, at Bear Paw Mountain, the Army under Colonel Miles again caught up with Chief Joseph and his band of Nez Perce Indians. After five days of fighting, the Nez Perce surrendered, more from exhaustion than defeat. Of the 800 Nez Perce who had fought their way to within three miles of Canada, only 480 were still alive. It was after this battle that a war-weary Chief Joseph sent his now-famous statement to Colonel Miles: "From where the sun now stands, I will fight no more forever."

Interpretive markers. Free.

# Nebraska

Coronado's expedition claimed the Nebraska area for Spain in 1541, but later fur traders supported French claims. After the Louisiana Purchase in 1803, the Lewis and Clark Expedition explored the region. The Yellowstone Expedition of 1819 established Fort Atkinson, although Major Stephen H. Long called the area "a great desert." Later the rich Nebraska land brought a surge of immigrants, whose appearance was contested by the great war chiefs of the Sioux and Cheyenne. By 1876, the Indians had ceded their lands in Nebraska, although sporadic fighting continued until about 1890. The military forts in Nebraska served as a basis for frontier defense during the Civil War, although they were often manned by volunteers or "Galvanized Yankees," Confederate soldiers who chose western duty rather than Union imprisonment.

★ ★ ★

# EXPLORING MILITARY AMERICA

## BELLEVUE

STRATEGIC AIR COMMAND MUSEUM, 2510 Clay St.

The SAC Museum covers the history of the Strategic Air Command and the United States Air Force from Kitty Hawk to human ascent into space. A five-screen reenactment shows what actually happens during a SAC red alert.

Museum, outdoor displays. Admission.

## BURWELL

FORT HARTSUFF STATE HISTORICAL PARK.

Duty at this fort was considered one of the more pleasant assignments in the Department of the Platte from 1874–1881. The major encounter with hostile Indians occurred in 1876 at the Battle of the Blow-Out with the Sioux.

Museum, guided tours. Apr.–Oct. Free.

## CRAWFORD

FORT ROBINSON STATE PARK, 3½ mi. w. on US 20.

The fort was built in 1874, about a mile from the Red Cloud Indian agency, and the troops at the post were active during the 1876 Sioux campaign. In 1877 Chief Crazy Horse of the Oglala Sioux was killed at Fort Robinson, fighting imprisonment. The garrison at Fort Robinson was also involved in the tragic Cheyenne escape attempt from the fort. The Cheyenne were killed against the bluffs behind the fort, choosing death over returning to the Oklahoma Reservation from which they had fled. In 1890, troops from Fort Robinson rode against the Sioux in the Ghost Dance uprisings, an Indian religious movement, which included the belief that wearing the ghost dance shirt made a warrior magically bulletproof. Fort Robinson was not abandoned at the end of the Indian wars but continued in existence as a remount depot and in World War II as a German POW camp.

Restored fort, museum, tours to nearby Red Cloud Indian Agency. Apr. 1–Nov. 15, or by appt. rest of year. Free.

# NEBRASKA

In the town of Crawford in the City Park is the CRAZY HORSE MUSEUM with Sioux Indian relics. Free.

## FORT CALHOUN

FORT ATKINSON STATE HISTORICAL PARK, off US 73, 1 mi. e. of town of Fort Calhoun, also n. of Omaha.

In 1804 the Lewis and Clark expedition camped at Council Bluffs, site of the fort. The Yellowstone Expedition, exploring the Rocky Mountain region, spent the winter of 1819–20 here; during the winter over 100 members of the expedition died. A flood forced movement of the fort from the original to present site. At one time the fort was the largest post in the West, with a garrison of over 1,000 soldiers.

Archaeological excavations at fort site. Museum at Fort Calhoun. Free.

## OMAHA

GENERAL GEORGE CROOK HOUSE, Fort Omaha, on Fort St. off 30th or I-680 30th St. Exit s. to Fort.

General Crook was one of the greatest Indian fighters the Army ever had. He fought the Apaches in Arizona, the Sioux in the Black Hills and the Paiute Indians in the Pacific Northwest. He was also one of the few military men who tried to treat the Indians fairly, protecting them when he could. Red Cloud said of General Crook, "He never lied to us. His words gave the people hope."

General Crook's home at Fort Omaha has been made into a museum with artifacts demonstrating the life style of the Commanding Officer of a major frontier post. There are also exhibits on the history of Fort Omaha, built in 1868.

Thurs.–Sun. afternoons only, or by appt. Admission.

# Nevada

Nevada was the last area within the boundaries of the lower forty-eight states to be explored. In 1776, Spanish missionaries are believed to have crossed southern Nevada, and in the early 1800s, fur trapper Jedediah Smith and explorers Joseph Walker and John Charles Fremont led expeditions in the area. In 1848, Mexico ceded the Nevada area to the United States. Settlers moving into the area combined with an uprising of the Paiute Indians, led to the establishment of Fort Churchill, which also acted as a supply depot for the Union in the Civil War.

★ ★ ★

### LAS VEGAS

LAS VEGAS MORMON FORT, 900 Las Vegas Blvd. North.

Only part of original structure remains of this fort, which was established as a halfway station on the Mormon trail in 1855. Eight houses were built within its walls. The Mormons abandoned the fort when they returned to Utah.

Museum of early Nevada history. Free.

# NEVADA

## NIXON

PYRAMID LAKE WAR MARKER, across street from Nixon post office.

Warfare broke out between the Paiute Indians and white miners and traders when two Indian girls were abducted. The miners organized into a volunteer company and marched north into Paiute country around Pyramid Lake and into an ambush that killed 46 of the volunteers. Later, regular troops fought the Paiutes in a three-hour battle, and Fort Churchill was established to prevent further Indian problems. The battle area is 4 miles southwest of the lake and south of Nixon and is largely unchanged. Free.

## SILVER SPRINGS

FORT CHURCHILL HISTORIC STATE MONUMENT, 8 mi. s. of Silver Springs off US 95 Alt.

Fort Churchill served as a home base for frontier soldiers between expeditions against the Indians and was also a station on the Pony Express Route and a supply depot during the Civil War. The outpost was abandoned in 1871, and the adobe buildings of the fort fell into picturesque ruins.

Visitor center, exhibits. Free.

# New Hampshire

The first European explorers and settlers in New Hampshire were English. In the early 1700s they built forts for protection against French and Indian attacks but the raids ceased only when Robert Rogers of New Hampshire and his Rogers Rangers wiped out the St. Francis Indian village in Quebec. New Hampshire struck an early blow for independence in 1774, even before the battles of Lexington and Concord, by capturing the British Fort William and Mary. In the War of 1812, New Hampshire recruited 35,000 men and outfitted 14 privateer ships. The state sent 39,000 men to fight for the Union in the Civil War, three times its required quota.

★ ★ ★

**CHARLESTOWN**

OLD FORT NO. FOUR, SR 11, 1 mi. n. of Charlestown.

In 1744, the settlers at what is now Charlestown built a log fort enclosing many of the town's dwellings. This sheltered them during the Indian raids of 1746. During the King George's War, the fort,

# NEW HAMPSHIRE

garrisoned by a troop of militia, was besieged by a large force of French and Indians, who were beaten off after a three-day battle.

Replica of stockade, historic buildings and great hall, exhibits, tours. Mid-June–Labor Day. Weekends, preseason from mid-May and postseason to mid-Oct. Admission.

## CONCORD

STATE HOUSE, Main St.

The rotunda of the State House has a display of battle flags and portraits of New Hampshire officers who served in the Civil War. New Hampshire had a landslide of volunteers for the Union Army; the Fifth New Hampshire Volunteers had more casualties than any other regiment in the Union Army. Closed weekends. Free.

## DOVER

WAR MEMORIAL ROOM, Woodman Institute, 182 Central Ave.

Exhibits from all American wars in which New Hampshire men and women have been engaged. Free.

## HAMPTON BEACH

NEW HAMPSHIRE MARINE MEMORIAL.

A shrine to the memory of New Hampshire sons and daughters who lost their lives at sea, serving their country.

## NEW CASTLE

FORT CONSTITUTION, near intersection of SR 1-B and Wentworth St.

First constructed for protection against pirates in the seventeenth century and originally called Fort William and Mary, in December 1774, this fortress saw one of the earliest armed encounters of the Revolutionary War. Several hundred "Sons of Liberty" overpowered the British garrison at the fort and carried off 100 barrels of gunpowder, some of which was used at the battle of Bunker Hill. During

# EXPLORING MILITARY AMERICA

the war, the fort's name was changed to Fort Hancock, then Fort Constitution. During the War of 1812, a brick Martello tower was built overnight at Fort Constitution, which scared off three British warships. The fort was garrisoned and enlarged during the Civil War and continued to be garrisoned through World War II. The Coast Guard has taken over the historic fort and access to Fort Constitution may be obtained from the staff at the Coast Guard Station. Free.

## RINDGE

CATHEDRAL OF THE PINES WAR MEMORIAL, 2 mi. n.e.

Two national war memorials, the Altar of the Nation, a national memorial for all American war dead, and the Memorial Bell Tower, a national memorial specifically honoring all women war dead, may be visited May through November. Free.

# New Jersey

Beginning in 1524, the French, then Dutch, then Swedish flags flew over New Jersey; but in 1664, the British acquired the colony. In the mid-1750s, the French and Indian War unified the American colonists and the British military against their common enemies, the French and French-allied Indians. In 1774, New Jersey started the American Revolution early, burning a British tea ship at the mouth of the Delaware River, an event called "the Greenwich Tea Party." Nearly 100 Revolutionary War battles and skirmishes were fought in New Jersey. Although there was dissension in the state in the Civil War, New Jersey had abolished slavery in 1846, and volunteer recruitment made a military draft unnecessary.

★ ★ ★

**DOVER**

PICATINNY ARSENAL AMMUNITION MUSEUM, Picatinny Arsenal, SR 15,
\*    1 mi. to entrance.

# EXPLORING MILITARY AMERICA

Collection presents a history of American and foreign-made ammunition from early to modern-day wars.

Friday only or by appointment. Free.

## FORT LEE

FORT LEE HISTORIC PARK, Hudson Ter. in Palisades Interstate Park, just south of the George Washington Bridge.

Fort Lee was part of the fortifications erected by order of George Washington for the defense of New York and the Hudson River. After a large British force captured nearby Fort Washington in November, 1776, Washington realized that Fort Lee had to be abandoned or its troops would suffer the same fate. The Continentals stationed at Fort Lee just managed to escape before the arrival of the British, leaving most of their supplies and artillery behind. The disastrous fall of Fort Lee marked the start of the British invasion of New Jersey and Washington's retreat to Pennsylvania.

Historic fort, visitor center, exhibits, tours. Free.

## FORT MONMOUTH

U.S. ARMY COMMUNICATIONS-ELECTRONICS MUSEUM, in Myer Hall, Avenue of Memories, Fort Monmouth, 50 mi. s. of New York City off Route 35 and Garden State Pkwy.

The collection covers the history of military communications from the primitive flag and mirror system used during the Revolution to the sophisticated electronics communications used by the U.S. Army Signal Corps today. Closed weekends. Free.

## FREEHOLD

MONMOUTH BATTLEFIELD STATE PARK, n.w. on SR 522.

One of the best-preserved of the Revolutionary War battlefields, Monmouth was the last major battle fought in the North and was a turning point of the American Revolution. British General Clinton had abandoned Philadelphia and marched toward the New Jersey

# NEW JERSEY

coast with General Washington in close pursuit. The two armies met on the fields around Monmouth Courthouse on June 28, 1777, in the longest sustained action of the war. Although Clinton managed to escape, the American continental soldier proved he was the equal of the British regular.

Battlefield, visitor center, exhibits. Free.

Several historic sites are located near the battlefield, including the VILLAGE INN at Englishtown, which was Washington's headquarters during the battle, the OLD TENNENT CHURCH, which served as a temporary hospital and burial ground, and COBB HOUSE, which now is an information center with an electrified topographical map of the troop movements during the battle. On the north side of SR 522, near the battlefield, is the legendary Molly Pitcher's spring and well. Molly carried water to the soldiers during the battle, and when her husband fell wounded, she took his place firing the cannon.

## HACKENSACK

U.S.S. LING, NEW JERSEY SUBMARINE MEMORIAL, Borg Park on the Hackensack River, intersection of Court and River Sts.

*U.S.S. Ling* is one of the fleet-type submarines that patroled our shores during World War II. The U.S. Navy had a total of 288 submarines in operation during the war, of which 52 were lost.. The *U.S.S. Ling* is maintained as a memorial to submariners throughout the world.

Tour, museum, outdoor display of naval military equipment. Admission.

## MORRISTOWN

MORRISTOWN NATIONAL HISTORICAL PARK.

During the winters of 1776–77 and 1779–80, Washington struggled desperately to hold his ragged Continental Army together in the bleak hills around Morristown. The winter of 1779–80 was the worst in a century. Food supplies dwindled, and starvation confronted the beleaguered army. Primitive huts offered little protection against the cold, and sickness added to the ordeal. The hard winter so destroyed the morale of both officers and enlisted men that a mutiny occurred, and the soldiers marched on the Continental Congress in Philadelphia, demanding food and pay. Somehow the army managed to survive and fought again in the spring.

Reconstructed encampment, fort, historic homes, museum. Free.

## NATIONAL PARK

RED BANK BATTLEFIELD, 1 mi. from the town of National Park. Take National Park exit from I-295, 2 mi. to battlefield.

On an October afternoon in 1777, the largest Revolutionary battle in South Jersey took place on a high bluff overlooking the Delaware River. The British had occupied Philadelphia (at that time the capital of America); but Fort Mercer on the New Jersey side and Fort Mifflin on the Pennsylvania side of the Delaware prevented enemy supplies from reaching Philadelphia. A brigade of 1200 Hessian soldiers attacked Fort Mercer, but a 19-year-old blacksmith, Jonas Cattell, had run nine miles to warn the fort of the enemy approach. Consequently, the commander had time to build a new "surprise" wall and trenches inside the fort, along with an abatis of sharpened tree trunks. Because of Cattell's warning, the defenders of the fort killed or wounded over 500 Hessians, and suffered only 36 casualties themselves. Although the British eventually captured Fort Mercer after heavy bombardment, the victory at Red Bank raised the morale of Washington's army and encouraged the French to enter the war as an ally of America.

Battlefield, interpretive markers, museum. Free.

## PRINCETON

PRINCETON BATTLEFIELD STATE PARK, SR 583.

Washington's surprise attack on the British on January 3, 1777, occurred on the south edge of the town of Princeton. The fighting was so fierce that one British regiment sought refuge at nearby Prince-

# NEW JERSEY

ton University's Nassau Hall. The hall was used during the war as a barracks and hospital. The battle area at Princeton has been preserved, and Clark House still stands at the edge of the field. It was at this house that General Hugh Mercer died of wounds suffered in the battle. A memorial arch marks the burial site of unknown American soldiers killed in the battle.

Interpretive markers, historic house. Free.

## SALEM

FORT MOTT STATE PARK, 3 mi. n.w. on SR 49.

The fort was used during the Civil War for the defense of the Delaware River and Philadelphia. Gun mounts and underground fortifications may still be seen. Adjacent to the fort is Finns Point National Cemetery, which contains the graves of more than 2,000 Confederate prisoners of war. Free.

## TRENTON

THE OLD BARRACKS, South Willow and Front Sts.

Five fieldstone barracks were built in New Jersey to house British soldiers during the French and Indian War. The barracks at Trenton is the only one to survive. British troops, Hessian mercenaries and American soldiers were all billeted at the Old Barracks during the Revolutionary War, as the war moved back and forth across the state. Hessian soldiers were at the Old Barracks when the Battle of Trenton was fought not far from the barracks in the early hours of December 26, 1776.

Restored eighteenth-century barracks, museum. Admission.

WASHINGTON CROSSING STATE PARK, 8 mi. n.w. of Trenton on SR 29 on the banks of the Delaware River.

On Christmas night, 1776, in a bold surprise move, General Washington crossed the Delaware River with 2,400 men. The next morning they routed the British garrison in winter quarters at Trenton, capturing over 900 Hessian mercenaries. This brilliant victory, along

# EXPLORING MILITARY AMERICA

with Washington's successful attack on Princeton a few days later, brought new hope to the patriot cause. The point where Washington's troops made their historic crossing is now a state park, and the Continental Lane, over which American troops marched on that memorable night from the ferry landing, may be retraced.

Flag museum and ferry house. Hours vary. Free.

# New Mexico

In the sixteenth century, Spanish explorers invaded New Mexico; they founded Santa Fe in 1610. Later in the seventeenth century, the Indians forced the Spanish from New Mexico, but the Spanish returned with a stronger military force and the reconquest was completed by 1696. In 1821, New Mexico became part of the new Mexico Republic, and in the same year the first wagon trains arrived in Santa Fe from Missouri. New Mexico became a part of the United States in 1848, after the Mexican War. The area was kept on the Union side in the Civil War by the defeat of Confederate forces at Glorieta Pass. In 1916 Mexican revolutionary Pancho Villa attacked Columbus, New Mexico, which brought about the unsuccessful punitive American expedition after Villa into Mexico. In 1945, the world's first atomic bomb, forecasting the terror of future weapons and warfare, was test-exploded in the White Sands area.

★ ★ ★

# EXPLORING MILITARY AMERICA

## ALAMOGORDO

INTERNATIONAL SPACE HALL OF FAME, 2 mi. n.e.

Exhibits honor military and civilian space pioneers from every nation involved in rockets and space exploration. Outdoor displays are offered of space launch vehicles and spacecraft. Admission.

## ALBUQUERQUE

NATIONAL ATOMIC MUSEUM, Bldg. 358, Main Street, Kirtland AFB, southeast section of Albuquerque.

This unique museum has a permanent exhibit of nuclear weapons from their beginning at the first man-made atomic explosion near Alamogordo in July, 1945.

Free.

RESCUE MEMORIAL MUSEUM, Chapman Hall, Kirtland AFB.

One of the newest military museums, the collection includes exhibits of Air Force rescue units and activities dating back to the Korean conflict. Closed weekends. Free.

## COLUMBUS

PANCHO VILLA MUSEUM, Pancho Villa State Park.

The Mexican insurgent "Pancho" Villa made a surprise attack on the town of Columbus in March, 1916. General John Pershing was sent on a punitive expedition into Mexico after Villa. The expedition never did catch Villa, but it did give many army officers field experience and a chance to experiment with such new military novelties as field radios and airplanes. The First Aero Squadron was formed during this expedition. The military experience gained in Mexico proved useful in World War I.

Museum. Admission.

## FORT SUMNER

FORT SUMNER, 6 mi. e. on US 60.

In 1862, captive Navajos were marched about 400 miles to the infamous Bosque Redondo Reservation at Fort Sumner, a march that

# NEW MEXICO

is still referred to by the Navajos as the "Long Walk." Life at the reservation for the Indians was harsh, and thousands died. Finally, in 1868, the Navajos were allowed to return to their homeland.

Visitor center, exhibits. Admission.

## HOBBS

CONFEDERATE AIR FORCE MUSEUM (NEW MEXICO WING). Lea County and Hobbs Airport.

A display of World War II aircraft, which are not only exhibited but actually flown. Free.

## LAS CRUCES

WHITE SANDS MISSILE RANGE, 27 mi. n.e. on SR 70.

It was at White Sands Missile Range that the first man-made atomic explosion took place, moving warfare into the atomic age. Missile Range open daily with guided tours during the summers on Saturdays at 2 p.m. Free.

## LAS VEGAS

ROUGH RIDERS MEMORIAL AND CITY MUSEUM, Municipal Bldg.

Theodore Roosevelt and his Rough Riders, along with two black cavalry regiments, rode into history when they made their famous, successful charge up San Juan Hill (actually Kettle Hill) in Cuba during the Spanish American War. The battles of San Juan Hill and El Caney were the two decisive land battles of that war. Mementos of President Roosevelt and the Rough Riders are part of this museum collection. Free.

## MOUNTAINAIR

QUARAI STATE MONUMENT, 8 mi. n.w. on SR 14 and 1 mi. w.

Built in 1630, the Spanish mission here was abandoned in 1672 after numerous Apache raids. Unlike the Pueblo Indians, the Apaches

# EXPLORING MILITARY AMERICA

never accepted the Christian religion, but they did adopt quickly one Spanish import, the horse, which made the Apaches a deadly military threat to the Spanish and later the American army.

Visitor center, museum. Free.

## SANTA FE

MISSION OF SAN MIGUEL OF SANTA FE, Old Santa Fe trail and East De Vargas Sts.

When the Spanish military came into New Mexico, the Franciscan priests came too. They set up fortresslike missions and attempted to convert the Indians to Christianity. One of the first such missions was at Santa Fe in 1610. The thick adobe walls, however, did not stop the mission from being burned by the Pueblo Indians in the Rebellion of 1680, which temporarily drove the Spanish out of New Mexico.

Restored mission. Free.

GLORIETA PASS BATTLEFIELD, 10 mi. s.e. of Santa Fe on US 84-85.

The battle at Glorieta Pass in March 1862 ended the Confederate invasion of New Mexico. Union forces destroyed a Southern wagon train and supplies. Key positions of the battle site are still visible. Interpretive markers. Free.

## TAOS

MISSION SAN GERONIMO DE TAOS, 2½ mi. n. of Taos Plaza.

The walled mission of San Geronimo de Taos was burned in the 1680 Pueblo Rebellion, along with other Spanish missions in New Mexico. The mission was rebuilt by the Spaniards, but it was later destroyed again, this time by U.S. troops during the Mexican War.

Mission ruins. Free.

One block north of Taos Plaza is the GOVERNOR BENT HOUSE, which was the scene of a skirmish during the Mexican War. Led by Mexican insurgents, a group of Taos Indians revolted against the newly established American rule and killed and scalped Governor Bent in his home. Admission.

# NEW MEXICO

**WATROUS**

FORT UNION NATIONAL MONUMENT, 8 mi. n. of I-25 at the end of SR 477.

The Apaches, Kiowas and Comanches had long been formidable military foes of the Spanish and Mexicans. After New Mexico was ceded to the United States at the close of the Mexican War, the Indians fought just as fiercely against the Americans. As a result, Fort Union was built in 1851; it soon became one of the most important army posts in the Southwest. From it the army launched extensive military campaigns including Colonel Cooke's battle against the Apaches in 1854, and Colonel Kit Carson's battle with the Navajos at Canyon de Chelly. General Sheridan used mounted riflemen from Fort Union in 1868 as part of the Red River War on the Staked Plains. During the Civil War, Confederate forces tried to capture Fort Union but were stopped at Glorieta Pass, leaving New Mexico in Union hands.

Ruins of fort, museum, tours. Free.

# New York

Before the coming of the white man there was in the New York area a Confederacy made up of the Five Indian Nations of Seneca, Mohawk, Cayuga, Oneida and Onondaga tribes. Into these Indian lands came the French in the sixteenth century, followed by the Dutch and English in the seventeenth century. By 1674, English control was dominant, but their settlements and forts were challenged by fierce French and Indian attacks, both before and during the French and Indian War. Almost one-third of the battles of the Revolutionary War took place in New York State, and during the War of 1812, New York was attacked again, both by land and sea. In spite of violent draft riots in New York City during the Civil War, the state sent 500,000 men to the Union Army; one tenth of them died in service.

★ ★ ★

# NEW YORK

## ALBANY

SARATOGA NATIONAL HISTORICAL PARK, 30 mi. n. of Albany on US 4 and SR 32. 8 mi. s. of Schuylerville on US 4. Travelers using I-87 should take Exit 12.

Between September 19 and October 17, 1777, British General Burgoyne's army invaded New York from Canada. His British regulars and German mercenaries were defeated at the battle of Saratoga by American continentals and militia under General Horatio Gates. One of "the turning points of the Revolutionary War," the victory at Saratoga brought the surrender of Burgoyne's army and encouraged French support for the American cause.

Visitor center on Fraser Hill, exhibits, Saratoga Battle Monument, battlefield, General Philip Schuyler House, guided and self-guided tours. House open June 15–Labor Day. Admission. Saratoga National Historical Park open all year. Free.

NEW YORK STATE MILITARY MUSEUM, 2nd floor of the State Capitol in Albany.

One of the largest collections of Civil War relics, battle flags and regimental colors in the country. Closed weekends. Free.

## BROOKLYN

HARBOR DEFENSE MUSEUM, Fort Hamilton. Take I-278 to the last exit before the Verrazano Bridge.

Museum is housed in the battery of the original Fort Hamilton (1825), a seacoast defense fort. Exhibits tell story of coastal defense in the United States from the seventeenth century to present day.

Afternoons only. Free.

## BUFFALO

NAVAL AND SERVICEMEN'S PARK, Waterfront at Maine St. and S. Park Ave.

Self-guided tours of the *U.S.S. The Sullivans,* a World War II destroyer, and the *U.S.S. Little Rock,* a World War II cruiser.

May 1–mid-Oct. Admission.

# EXPLORING MILITARY AMERICA

## CHERRY VALLEY

CHERRY VALLEY MUSEUM, 45 Main St.

In November, 1778, 700 Tories and Seneca Indians attacked the Cherry Valley settlement, killing 48—including women and children as well as Continental soldiers—and taking forty captives. More children would have been killed but for the heroism of slaves who carried a number of children to safety in the nearby forest.

Museum, monuments marking mass grave of settlers killed. Memorial Day–Oct. 15, by appt. rest of year. Admission to museum.

## CROWN POINT

FORT CROWN POINT STATE HISTORICAL SITE, Crown Point Reservation, 7½ mi. n.e. on SR 8 w. of the s. end of Lake Champlain Bridge.

Fort Crown Point is considered one of the best existing examples of eighteenth century military engineering in America. Included in the Crown Point Reservation are the ruins of Fort Crown Point and Fort St. Frederic (built by the French in 1731). The British captured the French fort in 1759 and began construction of a British fort, called Fort Amherst, or Crown Point. During the American Revolution, the Sixth Pennsylvania Battalion occupied the fort until forced to withdraw to Fort Ticonderoga by General Burgoyne. Most of the cannon that the Americans captured at Fort Ticonderoga and sent to help Washington's siege of Boston were originally from Crown Point.

Well-preserved remains of fort, visitor center, museum. Mid-May–Oct. 15, rest of year by appointment. Grounds open all year. Free. Also, ruins of Fort St. Frederic and museum, located junction of SR 8 and 9 N, Crown Point.

## FORT EDWARD

OLD FORT HOUSE, 29 Lower Broadway, ½ mi. s. on US 4.

Fortified house (1772) was headquarters for Generals Schuyler, Arnold, Washington, Burgoyne and Stark. July 1–Aug. 31; by appointment rest of year. Donations.

# NEW YORK

## FORT JOHNSON

OLD FORT JOHNSON, SR 5 w. of jct. SR 67.

Fortified stone home of Sir William Johnson, 1749–63, British Indian commissioner and commander of 1755 expedition against Crown Point, halting French invasion of New York. His son was a Loyalist during the American Revolution, and patriots seized the home and stripped the lead roof for bullets.

Museum. May 1–Oct. 31. Admission.

## FORT PLAIN

FORT PLAIN MUSEUM. Take exit 29, New York State Thruway (Interstate 90) at Canajoharie, then w. 2 miles.

Museum includes model of blockhouse, artist's representation of the Revolutionary War fort and archaeological excavation. Admission.

## HERKIMER

HERKIMER COUNTY HISTORICAL SOCIETY, 400 N. Main St.

Museum of military relics from Colonial, Revolutionary, Civil Wars and both World Wars. Closed weekends. Free. Also at Herkimer is REPLICA OF 1776 FORT DAYTON, where forces under General Herkimer gathered before Battle of Oriskany in 1777.

## HUNTINGTON

NATHAN HALE MEMORIAL MONUMENT, 1 mi. n. of SR 25A on SR 110, Long Island.

Monument marks spot where patriot spy was captured during the Revolutionary War, September 21, 1776, and hanged the following morning. His last words are said to have been, "I only regret that I have but one life to lose for my country."

# EXPLORING MILITARY AMERICA

## JOHNSTOWN

JOHNSON HALL STATE HISTORIC SITE, ¼ mi. w. on Hall Ave.

Sir William Johnson, British Indian Commissioner, held council with six Iroquois Indian Nation tribes on grounds of this house. To the north is site of Battle of Johnstown, fought in October, 1781.

Museum, stone blockhouse. Free.

## KINGS POINT

UNITED STATES MERCHANT MARINE ACADEMY, Steamboat Road, facing Long Island Sound.

This training institute for Merchant Marine and Naval Reserve has on its grounds the United States Merchant Marine Memorial Chapel and Merchant Marine Museum, which includes commemoration of over 700 ships sunk in enemy action and over 5,000 merchant marines killed in World War II.

Museum. Free.

## LAKE GEORGE VILLAGE

FORT WILLIAM HENRY, ½ mi. s. on US 9.

This fort was built in 1755 after a bloody fight between English and French Indians for the area. French General Montcalm sent troops to attack the fort in March, 1757, but they were defeated by deep snows. The French attacked again later in 1757, with 8,000 men from Fort Carillon, and the fort surrendered after a six-day siege. Despite Montcalm's efforts, the English garrison of Fort William Henry was massacred by Montcalm's Indian allies from 33 different Indian nations. During the American Revolution, both British and American troops camped in the ruins of the fort. General George Washington in 1783 made a remark at the site that there was "a lot of history under this ground."

Reproduction 1755 fort, museum. May 1–Oct. 10. Admission.

# NEW YORK

LAKE GEORGE BATTLEFIELD PARK, ½ mi. s. off US 9.

In battle in September 1755, British Sir William Johnson defeated French Canadians and Indians at this site, and in 1759, General Amherst erected Fort George and was eventually successful in capturing Fort Ticonderoga. The Americans captured Fort George in 1775, and in that same year, Benjamin Franklin and several other Americans left from here to try, unsuccessfully, to win Canadians as allies in the American Revolution. In 1780, the British captured the fort, but abandoned it after the British defeat at Yorktown.

Ruins of Fort George, monuments. Memorial Day–Labor Day. Admission.

## NARROWSBURG

FORT DELAWARE, ¾ mi. n. on SR 97.

All that remains of the fort is a stockade with blockhouse enclosing three log cabins and various fort buildings, including an armory and gun platform. The fort was the first stockaded settlement in the Upper Delaware Valley, 1755–85.

Remains of stockade town, museum, June 27–Sept. 3. Admission.

## NEWBURGH

NEW WINDSOR CANTONMENT STATE HISTORIC SITE, 1 mi. n. of Vails Gate on Temple Hill Rd.

A winter encampment of American forces in the Revolution, including reconstructed camp and exhibits. Apr. 15–Oct. 31. Free. Also at Newburgh is KNOX HEADQUARTERS, 4½ mi. s.w. on SR 94, occupied by Generals Washington, Knox and Gates during the American Revolution, and WASHINGTON HEADQUARTERS STATE HISTORIC SITE, Washington and Liberty Sts. The Army disbanded at the end of the Revolution at this site and grounds contain the Tower of Victory and State Museum. Both Knox and Washington Headquarters are free.

# EXPLORING MILITARY AMERICA

## NEW YORK CITY

CASTLE CLINTON NATIONAL MONUMENT, Battery Park, Manhattan.

This fort was completed in 1811 in the midst of the "fortification fever" that swept New York at the time the British were seizing American ships and impressing seamen. Five new forts were built: Fort Wood on Bedloe's Island, Fort Gibson on Ellis Island, Castle Williams on Governors Island, Southwest Battery at tip of Manhattan Island, and North Battery at foot of Hubert Street. Castle Clinton, then called West Battery, was U.S. Army headquarters in War of 1812.

Reconstructed fort, exhibits. Memorial Day–Labor Day. Closed Fri. and Sat., rest of year. Free. Also at Battery Park, EAST COAST MEMORIAL, with names of thousands of American military who died at sea in World War II.

MORRIS-JUMEL MANSION, 160th St. and Edgecombe Ave.

This pre-Revolutionary War mansion is the major surviving landmark of the Battle of Harlem Heights, New York, September 1776, in which the British were forced to retreat. House was Washington's headquarters during battle. Restored home. Admission.

FRAUNCES TAVERN, 54 Pearl St. (Pearl and Broad Sts.)

Tavern scene of Washington's farewell to officers of the Continental Army, December 7, 1783. Museum, 2d fl. of restaurant. Free.

## NORTH HOOSICK

BENNINGTON BATTLEFIELD, 2¼ mi e. on SR 67.

Revolutionary General John Stark and New England militia in 1777 captured British Hessian force here. Markers. Early Spring–late Fall. Free.

## OSWEGO

FORT ONTARIO STATE HISTORIC SITE, 3 blocks n. of SR 104 on E. 7th.

First built by the British in 1755, captured by the French in 1756, then rebuilt by the British, the fort served as base for the

# NEW YORK

British in the French and Indian War and Revolutionary War. The present fortification, the third on the site, was built in 1839, constructed of cut stone blocks, pentagonal in plan with arrow-shaped bastions at each corner. The fort remained active until 1946.

Restored fort, visitor center, exhibits. Apr. 15–Oct. 31. Admission.

## OYSTER BAY

RAYNHAM HALL, 20 W. Main St., Long Island.

British headquarters during the Revolution, winter of 1778, this was the home of Samuel Townsend. Townsend was partly responsible for the capture of British spy Major Andre and for discovering Benedict Arnold's plan to betray West Point to British. Admission.

## PLATTSBURGH

KENT DELORD HOUSE, 17 Cumberland Ave. and Museum, 3rd fl. City Hall.

The Battle of Valcour, during the Revolutionary War, took place 5 miles south of Plattsburgh, an American defeat that nevertheless prevented a British advance. During the War of 1812, the first full-scale naval battle took place in Plattsburgh Bay in September, 1814. General Macomb fought a superior British force on land while the American fleet of Commodore MacDonough defeated the British on the lakes. The Kent DeLord House was British headquarters during the War of 1812. Admission to house/museum. At CITY HALL MUSEUM exhibits on Battles of Valcour and Plattsburgh. Limited hours. Free. MACDONOUGH MONUMENT, commemorating hero of naval battle, open May 15–Oct. 15. Free.

## RENSSELAER

FORT CRAILO, 9½ Riverside Ave. s. of Aiken Ave.

Fortified Dutch Manor House (1704) was used by British dur-

# EXPLORING MILITARY AMERICA

ing French and Indian War as training center. According to legend, words to "Yankee Doodle" were composed here in 1758.

Museum. Free.

## ROME

FORT STANWIX NATIONAL MONUMENT, Dominick, Spring, Liberty, James Sts.

Originally British (1758), Fort Stanwix was rebuilt and garrisoned by George Washington in 1776; it was attacked in August 1777 by British, Tories and Indians. A relief force from Saratoga, under Benedict Arnold, arrived after an earlier relief force of militia was ambushed at Oriskany. In 1784, the fort was the site of a treaty that ended fighting with the Iroquois.

Reconstructed fort, museum at 207 N. James St. in City Hall. Admission to museum. Fort free.

ORISKANY BATTLEFIELD, 5 mi. e. of Rome, 2 mi. w. of Oriskany on SR 69.

In the summer of 1777, the British planned to attack Albany but met resistance at Fort Stanwix. General Herkimer, commander of the Mohawk Valley militia, set forth with 800 men to relieve the fort. Herkimer's men were ambushed by a large force of Tories, and for six hours fought what has been called "the bloodiest battle of the Revolution." The Tories won, but had to return to Fort Stanwix.

Exhibits, tours. Free.

## ROUSES POINT

FORT MONTGOMERY (FORT BLUNDER) 1 mi. s. of Canadian border on Island Point.

Fort Montgomery was more aptly named Fort Blunder because the fort's construction was abandoned in 1819 when it was learned that the site at that time belonged to Canada. Fort ruins. Free.

# NEW YORK

## SACKETS HARBOR

SACKETS HARBOR BATTLEFIELD STATE HISTORIC SITE.

Here American forces under Brigadier General Jacob Brown repulsed a British landing and attack under Sir George Prevost, Governor-General of Canada, in the War of 1812. A later attempt from here, under American Major General James Wilkinson, to seize Montreal was a fiasco.

Museum, tours. Admission.

## ST. JOHNSVILLE

FORT KLOCK, 2 blocks e. on SR 5.

The fortified fur-trading post built by John Klock was used as refuge by Mohawk Valley settlers in the Revolution. Battle of Klock's Field was fought nearby in October, 1780, with Indians and British raiders driven off by American militia under General Van Rensselaer.

Restored fortified house. Admission.

## SCHOHARIE

OLD STONE FORT, 1 mi. n. on N. Main St.

This church was fortified during the Revolution to protect settlers. Blackened hole in wall is a memento of bloody attack in 1780 by 800 British, Tories and Indians.

Museum in church. May 1–Oct. 31. Admission.

## STATEN ISLAND

CONFERENCE HOUSE, foot of 7455 Hylan Blvd., Tottenville.

In September 1776, British and American representatives met here with British Lord Howe in the only peace conference of the Revolution. Howe offered peace and amnesty if America dissolved its armies and withdrew the Declaration of Independence. The American representatives, including Benjamin Franklin and John Adams, refused. Admission.

# EXPLORING MILITARY AMERICA

BATTERY REED (FORT RICHMOND), Fort Washington Reservation.

This nineteenth century fort, constructed of slabs of granite, was garrisoned during the Civil War; mounting 150 cannon, it was one of the most powerful forts on the eastern seaboard. Free.

## STONY POINT

STONY POINT BATTLEFIELD STATE HISTORIC SITE, 3¼ mi. n.e. off US 9W.

American General "Mad" Anthony Wayne led a "cold steel" bayonet charge of this British stronghold July 16, 1779 and captured the garrison of 575 soldiers.

Museum, earthworks. June 1–Oct. 31. Free.

## TAPPAN

GEORGE WASHINGTON MASONIC SHRINE, Livingston Ave. and Oak Tree Rd.

This building was used several times as army headquarters of General Washington during the Revolution. Nearby is '76 HOUSE where British spy Major Andre was imprisoned and the TAPPAN REFORMED (DUTCH) CHURCH where his court-martial trial was held. Free.

## TICONDEROGA

FORT TICONDEROGA (FORT CARILLON), entrance 1 mi. n.e. of village of Ticonderoga on SR 74, 20 mi. e. of Exit 28, I-87.

In 1755, the French built Fort Carillon and two years later General Montcalm used the fort for preparing a French and Indian attack on British Fort William Henry. In 1758, British General Abercromby led 13,000 men against the fort and was defeated, but in 1759, British General Amherst captured the fort, after a four-day siege, and renamed it Fort Ticonderoga.

Early in the Revolution, Ethan Allen, "In the name of the Great Jehovah and the Continental Congress," with his Green Mountain

# NEW YORK

Boys captured the fort without firing a shot. The British retook the fort in 1777, but not before its cannon were transported to American patriots in Boston. Between 1755 and 1777, Ticonderoga was attacked six times, three times successfully.

Restored fort, museum, marked battleground, guided tours. July 1–Oct. 15. Admission.

FORT MOUNT HOPE, ½ mi. e., following signs, to Ticonderoga.

French and Indian War fortification outpost of Fort Ticonderoga. Reconstructed blockhouse and exhibits. May 23–Oct. 31. Donations.

MOUNT DEFIANCE, 1 mi. s.e. off SR 22 and 73, Ticonderoga.

Overlook, now part of Fort Ticonderoga, where British General Burgoyne placed cannon to force American evacuation. Free.

MOUNT INDEPENDENCE, linked to Fort Ticonderoga by boat bridge.

Least disturbed of any Revolutionary War site, with military roads, gun emplacements, foundations and graves of American soldiers virtually untouched. Free.

## WATERVLIET

WATERVLIET ARSENAL, 5 mi. n. of Albany, SR 32, Watervliet.

Museum at arsenal portrays use of cannon throughout history, with the earliest cannon in the collection dating from 1842.

Open by appointment.

## WEST POINT

U.S. MILITARY ACADEMY, on the west bank of the Hudson River, 50 mi. n. of New York City at West Point off I-87 or I-84. The museum is in Thayer Hall, 1 mi. from main entrance.

The U.S. Military Academy for the training of Army Officers was formally opened in 1802, but a military post had existed at West Point since 1778. The Academy is open to visitors, except for the cadet barracks and academic buildings. Of particular interest is the Old Cadet Chapel (1836), commemorating with shields American

# EXPLORING MILITARY AMERICA

generals of the Revolutionary War. There is a shield for Benedict Arnold who attempted to betray West Point to the British during that war. The WEST POINT MUSEUM, entrance on Cullum Road, has one of the most extensive collections of military artifacts in the world. Earthworks of FORT CLINTON are north and east of the Parade Ground with a monument to General Kosciuszko. TROPHY POINT has war relics from Revolution.

Museum, monuments, visitor center inside South Gate. Free.

BEAR MOUNTAIN HISTORICAL MUSEUM STATE PARK, 5 mi. s. of West Point, off US 9W, near Bear Mountain Bridge.

British General Sir Henry Clinton captured Forts Clinton and Montgomery in Hudson River Valley in October, 1777 and broke a defensive boom strung across the Hudson River. Bear Mountain Historical Museum, on the site of Fort Clinton, has exhibits on history of both forts. Excavated ruins of Fort Montgomery. Free.

## YOUNGSTOWN

OLD FORT NIAGARA STATE PARK, n. of Youngstown on SR 18.

On this site in 1648 explorer LaSalle set up a fort, and nine years later, the French built another fort. During the winter of 1688, only 12 survived of a garrison of 100. In 1726, the French pretended to the Iroquois Indians to be building a fur storage area but instead built a massive "French castle" fort, calling it Fort Niagara. After several attacks in the 1750s, the British, with Indian allies, finally captured the fort. During the American Revolution, the British sent Indian raids from the fort into Cherry Valley, New York, and Wyoming, Pennsylvania. During the War of 1812, the British again captured Fort Niagara, returning it after the war.

Restored features of the fort include fortified "French castle," moat, drawbridge and blockhouse and pre-Revolutionary War buildings.

Admission.

# North Carolina

Sixteenth-century French and Spanish explorers came into this area, but the English were the first to try to colonize it. The first settlements, including the Lost Colony of Roanoke, were failures, but a permanent settlement was started north of Albemarle Sound in 1660. The early settlements endured not only Indian attacks and pirate raids but oppressive British taxes on tobacco so that by the time of the American Revolution, North Carolina was the first to vote for separation from England. During the war, North Carolina militia had to fight Tories and Cherokee Indians as well as British. In the War of 1812, over 7,000 North Carolina men served on land and sea. In the Civil War, although last to secede, North Carolina sent more than 175,000 men to the Confederacy, losing more men than any other Southern state.

★ ★ ★

**The Air Force Museum,** Wright-Patterson Air Force Base, Dayton, Ohio, is the largest military aviation museum in the world and plays host to one million visitors annually. Among its more than 145 aircraft on exhibit is the B-24 Liberator, a bomber employed in every combat theater in World War II.
UNITED STATES AIR FORCE MUSEUM, WRIGHT-PATTERSON AIR FORCE BASE, DAYTON, OHIO

**Fort Recovery** at Fort Recovery, Ohio, is a partial reconstruction of the 1793 fort used in the campaign against Indians in the Northwest Territory. Near the fort is the site of the 1791 Maumee Indian victory over General Arthur St. Clair's 1,400 soldiers. The 900 soldiers slain was a greater number than in any Revolutionary War battle. THE OHIO HISTORICAL SOCIETY, INC., COLUMBUS, OHIO

**The Pennsylvania Military Museum,** US 322, just east of State College Boalsburg, Pennsylvania, offers exhibits on eight major wars. One of the outstanding exhibits is the reconstruction of a World War I battlefield, including trenches, ambulances, barbed wire, tanks and guns. THE PENNSYLVANIA MILITARY MUSEUM, BOALSBURG

**Gettysburg National Military Park,** Gettysburg, Pennsylvania, commemorates the July 1863 battle between Union and Confederate forces that cost 51,000 casualties. One Confederate soldier in every four who fell in the battle was a North Carolinian, and this North Carolina State Monument is one of a multitude of monuments and markers on the battlefield. GETTYSBURG TRAVEL COUNCIL, GETTYSBURG, PA.

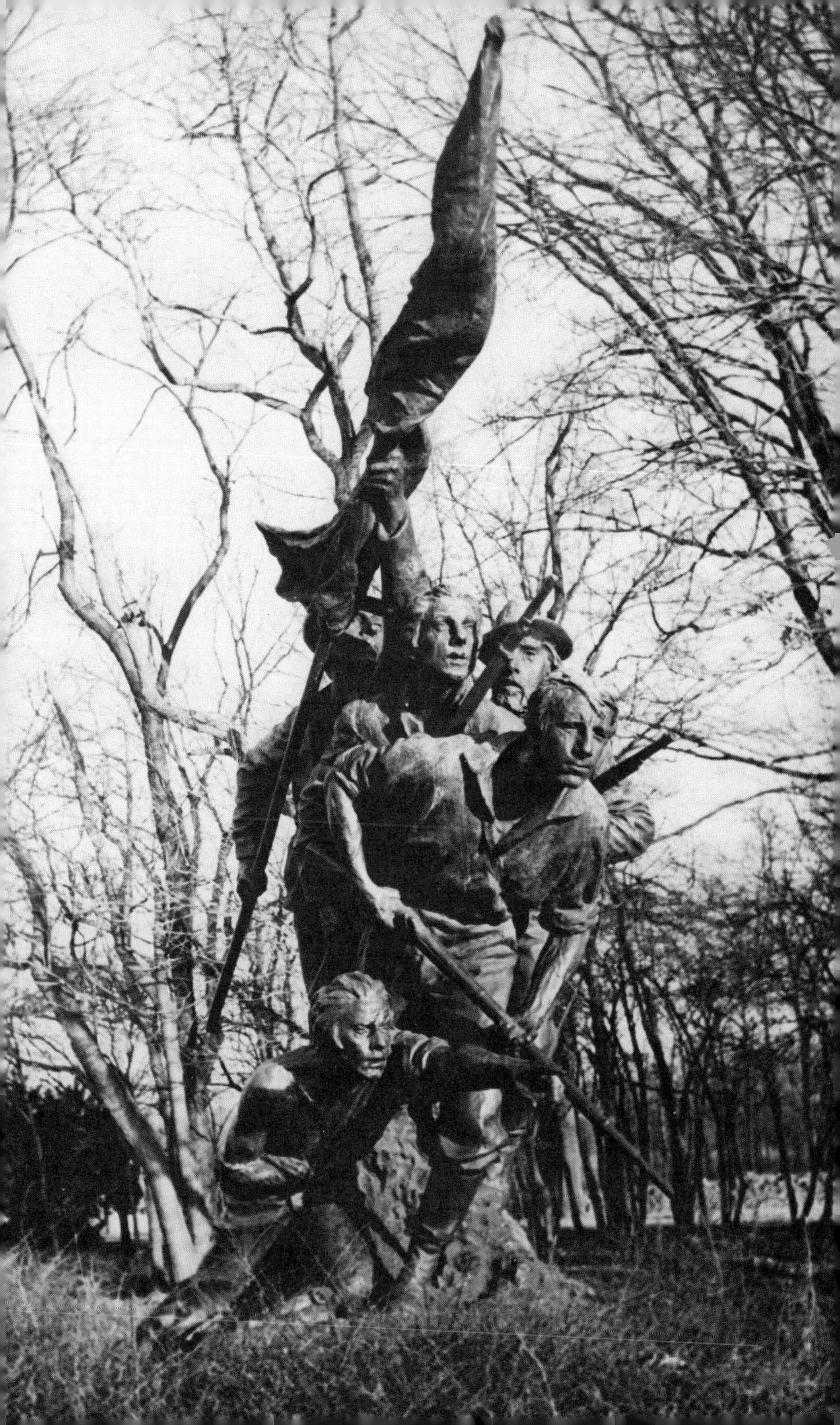

The **U.S.S. Olympia** and the **U.S.S. Becuna,** Penn's Landing, Philadelphia, symbolize American naval history. The cruiser *Olympia* was Commodore Dewey's victorious flagship in the devastation of the Spanish fleet off the Philippines, May 1, 1898, and flagship in the North Atlantic in World War I. The *Becuna* was submarine flagship of the Southwest Pacific fleet in World War II and served also in the Korean and Vietnam conflicts. CRUISER OLYMPIA ASSOCIATION, PHILADELPHIA

**Rose,** Newport Harbor, Rhode Island, is the only reconstructed Revolutionary War frigate afloat. The original frigate of 24 guns, built in 1756, saw Revolutionary War service, and on board this reconstruction are Colonial and Revolutionary exhibits and a fully furnished great cabin.
PHOTO BY JOHN F. MILLAR, COURTESY OF NEWPORT COUNTY CHAMBER OF COMMERCE

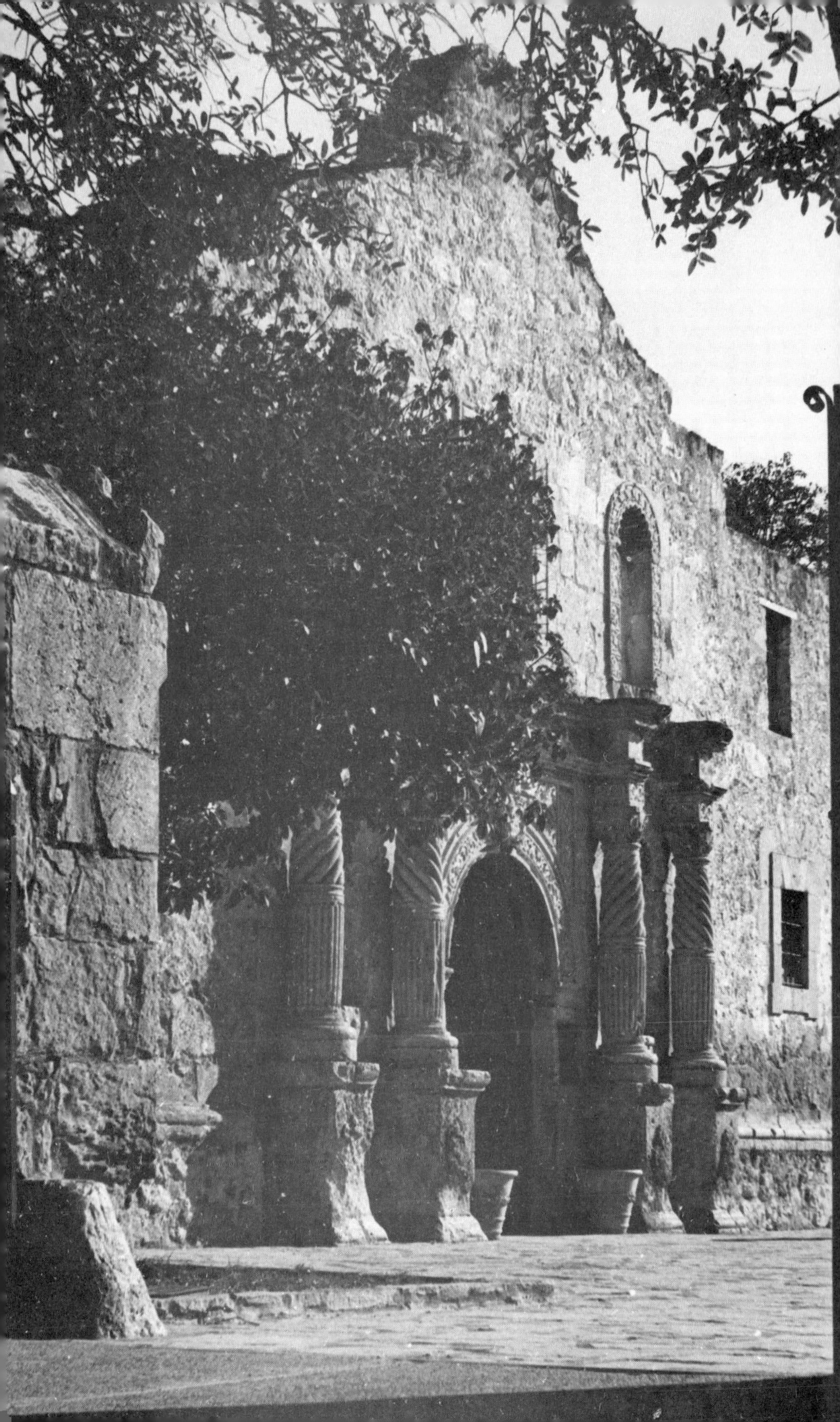

**James Fort,** Jamestown, Virginia, is reconstructed as built in 1607. First permanent English colony in the United States, it has undergone excavation for almost 50 years. Replicas of vessels that brought the first settlers are moored nearby.
JAMESTOWN-YORKTOWN FOUNDATION, WILLIAMSBURG, VA.

**The Alamo,** San Antonio, Texas, served six armies and the Indians for ten battles and many skirmishes in its 250-year history. The famous February 23 to March 6, 1836 siege of the Alamo by Mexican General Santa Anna's forces ended in the death of 188 Texan defenders. S.W. PHOTOS, COURTESY OF DAUGHTERS OF THE REPUBLIC OF TEXAS, CUSTODIANS OF THE ALAMO, SAN ANTONIO, TEXAS

In the circular exhibit hall of the Hall of Valor, **New Market Battlefield Park,** Virginia, the 1860–65 Civil War history is given, from the first shot at Fort Sumter to the final peace at Appomattox. Two award-winning films tell of the 1864 Battle of New Market and trace Stonewall Jackson's Shenandoah Valley Campaign of 1862. NEW MARKET BATTLEFIELD PARK, NEW MARKET, VA.

**Richmond National Battlefield Park** near Richmond, Virginia, aids understanding of the Civil War operations and battles near the capital of the Confederacy. Seven drives on Richmond failed but Grant's 1864 assault, sliding off to Petersburg, eventually resulted in Confederate surrender at Appomattox. VIRGINIA STATE TRAVEL SERVICE, RICHMOND, VA.

**The U.S.S. Missouri,** at Puget Sound Naval Shipyard, Bremerton, Washington, is the battleship on which the Japanese signed the Instrument of Surrender ending World War II, September 2, 1945, in Tokyo Bay. In World War II, the ship participated in operations against Iwo Jima, Okinawa and the Japanese mainland. She served also in the Korea War as part of the United Nations forces. NAVAL INACTIVE SHIP MAINTENANCE FACILITY, PUGET SOUND NAVAL SHIPYARD, BREMERTON, WASHINGTON

**Fetterman Massacre Monument,** overlooking US 87 near Story, Wyoming. In December 1866, Lt. Colonel Fetterman's troops of more than 80 men were ambushed and killed near Fort Phil Kearny by a force of 2,000 Sioux, Cheyenne and Arapaho under Chief Red Cloud. The troops were coming to the aid of a wagon train. WYOMING TRAVEL COMMISSION, CHEYENNE, WYOMING

**Fort Caspar,** Caspar, Wyoming, built 1857, witnessed mountain men of the fur trade, wagon emigrants to Oregon, "Forty-Niners" to California, Mormons to Salt Lake, Indians to Fort Laramie treaty grounds, Pony Express riders and passengers on the first transcontinental stage coaches. Near the fort were fought several Indian battles. WYOMING TRAVEL COMMISSION, CHEYENNE, WYOMING

ON THIS FIELD ON THE 21ST DAY OF
DECEMBER, 1866,
THREE COMMISSIONED OFFICERS AND
SEVENTY SIX PRIVATES
OF THE 18TH U.S. INFANTRY, AND OF THE
2ND U.S. CAVALRY, AND FOUR CIVILIANS,
UNDER THE COMMAND OF CAPTAIN BREVET-
LIEUTENANT COLONEL WILLIAM J. FETTERMAN
WERE KILLED BY AN OVERWHELMING
FORCE OF SIOUX, UNDER THE COMMAND OF
RED CLOUD.
THERE WERE NO SURVIVORS.

# EXPLORING MILITARY AMERICA

## ATLANTIC BEACH

FORT MACON STATE PARK, 2 mi. e. on SR 58.

One of the oldest military sites in North Carolina, the fort stands in an area fought over by the Spanish and English. Fort Hampton, built in 1808, was replaced by Fort Macon in 1826. At the start of the Civil War, the fort was seized by the Confederacy, but one year later, after heavy bombardment by Union forces, the fort fell into Union hands. For the remainder of the war, the North Carolina coast was blockaded by Federal forces from Beaufort to the Virginia line. The fort was garrisoned again during the Spanish American War.

Restored fort, museum. Free.

## BURLINGTON

ALAMANCE BATTLEGROUND, 6 mi. s. of SR 62 (marked exits from I-85).

During the years before the American Revolution, excessive taxes and government abuses caused conflict in North Carolina between colonists known as "Regulators," and the royal government. The War of Regulation broke out, and the two forces met and fought near Alamance Creek in May, 1771. The Regulators were no match for the better-trained royal militia. Although the battle ended in defeat for the Regulators, the armed resistance of the colonists against royal authority was a forerunner of the War of American Independence.

Battle site, visitor center, exhibits. Free.

## CAROLINA BEACH

BLOCKADE RUNNERS OF THE CONFEDERACY MUSEUM, 1 mi. n.w. on US 421.

During the Civil War, the coast of the Confederate States was so effectively blocked by Union naval forces that vitally needed supplies for the Confederate Army could only be slipped through the blockade by daring vessels called "blockade runners." Many of the blockade

## NORTH CAROLINA

runners fell victim to Union patrol boats and were sunk or captured without ever reaching port.

Museum, scale model of Fort Fisher. Admission.

## DURHAM

BENNETT PLACE STATE HISTORIC SITE, 4 mi. n.w. off US 70 and I-85.

It was at this simple farmhouse that General Johnston and General Sherman signed the surrender papers, ending the Civil War for Confederate forces still in the field on April 25, 1865. The surrender of General Lee at Appomattox had taken place on April 9. Free.

## FAYETTEVILLE

FORT BRAGG is 5 mi. n.w. of Fayetteville. From I-95/SR 301, take SR 24 n. 14 mi. to main gate of the fort.

SPECIAL WARFARE MUSEUM, Gruber Rd. and 12th St., 3 mi. from main gate of Fort Bragg.

History of special warfare units, such as the Green Berets, may be seen at this museum. Free.

EIGHTY-SECOND AIRBORNE DIVISION WAR MEMORIAL MUSEUM, Ardennes Rd. at Gela St., Fort Bragg.

The history and campaigns of this famous airborne division are traced from World War I through Vietnam. Free.

## GREENSBORO

GUILFORD COURTHOUSE NATIONAL MILITARY PARK, 6 mi. n. off US 220 on New Garden Rd.

On March 15, 1781, an American army commanded by General Nathanael Greene made its stand at Guilford Courthouse to contest the invasion of North Carolina by the British forces of Lord Cornwallis. After a fierce two-hour engagement, Greene withdrew his troops but left behind over 500 dead and wounded British soldiers. So costly was the British victory that Cornwallis was unable to pur-

# EXPLORING MILITARY AMERICA

sue the retreating rebels, and his later surrender at Yorktown was due partly to the serious loss of manpower he suffered at Guilford Courthouse.

Battleground, monuments, visitor center, exhibits, tours. Free.

## KINSTON

C.S.S. NEUSE, at Caswell/Neuse State Historic Site, w. of Kinston on US 70A.

The *Neuse* was one of 22 ironclad ramming vessels built by the Confederacy. When Union forces advanced along the Neuse River in March, 1865, the *Neuse* shelled the oncoming troops, then, to avoid capture, the boat was blown up and sunk in the river. She stayed submerged for 96 years, until her recent excavation. Artifacts recovered from the ship may be seen in a nearby visitor center. Free.

## KURE BEACH

FORT FISHER, 3 mi. s. of Kure Beach on US 421, or 18 mi. s. of Wilmington on US 421.

Until the last months of the Civil War, Fort Fisher, overlooking Cape Fear River, kept the valuable port of Wilmington open to the Confederate blockade runners that supplied the Confederate Army. In January 1865, the fort was attacked by a Union naval bombardment of over two million pounds of projectiles. Then land forces broke into the fort; and after bloody hand-to-hand combat, the fort was forced to surrender. The fight for Fort Fisher was the heaviest land–sea battle fought in the Civil War and helped seal the fate of the South.

Remains of fort, visitor center, exhibits. Free.

## NEWTON GROVE

BENTONVILLE BATTLEGROUND, 3 mi. n. on US 701, then 2 mi. e. of SR 1008. (Newton Grove is s.w. of Goldsboro on US 13.)

In a last ditch attempt to halt Union forces in North Carolina, General Joseph Johnston's Confederates opposed General Sherman's

# NORTH CAROLINA

Union troops at Bentonville in March of 1865. This last major battle in North Carolina was a defeat for the greatly outnumbered Confederates; and on April 26 at the Bennett farmhouse near Durham, General Johnston surrendered to General Sherman. During the Bentonville battle, many of the wounded from both sides were taken to the Harper farmhouse nearby, which served as a hospital.

Descriptive markers on battlefield, Harper House, visitor center, exhibits, tours. Free.

## ROANOKE ISLAND

FORT RALEIGH NATIONAL HISTORIC SITE, on US 158, 4 mi. n. of Manteo on Roanoke Island.

England's first attempt to colonize eastern America was a military venture, sent to America in 1585 by Sir Walter Raleigh. Fort Raleigh was built on Roanoke Island, and a second colony, including women and children, was sent out in 1587. By 1590, although the primitive fort still stood, the colony had mysteriously disappeared, and no trace was ever found of any survivors.

Restored fort, visitor center, exhibits. Free.

## STATESVILLE

FORT DOBBS, US 21 exit off I-40, n. 1 mi. on US 21 to SR 1930, w. 1½ mi. on SR 1930.

Fort Dobbs (1756) was built by a company of provincial rangers to protect settlers during the French and Indian War. During periods of danger, the settlers camped near the protection of the log walls of the fort. On the night of Feb. 27, 1760, a raiding party of Cherokee Indians attacked, but the fort was successfully defended. After the war, the fort was abandoned and fell into ruins.

Excavated fort, exhibits. Free.

## WILMINGTON

BRUNSWICK TOWN (FORT ANDERSON) midway between Wilmington and Southport, off SR 133 (adjacent to Orton Plantation).

# EXPLORING MILITARY AMERICA

The colonial port town of Brunswick was first settled in 1726. In 1748 it was captured for three days by Spanish privateers. In 1765 the citizens of Brunswick, in one of the first incidents of armed resistance to British authority, placed the royal British governor under arrest. In 1776 the town was burned by the British. The Confederates built Fort Anderson at Brunswick to protect Wilmington. Bombarded by the Union navy in February, 1865, the Confederates were forced to abandon the fort.

Preserved earthworks, ruins of Brunswick town, visitor center, exhibits, tours. Free.

FORT ANDERSON STATE HISTORIC SITE on Cape Fear River, 19 mi. s. of Wilmington via US 17 and SR 133.

The earthwork fortifications of Fort Anderson came under Federal attack after the fall of Fort Fisher during the Civil War. The fort held out for 30 days against heavy bombardment but finally was abandoned by the Confederates on February 19, 1865.

Earthworks of fort, visitor center, exhibits. Free.

MOORES CREEK NATIONAL BATTLEFIELD, 20 mi. n.w. of Wilmington, via SR 11 or US 421 and SR 210.

On February 27, 1776, patriots and loyalists clashed at Moores Creek Bridge. Patriot militia threw back a larger loyalist force, and the victory helped prevent a full-scale invasion of the South. Historians have said that if the South had been conquered in 1776, it is possible the rebellion would never have turned into a revolution.

Battleground, visitor center, exhibits, tours. Free.

U.S.S. NORTH CAROLINA BATTLESHIP MEMORIAL, s. on US 17, 74, 76 and 421 on Cape Fear River.

The interior of this World War II battleship may be toured as well as a museum of naval exhibits that includes a film of the Pacific campaigns in which the *U.S.S. North Carolina* participated. From June 8–Labor Day, a sound and light production of the ship's naval history is given nightly at 9 p.m. Admission.

# North Dakota

Beginning in 1738, French, British, Canadians and Spanish came to North Dakota in search of furs. The United States acquired the area with the 1803 Louisiana Purchase; and the Lewis and Clark Expedition spent the winter of 1804–05 at Fort Mandan raising the first American flag over the territory. Pembina, site of 1812 British Fort Daer, was the first settlement. The Dakota Territory was the scene of Sioux Indian warfare in the early 1860s. The war spread throughout the northwestern plains, forcing the military to keep North Dakota forts garrisoned during the Civil War. It was at Fort Buford that Chief Sitting Bull of the Sioux surrendered in 1881.

★ ★ ★

**ABERCROMBIE**

FORT ABERCROMBIE STATE HISTORIC SITE, ¼ mi. e. of Abercrombie on US 81 (35 mi. s. of Fargo.)

The first permanent military fort in North Dakota (1857), this fort was most active during the Sioux uprising in 1862. The Civil War had pulled many of the regular troops from the fort, and for

# EXPLORING MILITARY AMERICA

two months the undermanned fort was besieged by the Sioux Indians, who had already struck terror throughout Minnesota. At the time of the siege, the fort had no stockade. Piled-up cordwood, placed around the barracks and three 12-pound howitzers were all the protection the fort had.

Original buildings and reconstructed fort buildings, museum, tours. May 1–Sept. 15. Admission.

## BISMARCK

CAMP HANCOCK MUSEUM, First and Main Sts.

Built as a supply and infantry post in 1872, to protect settlers and railway survey crews, the camp subsequently became a quartermaster's depot, signal station and weather station.

Museum. May 1–Sept. 15. Free.

## DEVIL'S LAKE

FORT TOTTEN HISTORIC SITE, 12 mi. s.w. on SR 57.

Although never under attack, the soldiers at Fort Totten were decimated by disease, the extreme cold and the hazards of life on the frontier. Nevertheless, they found recreation in hunting and even formed theater groups. Fort was turned over to the Bureau of Indian Affairs in 1890.

Original fort buildings, museum. June 1–Oct. 31, rest of year by appointment. Free.

## ELLENDALE

WHITESTONE HILL BATTLEFIELD, 22 mi. w. of Ellendale on SR 11, 8 mi. n. of SR 56, then 2 mi. e. on gravel road.

When General Sully and the cavalry attacked the Sioux Indian camp at Whitestone Hill in September 1863, the Indian women and children were placed in the central square formed by the warriors. The battle lasted two hours, and 150 Indians died before darkness ended the battle. The battle had been fought as a reprisal for the

# NORTH DAKOTA

Minnesota Great Sioux uprising of 1862, but history has shown that none of the Sioux at Whitestone were involved in the fighting in Minnesota.
Museum, interpretive exhibits. May 1– Sept. 30. Free.

## KILLDEER

KILLDEER MOUNTAIN BATTLEFIELD, 11 mi. n.w.

In the summer of 1864, General Sully fought the last battle in his campaign against the Sioux on this site. Interpretive markers and gravestones.

## MANDAN

FORT RICE, 22 mi. s. of Mandan, or 8/10 mi. s. of town of Fort Rice.

It was from Fort Rice (1864) that General Sully left with his troops for his campaigns in the Badlands and the Killdeer Mountains against the Sioux. It was also at Fort Rice that one of the largest, least-publicized Indian peace parlays was held, the great Laramie Treaty Council of 1868.

Partially reconstructed fort, descriptive markers. Free.

FORT ABRAHAM LINCOLN STATE PARK, 5 mi. s. of Mandan on SR 1806.

It was from this fort that Colonel Custer led more than 250 soldiers of the Seventh Cavalry to their deaths in the Battle of the Little Bighorn in 1876. Aside from occasional skirmishes with the Indians, life at Fort Lincoln was monotonous, although Colonel Custer kept packs of hounds for hunting and the sutler's store had a billiard parlor. The remnants of the Seventh Cavalry left Fort Lincoln for Yellowstone country and the Nez Perce Indian War, and the fort was abandoned in 1891.

Reconstructed fort, interpretive markers, museum. June–Aug. Free.

## PEMBINA

PEMBINA STATE HISTORIC SITE AND MUSEUM, 1 block e. in Pembina State Park.

# EXPLORING MILITARY AMERICA

The area was a hub of several fur trader posts and considered British territory until 1818. Museum marks site of 1812 British Fort Daer.

Museum. Memorial Day–Labor Day. Free.

## WASHBURN

FORT MANDAN, 3 mi. w. via SR 17.

The original Fort Mandan was washed away by the Missouri River. Members of the Lewis and Clark expedition spent the winter of 1804–05 at the fort. It was while the expedition was at Fort Mandan that the Indian girl, Sacajawea, joined the expedition.

Reconstructed fort, exhibits. Free.

## WILLISTON

FORT BUFORD STATE HISTORIC SITE, 9 mi. w. of Williston on US 2, then 16 mi. s.w. by signs.

Unlike other western forts, Fort Buford had a twelve-foot-high stockade and such luxuries as a post library and theater. During its first four years, the fort was under almost continuous siege by the Sioux; in the 1870s and '80s, it served as a supply base for other western forts. The fort was the site for the surrender of Chief Sitting Bull in 1881. The all-black Twenty-fifth Infantry and Tenth Cavalry served at the fort until its abandonment in 1895.

Several original fort buildings, museum. May 1–Sept. 30, rest of year by appointment. Admission.

# Ohio

The French were the first Europeans to explore and trap furs in the Ohio Valley. They arrived in the seventeenth century. Competition from British fur traders and American settlers brought about conflicts, leading eventually to the French and Indian War, followed by Chief Pontiac's Rebellion. Even after England gained control of the Ohio territory, Indian fighting continued in Lord Dunmore's War of 1774. During the Revolution, there were six years of savage fighting between settlers on the Ohio frontier and Indians supported by Tories and British. The 1794 Battle of Fallen Timbers in the Maumee Valley finally broke Indian resistance.

The War of 1812 was strongly supported in Ohio, and the most famous naval victory of that war, Admiral Perry's defeat of the British fleet, took place on Lake Erie. Although little Civil War fighting occurred in Ohio, the state sent more than 300,000 men to the Union forces.

★ ★ ★

# EXPLORING MILITARY AMERICA

## BOLIVAR

FORT LAURENS STATE MEMORIAL, Jct. I-77 and SR 212.

Fort Laurens was the only Revolutionary War fortification in Ohio and is a site of a Tomb of an Unknown Soldier from the American Revolution. The Revolutionary War on the frontier was a bloody confrontation between frontier settlers and Indians supplied with arms by the Tories and British.

Museum. Apr. 1–Oct. 30. Admission.

## DAYTON

THE UNITED STATES AIR FORCE MUSEUM, 4¾ mi. n.e. at Old Wright Field (now part of Wright-Patterson Air Force Base) on Springfield St.; 1¼ mi. s. of SR 4 via Harshman Rd. Exit.

Over one hundred military aircraft, historic and modern, are included in this indoor collection, the oldest and largest military aviation museum in the world. In addition, there are hundreds of aeronautical items and exhibits covering the U.S. Air Force's colorful history from its unofficial beginning in 1908 when Orville Wright tried to sell his first plane to the U.S. Army. Free.

## DEFIANCE

FORT DEFIANCE, City Park.

Descriptive markers, stones and old earthworks are the only visible remains of Fort Defiance, one of the outposts built by General Wayne in 1794 in the Maumee Valley. It was from such outposts that Wayne conducted scouting parties against the Indians until their final defeat in the Battle of Fallen Timbers in 1794, near present-day Toledo. The site of FORT WINCHESTER, built in 1812 by General Harrison, may also be seen at Defiance. Free.

## EATON

FORT ST. CLAIR STATE MEMORIAL, 1 mi. w. off SR 122.

Monument marks site of battle between Kentucky soldiers and the Miami Indians at Fort St. Clair. Free.

# OHIO

## FORT JEFFERSON

FORT JEFFERSON STATE MEMORIAL, SR 121 just s. of village of Fort Jefferson.

A monument and marked archaeological excavations may be seen at the site of Fort Jefferson, one of the frontier outposts built by General Anthony Wayne. Free.

## FORT RECOVERY

FORT RECOVERY in the town of Fort Recovery on SR 49.

Fort Recovery was built in 1793 and included two blockhouses connected by a blockade wall. It was near Fort Recovery that General Arthur St. Clair and his 1,400 men were surprised by an attack of Maumee Indians in 1791. In his retreat, 900 of his men were killed or wounded, one of the most disastrous defeats ever suffered by American government troops at the hands of the Indians, with a greater number slain than in any Revolutionary War battle. It was after the terrible defeat near Fort Recovery that President Washington placed General "Mad" Anthony Wayne in command of the campaign against the Indians in the Northwest Territory. Wayne built a series of forts, including Fort Recovery, and conducted scouting expeditions against the Indians.

Partially restored fort, museum, tours. Apr.–Oct. Free.

## FREMONT

FORT STEPHENSON MUSEUM in the Public Library in Fort Stephenson Park.

One cannon and 150 American soldiers successfully defended Fort Stephenson against the attack of 400 English soldiers and 300 Indians in 1813. Although the fort no longer stands, the museum has displays of military and Indian relics from the War of 1812.

Free.

# EXPLORING MILITARY AMERICA

## GREENVILLE

GARST MUSEUM, 205 N. Broadway.

Fort Greene Ville—site on E. Water Street, with descriptive marker—was one of a series of forts built by General Wayne in Ohio. After Wayne defeated the Indians at the Battle of Fallen Timbers, he led his army back to Fort Greene Ville where in 1795 a treaty of peace with the Confederated tribes of Indians was signed. Under the treaty, the Indians ceded to the United States all Ohio lands south to the Greene Ville treaty line.

The Garst museum has exhibits and artifacts from the Indian Wars in Ohio. Of special interest is the Treaty Room, which shows the trail taken by General St. Clair and General Wayne from Fort Washington to Fort Recovery, along with memorabilia from the other forts built during the Indian Wars. Free.

ALTAR OF PEACE, Memorial Drive.

A perpetual flame burns, commemorating the council fire kept burning by General Wayne until all the Indian tribes of the Confederation had signed the Treaty of Greene Ville in 1795.

## MARIETTA

CAMPUS MARTIUS STATE MEMORIAL MUSEUM, Washington and 2nd Sts.

The museum encloses a section of the original fortification built to protect Marietta, the first organized settlement in the Northwest Territory. Displays include exhibits of military equipment. Admission.

## MAUMEE

FALLEN TIMBERS BATTLEFIELD, 2 mi. w. on US 24.

In August of 1794, General Wayne and an army of 3,000 marched against Indian tribesmen, who were aided by the British and Canadians. Wayne met the Indians in an area where trees had been overturned by a storm, along the Maumee River. The battle was a decisive victory for Wayne and established American control

# OHIO

over the old Northwest Territory and led to the Treaty of Greene Ville (Greenville) in 1795.

Descriptive markers. Free.

## PERRYSBURG

FORT MEIGS, on SR 65, 1 mi. s.w. of jct. SR 25.

Built by General William Henry Harrison in 1813, Fort Meigs is the largest reconstructed walled fort in America. It was under siege by British troops and Chief Tecumseh's warriors twice during the War of 1812. Once the garrison ran so low on ammunition that the Americans retrieved British cannonballs fired against them and used them for return fire. The successful defense of Fort Meigs, and General Harrison's later victory at the Canadian Thames, shattered the enemy threat to the western frontier in the War of 1812.

Restored fort, exhibits. Apr. 1–Oct. 31. Admission.

## PIQUA

MUSEUM OF THE OLD NORTHWEST FRONTIER, 3 mi. w. on SR 66, then 2½ mi. n. on Hardin Road.

The museum has an exceptional collection of French and Indian war maps, documents, military artifacts and other memorabilia, which tell the story of this war, as well as other battles fought in America during this period. May–Oct. Admission.

## PUT-IN-BAY

PERRY'S VICTORY AND INTERNATIONAL PEACE MEMORIAL at Put-in-Bay on South Bass Island in Lake Erie. Reached during summer by automobile ferries from Catawba or Port Clinton.

In the Battle of Lake Erie in September of 1813, Commodore Oliver Hazard Perry won a decisive victory over a much larger British naval squadron. It was after this battle that Perry sent his famous message: "We have met the enemy and they are ours." The victory gave America control over Lake Erie and made possible a successful American advance into Canada.

The pink granite memorial is one of the world's greatest battle monuments. Observation platform. Late April–late Oct. Free.

## WEST POINT

JOHN H. MORGAN SURRENDER SITE, 3 mi. w. on SR 518.

On July 20, 1863, Confederate cavalry officer General John Hunt Morgan attempted to cross the Ohio River to return to Confederate territory. The day before, on Buffington Island near Pomeroy (state monument on SR 124 and Ohio River), Morgan's raiders had fought Union forces in the only Civil War battle in Ohio. Seven hundred Confederates were captured, and when Morgan was prevented from crossing the river, he turned inland. After a skirmish at Salineville, his force was captured near West Point.

Interpretive markers at sites.

# Oklahoma

In 1830, the U.S. Government decreed that all eastern Indian tribes were to be relocated west of the Mississippi River. The Five Civilized Tribes (Cherokees, Chickasaws, Choctaws, Creeks and Seminoles) were removed to the Indian Territory of Oklahoma, to land already occupied by the Osage and Quapaw tribes, among others. Indian unrest began and increased during the Civil War. Indians fought on both sides of the war, their lands invaded and devastated by both Confederate and Union troops. Some of the Five Tribes had been slaveowners and had Confederate sympathies. The U.S. government used this as a pretext to force more land concessions after the war. White settlers moved into the newly opened Indian lands, creating towns overnight. The western half of the area became white and the eastern half remained Indian territory, when the new state was created. More than 65 Indian tribes live today in Oklahoma.

★ ★ ★

# EXPLORING MILITARY AMERICA

## CHEYENNE

BATTLE OF WASHITA BATTLEGROUND, 2 mi. w. and n. of Cheyenne on SR 47 and SR 47A.

Site of Colonel Custer's November 1863 attack on the sleeping Cheyenne village of Chief Black Kettle on the bank of Washita River. Black Kettle, who had struggled to bring peace to his people, was the first to die at Washita, along with 38 Indians, mostly women and children. Free.

BLACK KETTLE MUSEUM, jct. of US 283 and SR 47.

The museum honors those massacred by Custer's Seventh Cavalry at Washita. Battlefield and museum. Free.

## COOKSON

FORT CHICKAMAUGA, ½ mi. n. on SR 82.

Recreation of an early-day horse cavalry post where soldiers in period costume maintain customs and styles of the 1870s army.

Original buildings. Admission.

## FORT GIBSON

FORT GIBSON, 1 mi. n., on SR 80.

The oldest military post in Oklahoma (1824). Life here was so harsh that in its first 11 years 570 men died. The fort earned the name, "Graveyard of the Army." Captured by the Confederates during the Civil War, the fort was later recaptured by Union troops.

Partially reconstructed fort, interpretive markers. Free.

## FORT TOWSON

FORT TOWSON, 1 mi. n.e., off US 70.

Ruins of 1824 army post whose garrison patroled the Red River and the border between U.S. and Mexico. In 1854, the fort became the capital of the Choctaw Nation. Occupied by Confederate troops, the

# OKLAHOMA

fort saw the surrender of the last Confederate general, Stand Waitie, in June of 1865.

Fort ruins, museum. Free.

## LAWTON

FORT SILL MILITARY RESERVATION, 5 mi. n., on US 62, 277 and 281.

Fort Sill was constructed in 1869 by black troopers of the Tenth Cavalry. It was from here that the Red River Campaign was launched against the southern Plains Indians in 1874, a war of attrition that destroyed the food supply of the Indians. The majority of the southern Plains Indians finally surrendered at the fort at the Old Stone Corral.

Today, Fort Sill is headquarters of the U.S. Army Field Artillery, but the old post area has been carefully preserved. So many famous Indian chiefs are buried at the Chiefs' Knoll that the Knoll has been called the "Indian Arlington."

FORT SILL MUSEUM, Old Post.

The museum is devoted both to the history of Fort Sill and the Army Field Artillery from colonial times to the present.

18TH FIELD ARTILLERY REGIMENT MUSEUM, Headquarters Battery.

Collection pertains to the history of the Eighteenth Field Artillery. Free guided tours available to Old Post. Museums: Free.

## MADILL

FORT WASHITA, 11 mi. e. of Madill on SR 199, or 10 mi. n.w. of Durant on SR 78–199.

This fort was built in 1824 and not only guarded wagon trains but protected the Five Civilized Tribes from the Plains Indians. Last occupied during the Civil War by the Confederates.

Partially restored fort. Free.

## OKLAHOMA CITY

FORTY-FIFTH INFANTRY DIVISION MUSEUM, 2145 N.E. 36th St.

Items relating to history of the Forty-fifth Infantry (Thunderbird) Division. Free.

# EXPLORING MILITARY AMERICA

## MUSKOGEE

FIVE CIVILIZED TRIBES MUSEUM, Honor Heights Park.

History of the five civilized tribes, whose military history is closely intertwined with America's military history. Admission.

U.S.S. BATFISH, ¾ mi. from Hyde Park exit of Muskogee turnpike, n.e. of Muskogee in War Memorial Park.

Continuous tours of a World War II submarine. Mar. 15–Sept. 30. Admission.

## RENTIESVILLE

HONEY SPRINGS BATTLEFIELD, n. off US 69.

A Civil War engagement was fought in July 1863, in Indian territory, between Confederate troops with Creek, Choctaw and Chickasaw allies, and Union troops including black infantry and two Indian regiments. The battlefield, in which the Union drove the Confederates across Elk Creek, has remained much as it was then.

Interpretive markers. Free.

# Oregon

Oregon land was claimed first by Spain in 1775, then by England, and finally in 1792 by the United States. The Lewis and Clark Expedition reached the mouth of the Columbia River, and in 1810, Fort Astoria was founded as an American fur trading post. After the War of 1812, the British Hudson Bay Company took over the fur trade in Oregon. The first great influx of American settlers, numbering about 900, arrived in 1843, causing conflict with the British over boundaries and with the Indians over whites taking more and more Indian land. The difficulties with England were settled when Oregon's boundary was set at the 49th parallel. The warfare with the Indians lasted through 1858, then flared up again in 1877 with the Nez Perce War. Fortifications to protect the Columbia River were built during the Civil War and continued in use into modern times.

★ ★ ★

# EXPLORING MILITARY AMERICA

## ASTORIA

FORT CLATSOP NATIONAL MEMORIAL, 4 mi. s.w. off US 101A.

When Lewis and Clark reached the end of their expedition from the Mississippi River to the Pacific Ocean, they wintered here, after building this fort, now reconstructed following Clark's original plans.

Fort, visitor center, museum, exhibits. Free.

FORT ASTORIA, Exchange and 15th Sts.

Permanent American outpost built in 1811. In the War of 1812, the fort and fur trade passed into British hands.

Restored corner of fort. Free.

FORT STEVENS STATE PARK, 9 mi. w. of Astoria, 4 mi. off US 101.

Built during the Civil War to protect the Columbia River against a Confederate invasion, the fort was originally surrounded by a moat with an entrance tunnel. The fort remained active until shortly after World War II, but today only the batteries, redoubts and some buildings remain. Fort Stevens was shelled by the Japanese in 1942 during World War II, the only fortification within the then-continental United States to be fired upon by an enemy since the War of 1812.

Original fort buildings, military exhibits, tour. June 1-Labor Day. Free.

## DAYTON

FORT YAMHILL BLOCKHOUSE, City Park, SR 221.

Fort built in 1855 to control Indians in the area. Phil Sheridan of Civil War fame served a tour of duty at the fort.

Interpretive marker. Free.

## THE DALLES

FORT DALLES MUSEUM, 16th and Garrison Sts.

Troops from Fort Dalles, the last post on the Oregon trail, fought in the Yakima Indian War of 1855-56. The former surgeon's quarters,

# OREGON

the only building remaining of the fort, is now a museum on the history of Fort Dalles and the surrounding area.

May 1–Sept. 30. Hours shortened rest of year. Free.

## KLAMATH FALLS

FORT KLAMATH PARK, Crater Lake Hwy 62, 26 mi. n.

Only a replica of the guardhouse is left of Fort Klamath (1863), which was the base of operations in the Modoc Indian War of 1873. Troops set out from here to move Captain Jack and his Modocs back on the Klamath Reservation. Captain Jack was tried and hanged at this fort in 1873. Historical exhibits relating to the fort may be seen at the KLAMATH COUNTY MUSEUM, 1451 Main St., Klamath.

Park: June–Sept. Free. Museum: Free.

## PILOT ROCK

BATTLE MOUNTAIN STATE PARK, 20 mi. s.w. US 395.

The last battle with the Indians in Oregon, the battle of Willow Spring in the Bannock War, took place here in 1878 between the Paiute and Bannock Indians and the U.S. Army.

Descriptive marker at site. Free.

## WALLOWA LAKE

OLD JOSEPH MONUMENT, n. end of Wallowa Lake near town of Joseph.

Memorial to Chief Joseph of the Nez Perce, one of the most respected Indian leaders, who is buried at this site. Free.

# Pennsylvania

William Penn received the land of Pennsylvania from the British Crown in 1681, although there had been some earlier colonization. Penn's honest dealings with the Indians are credited with saving Pennsylvania from warfare until the mid-1700s.

In 1754, however, French and Indian forces clashed with English and Colonials in western Pennsylvania, and the French Fort Duquesne, among other forts, was built to prevent further British settlements. British General Braddock's forces, which included the young Colonel Washington, were ambushed trying to capture Fort Duquesne. Later British victories, and the defeat of Chief Pontiac, allowed settlement of southwestern Pennsylvania.

In the Revolutionary War, the British occupied Philadelphia, at that time the capital of the United States, while Washington's army endured a bitter winter at Valley Forge. After the establishment of the new United States, the Whiskey Rebellion of 1794 erupted in western Pennsylvania and was put down by 15,000 troops.

# PENNSYLVANIA

As slavery was never entrenched in Pennsylvania, Civil War sentiment was strongly pro-Union. One of the decisive battles of the Civil War was fought at Gettysburg in 1863, with Lee's Confederate forces driven back south in retreat.

★ ★ ★

### BEDFORD

FORT BEDFORD MUSEUM, Fort Bedford Dr.

The original Fort Bedford was built in 1758 in the Allegheny Mountains. Today, a reproduction of the blockhouse of the fort serves as a museum, which includes a large-scale model of the fort and exhibits of military life from the eighteenth century.

Second Sun. in Apr.–last Sun. in Oct. Admission.

### BOALSBURG

PENNSYLVANIA MILITARY MUSEUM, US 322, just east of State College.

Interpretive exhibits concentrate on the individual serviceman and woman and the role they played in the eight major conflicts in which Pennsylvania was involved, from the colonial wars through World War II. One of the most fascinating exhibits is the reconstruction of a World War I battlefield complete with trenches and ambulance.

Admission.

TWENTY-EIGHTH DIVISION SHRINE, Pennsylvania Trail of History, US 322, just east of State College.

A park with monuments honoring the famous Twenty-eighth Division created in 1878; this division incorporated units that had their origin in the first years of American independence. Free.

# EXPLORING MILITARY AMERICA

## CARLISLE

HESSIAN GUARDHOUSE MUSEUM (also called HESSIAN POWDER MAGAZINE MUSEUM) Carlisle Barracks, 20 mi. w. of Harrisburg. Take SR 11 s. to gate.

The powder magazine at Carlisle Barracks was built in 1777 by Hessian prisoners captured at the Battle of Trenton. The magazine is now a museum of memorabilia and weapons, depicting the history of Carlisle Barracks from the French and Indian War to the present, including a large collection of Spanish American war relics. Carlisle Barracks is the second oldest Army post in the country.

May 15–Sept. 30. Free.

OMAR N. BRADLEY MUSEUM, Upton Hall, Carlisle Barracks.

The museum commemorates the military career of General Omar N. Bradley, World War II general and later Chief of Staff of the U.S. Army.

Closed weekends. Free.

## CHADDS FORD

BRANDYWINE BATTLEFIELD PARK, along US 1, e. of the bridge.

One of the most important battles of the Revolutionary War took place in September 1777, when British General William Howe marched his troops toward Philadelphia and clashed with Washington's Colonial forces on the east side of Brandywine Creek. After hard fighting, the British managed to cross the Brandywine and overran the Americans, who retreated in good order.

Battlefield, visitor center, exhibits. Restored headquarters of the Marquis de Lafayette and a reconstruction of Washington's headquarters may also be visited. Donations.

## ERIE

U.S.S. NIAGARA, foot of State Street.

During the Battle of Lake Erie, when Admiral Perry's flagship was destroyed, he transferred in a rowboat, under fire, to the *Niagara*.

# PENNSYLVANIA

The *Niagara* engaged and put out of action three British craft. The battle ended in a victory for the Americans and helped bring the War of 1812 to a successful conclusion for America. The fully restored *Niagara* may be toured as well as the prow of the first iron-hulled warship, the *U.S.S. Wolverine*. Free.

Also at Erie, on 3rd and Ash Sts., on the grounds of the Pennsylvania Home for Soldiers and Sailors, is the WAYNE BLOCKHOUSE. It is a replica of the one in which General Anthony Wayne, hero of the Revolution and Indian fighter, died in 1796.

Blockhouse open Memorial Day–Labor Day. Free.

## GETTYSBURG

GETTYSBURG NATIONAL MILITARY PARK, visitor center across from the National Cemetery on SR 134.

In July 1863, General Lee's Confederate Army of Northern Virginia invaded Pennsylvania, hoping to destroy the Union Army of the Potomac. At the small town of Gettysburg, the Union forces on Cemetery Ridge faced the Confederate forces on Seminary Ridge, and the three-day battle spelled disaster for the Confederates. Gettysburg was the war's bloodiest battle with 51,000 casualties, more than fell in any other battle fought in America, before or since. In Pickett's charge alone, 4,000 Confederates were wounded or killed. On November 19, 1863, President Lincoln dedicated the cemetery at the battlefield, where he gave his now famous Gettysburg Address.

Battlefield, marked battle sites, monuments, visitor center, exhibits, Cyclorama, tours.

Visitor center and battlefield entrance, free. Admission to Cyclorama. Charge for licensed guides and tape tour of battlefield.

NATIONAL GETTYSBURG BATTLEFIELD TOWER, ½ mi. s. on US 140 or SR 134, across from Gettysburg Park Visitor Center. Panoramic view of battlefield. Admission.

LEE'S HEADQUARTERS AND MUSEUM, ¾ mi. w. on US 30. Mar. 15– Nov. 30. Free.

# EXPLORING MILITARY AMERICA

SOLDIERS NATIONAL MUSEUM, ¾ mi. s. on US 140 near jct US 15 Bus Rt. Spring through fall. Admission.

GETTYSBURG BATTLE THEATER, 1¼ mi. s. on US 15 Bus Rt. Spring through fall. Admission.

NATIONAL CIVIL WAR WAX MUSEUM, Steinwehr Ave. at Culp St. Admission.

## GREENSBURG

BUSHY RUN BATTLEFIELD. Drive n. on SR 66 from US 30 at Greensburg and take 993 w. to park (near Jeannette). About 35 mi. from Pittsburgh.

A museum at Bushy Run Battlefield tells the story of the battle in which Colonel Bouquet broke Chief Pontiac's siege in August, 1763, during Pontiac's insurrection. At Bushy Run, Colonel Bouquet, a skilled Indian fighter, overcame superior Indian forces with a diversionary ruse and with the protection of flour bag "forts."

Museum. Admission.

## KINGSTON

109TH ARTILLERY HISTORICAL AND WAR MUSEUM, Kingston Armory, 280 Market Street.

Two hundred years of military history, dating from 1775, are collected in this museum. Admission.

## LIGONIER

FORT LIGONIER, jct. of Lincoln Highway East and SR 711.

The English were losing the French and Indian War until Sir William Pitt, Prime Minister of England in 1757, gave renewed support to the British forces in America. A campaign against the French-held Fort Duquesne was launched in 1758 from Fort Ligonier, which was used as a final staging area for the assault. At the approach of the British, the French burned and abandoned Fort Duquesne. Fort

# PENNSYLVANIA

Ligonier continued to be garrisoned by the British after the French and Indian War ended and served as a supply post during Pontiac's War. The fort was also used in 1774 as a refuge for settlers during the Indian raids of Lord Dunmore's War. By 1800, the fort had been abandoned.

Reconstructed fort, museum. Apr. 15–Nov. 15. Admission.

## NEW HOPE

WASHINGTON CROSSING STATE PARK, on SR 32 and 532, about 7 mi. s.e. of New Hope, on the Delaware River.

The Revolutionary War had come to Pennsylvania when General Washington crossed the Delaware River from Pennsylvania to New Jersey on Christmas night, 1776, with 2,400 soldiers. His victory at Trenton and his capture of Hessian mercenaries took place in New Jersey, but Pennsylvania has preserved Washington's embarkation point.

Memorial building, exhibits, McConkey Ferry Inn (where Washington dined before crossing the Delaware), Thompson–Neely House (where Washington held staff conferences). Admission to buildings.

## PHILADELPHIA

WASHINGTON SQUARE, 7th and Locust Sts.

Grave of the Unknown Soldier of the American Revolution.

FORT MIFFLIN, Island Ave. S. and Delaware River, back of airport.

Fort Mifflin (1772) prevented supplies from reaching British-occupied Philadelphia but fell after a six-day siege. Rebuilt in 1798 and again in 1860, the fort saw service as late as World War II.

Restored fort. Memorial Day–Labor Day, afternoons. Admission.

THE DANDY FIRST MUSEUM, 3205 Lancaster Ave.

Collection includes uniforms and exhibits from the Revolutionary War to the present. Free.

# EXPLORING MILITARY AMERICA

KOSCIUSZKO HOUSE, 301 Pine St.

Exhibits and multi-media presentations tell of Polish General Thaddeus Kosciuszko's invaluable contributions to the American Revolution. Free.

PEMBERTON HOUSE, 3rd and 4th on Chestnut St.

Reconstructed house with Army–Navy Museum, 1775–1800. Free.

MARINE CORPS MUSEUM AND MEMORIAL, New Hall, 4th and Chestnut Sts.

A reconstructed 1791 building contains exhibits on the Continental Marines in the American Revolution. Free.

INDEPENDENCE HALL, between 5th and 6th on Chestnut St.

It was here that the Declaration of Independence and Constitution were signed and George Washington was given the role of Commander-in-Chief of the colonial armies. *A Nation Is Born,* a sound and light program on the War of Independence, may be viewed. For information on program and tours of Independence Hall, there is a visitor center at 3rd and Chestnut Sts. Free.

THE WAR LIBRARY AND MUSEUM, 1805 Pine St.

One of the most prominent collections of Civil War memorabilia. Closed weekends. Admission.

U.S.S. OLYMPIA and the U.S.S. BECUNA, Penn's Landing Marina, Delaware Ave. and Spruce St.

One of America's most historic Naval vessels, the *U.S.S. Olympia,* was Admiral Dewey's flagship in the Battle of Manila Bay during the Spanish American war, a war that marked the beginning of the United States as a world power.

The guppy-class submarine, the *U.S.S. Becuna,* berthed with the *Olympia,* also boasts a colorful past; it served as the submarine flagship of the Southwest Pacific Fleet during World War II. Tours of both vessels. Admission.

# PENNSYLVANIA

## PITTSBURGH

FORT PITT MUSEUM, Point State Park, downtown Pittsburgh. Follow any major artery to the Point area and signs to museum.

After the French burned and abandoned Fort Duquesne, the British built Fort Pitt on the site in 1760, the largest outpost in North America at that time. The only major military action here occurred in 1763 during Pontiac's insurrection when the fort held out against an Indian attack, ending Indian resistance in western Pennsylvania. British troops left Fort Pitt in 1772, commenting, "The Americans will not submit to British Parliament, and they may now defend themselves." During the Revolution, the troops of George Rogers Clark set out from Fort Pitt to take the British outposts in the Illinois country. By the time Fort Pitt was abandoned in 1792, the booming town of Pittsburgh had grown up around the fort.

Fort Pitt blockhouse, museum with collection of French and Indian War materials, scale models of the three forts that have occupied this site. Admission.

SOLDIERS AND SAILORS MEMORIAL HALL, 5th Ave. and Bigelow Blvd.

Flags, weapons, uniforms from Civil War through World War II. Admission.

## SUNBURY

THE MAGAZINE, N. Front St.

All that remains of Fort August (1756), one of the largest of the Pennsylvania frontier forts, is the powder magazine.

Scale reproduction of fort, exhibits. Admission.

## UNIONTOWN

FORT NECESSITY NATIONAL BATTLEFIELD, 11 mi. e. on US 40.

After a brief skirmish with the French at Jumonville Glen (descriptive marker at Jumonville Rd., 3 mi. n. of SR 40), Colonel Washington anticipated a French attack and ordered the hasty erection of a small fort in Great Meadows, dubbed Fort Necessity. In the Battle of Great Meadows outside this fort—the first battle of the French and

# EXPLORING MILITARY AMERICA

Indian War and Washington's first military campaign—the young Washington and his raw, ill-supplied Virginia recruits were defeated by a larger French force on July 3, 1754.

Replica of Fort Necessity, information center, museum. Free.

BRADDOCK'S GRAVE, overlooking SR 40 (near Farmington). Fort Necessity is 2 mi. farther on US 40.

After their victory at Great Meadows, the French built Fort Duquesne. British General Braddock was wounded in an ambush, while attempting to take the fort in 1755. He died not far from Fort Necessity, where his grave may be visited today. Free.

## VALLEY FORGE

VALLEY FORGE NATIONAL HISTORICAL PARK. Visitor center at intersection of SR 363 and 23. There is a Valley Forge interchange on the Pennsylvania Turnpike.

Eleven thousand ragged, hungry men went into winter encampment with General Washington at Valley Forge in December 1777. Some 2,000 died of disease during the bitterly cold winter. The men lived in 900 primitive log huts and had little food and poor sanitation. They spent their days being drilled and disciplined by Baron Frederick von Steuben. By spring, what was left of the Continental Army had been turned into a well-trained force, able to defeat the British at the Battle of Monmouth.

Remains of major forts, earthworks, parade ground, reconstructed log huts, General Washington's and General von Steuben's headquarters, National Memorial Arch, visitor center, exhibits. Free.

WASHINGTON MEMORIAL CHAPEL AND MUSEUM, located on SR 23 within the park, has an outstanding collection of Revolutionary War mementos. Admission to museum.

## WASHINGTON

DAVID BRADFORD HOUSE, 173 S. Main St.

In 1792, in the Pittsburgh area, farmers rebelled against the new American government because of the federal excise tax on whiskey.

# PENNSYLVANIA

The so-called Whiskey Rebellion was suppressed when President Washington called out the militia. This stone mansion is where the Whiskey Rebellion began. Admission.

## WATERFORD

FORT LEBOEUF MUSEUM, US 19 and 31 High St.

Fort LeBoeuf was built by the French in 1753 to help establish its claim to the country west of the Alleghenies. The same year George Washington was sent to the fort to warn the French that they were trespassing on British soil.

Museum, with models of French forts, among other military exhibits. Admission.

# Rhode Island

Rhode Island's first European settlers were nonconformists, believers in freedom of conscience. Even with patient negotiation, however, the colony leader, Roger Williams, could not keep peace with the Indians at the time of the King Philip's War of 1675. Rhode Island was an early supporter of American independence from England and raised 1500 troops immediately after the battle of Lexington. Rhode Island ships served as privateers during the war, as they had in early colonial wars. The one land battle of the American Revolution in Rhode Island caused the evacuation of the British fleet from Newport. In the Civil War, Rhode Island contributed almost 24,000 men to the Union cause.

★ ★ ★

**NEWPORT**

FORT ADAMS STATE PARK, Ocean Drive.

One of the largest seacoast fortifications built in the United States, Fort Adams was constructed in 1799 to protect the entrance to Narragansett Bay. Over the entrance to the fort was inscribed, "Fort

# RHODE ISLAND

Adams, the Rock on which the Storm will beat." By the end of the War of 1812, the fort was in disrepair, and the burning of Washington D.C. during the war had shown the weakness of America's coastal defenses. Reconstruction work was begun on the fort so that it could defend against both land and sea attack, with three tiers of cannon and extensive earthworks. That the fort was never attacked is attributed to its formidable construction. Fort Adams was the command center for a complex of coastal batteries in the Northeast until the end of World War II.

Historic fort, guided tours. June 19–Sept. 5. Admission.

PROVIDENCE, moored at Fort Adams during the summer months.

This Continental 12-gun sloop, built in 1768, was the first naval command of John Paul Jones and is the ship from which U.S. Marines made their first amphibious landing.

Tours. Admission.

H.M.S. FRIGATE ROSE, Newport Harbor at King's Dock near the Treadway Inn.

Rhode Island resisted British naval forces as early as June 1765, attacking a British ship in Newport Harbor. In 1772, the British *Gaspee* was burned off Warwick. The frigate *Rose*, with 24 guns, was built in 1756, and served in the Revolutionary War era. The ship was reconstructed, partly of original wood, in 1969. The guns and great cabin are on display along with other Colonial and Revolutionary era exhibits.

Reconstructed ship, tours. Mid-Mar.–Nov. 30. Weekends the rest of the year. Admission.

ROCHAMBEAU STATUE AND MONUMENT, Kings Park.

Monument and statue commemorates the landing of the French allies at Rhode Island on July 10, 1780. During his stay in Newport in 1780, the French General Rochambeau used the VERNON HOUSE, 46 Clarke Street, at his headquarters. The French fleet with 4,000 troops had arrived to aid the Americans in dislodging the British from Newport. Friction between the American and French military leaders and a bad storm caused the French to withdraw. They were, however, heavily involved in the final big battle of the war at Yorktown.

NEWPORT ARTILLERY COMPANY ARMORY AND MUSEUM, 23 Clarke St.

The Armory houses an extensive collection of military uniforms as well as military artifacts from all parts of the world. The armory is headquarters for the Newport Artillery Company, organized in 1639 as a trained band against hostile Indians, the oldest militia organization with continuous service in America.

Apr.–Sept., afternoons. Rest of year by appointment. Donation.

NAVAL WAR COLLEGE MUSEUM, Founders Hall on Coaster's Harbor Island. Accessible through Gate No. 1 of the Naval Education and Training Center.

The U.S. Naval War College is the oldest naval war college in the world, founded in 1884. The museum covers the history of naval warfare and the history of the U.S. Navy in the Narragansett Bay area. The first naval engagement of the American Revolution took place in Narragansett Bay in June, 1775.

Free.

## PORTSMOUTH

BUTTS HILL FORT, off Sprague St.

The only major Revolutionary War land battle in Rhode Island was fought near Butts Hill Fort on August 29, 1778. Nearby Newport had been occupied by the British since 1776, and the recapture of Newport was planned as a joint American-French land and sea battle. The Americans seized Butts Hill on land, but the French ships were damaged by a storm and were never able to give battle. The American troops fought alone in what has been called "the best-fought battle of the war," and did force the eventual withdrawal of the British from Newport.

Fort redoubts, interpretive markers. Free.

MEMORIAL TO BLACK SOLDIERS, just to the left of the junctions of n. bound Routes 114 and 24.

# RHODE ISLAND

A monument, flag pole and descriptive marker commemorate the "desperate valor" of a regiment of Rhode Island black troops who at the Battle of Rhode Island repelled three furious assaults by Hessian regulars. The black troops in this engagement were the first black regiment to fight for the American flag.

# South Carolina

When the Spanish and French were unable to maintain a foothold in South Carolina, the English opened the area for settlement at Charles Town (present day Charleston) in 1670. Plagued by pirates, hostile Indians, slave uprisings, and threats of Spanish and French invasions, South Carolina nevertheless persisted as a royal colony. During the Revolutionary War, the state was overrun by British troops, and Charles Town was captured in 1780. After two years of fighting and several decisive battles, the British were driven out. In the Civil War, South Carolina was the first state to secede, and four months later, Confederate troops fired on Fort Sumter in Charleston harbor. The state put 62,000 in the field and 22 percent of them died. General Sherman's march across South Carolina in 1865 caused enormous destruction, including the burning of Columbia.

★ ★ ★

# SOUTH CAROLINA

## ALLENDALE

RIVERS BRIDGE CONFEDERATE MEMORIAL STATE PARK, 15 mi. e. of Allendale, SR 641, or 6 mi. sw of Eberhardt, via SR 36 and 641.

Fifteen thousand Confederate troops are said to have stood off Sherman's 22,000 Union troops for two days at this bridge, before they were outflanked and forced to withdraw.

Breastworks from battlefield. Museum of relics from the battle n.w. of Allendale off SR 641. Open by appointment. Free.

## BEAUFORT

THE BEAUFORT ARSENAL MUSEUM.

Built in 1776 of brick and tabby, the old arsenal is now a museum containing Revolutionary and Civil War relics.

Closed weekends. Donations.

FORT FREDERICK, on grounds of the Naval Hospital on SC 280, near Beaufort.

Built by the English in 1732 for defense against the Spanish, French and Indians, the fort fell into disrepair and was abandoned in 1758. Some of the old tabby walls remain. Interpretive marker.

PARRIS ISLAND MUSEUM, s. of Beaufort, off SR 17 or 21, Parris Island.

In 1562, Jean Rebault, a French Huguenot, established the fort that became Parris Island, a very early European settlement in North America. The island was captured by Union forces during the Civil War and used as a major port facility. After the war, a naval station was located on the island, largely because of the efforts of a black Congressman, Robert Smalls, ex-slave and Civil War hero. In 1915, the U.S. Marine Corps Recruit Depot was established on the island.

Museum of Marine Corps history. Free.

## CAMDEN

CAMDEN BATTLEFIELD, 5 mi. n. of Camden, w. of US 521 and 601.

Though the American Revolutionary army met serious defeat at Camden in August, 1780, the battle brought American General

# EXPLORING MILITARY AMERICA

Nathanael Greene to prominence. A skilled tactician, Greene's campaign cleared large portions of the South of British troops within a year. A portion of the Camden battlefield has been preserved. Thirteen other Revolutionary War battles took place near Camden, and a guidebook to the sites is available at the Camden Chamber of Commerce. Marked battlefields. Free.

## CHARLESTON

COLONIAL POWDER MAGAZINE, 79 Cumberland St.

This brick structure (1703) housed the public powder supply during Colonial days. When Charleston fell to the British in the Revolutionary War, the powder was removed secretly and hidden in a bricked-up portion of the Exchange on Broad Street. Ironically, the Exchange was also a notorious British prison where hundreds of Charleston's citizens were placed in cramped vaults for their patriot sympathies.

Powder Magazine and Exchange are now museums. Closed weekends. Admission.

North of Charleston is the FRANCIS MARION NATIONAL FOREST, whose low flat woods and coastal sands were once the battleground where the brilliant American general Francis Marion conducted successful guerrilla-like warfare against British troops.

THE BATTERY (White Point Gardens), Battery Park.

Some of the earliest fortifications defending Charleston were built at this point facing Charleston Harbor.

Cannons, monument. Free.

FORT JOHNSON POWDER MAGAZINE, James Island (Charleston Harbor).

Only eroded Confederate earthworks and 1765 powder magazine remain of this 1704 fort. A shell from Fort Johnson that exploded over Fort Sumter signaled the start of the Civil War. Free.

FORT SUMTER NATIONAL MONUMENT, Charleston Harbor. Can be reached only by boat leaving from the municipal marine dock, foot of Calhoun St.

# SOUTH CAROLINA

On April 12, 1861, the opening shot of the Civil War was fired against Union-held Fort Sumter. Federal troops had earlier, under cover of darkness, withdrawn from Fort Moultrie (across the channel) to Fort Sumter, which they considered more defensible. After a two-day bombardment, they were forced to surrender. The Confederacy controlled Fort Sumter until the end of the war despite frequent naval bombardments. By the end of the war, the fort was buttressed with sand and cotton as well as its own fallen masonry.

Fort, museum, tours. Free. Charge for boat ride to fort.

FORT MOULTRIE, part of the Fort Sumter National Monument, 1214 Middle St. on Sullivan's Island. Reached from Charleston via US 17 and SR 703.

In June 1776, the British attacked American-held Fort Moultrie, hoping to gain control over the southern colonies and quickly end the war. Colonel Moultrie and about 400 South Carolinians beat off a squadron of nine British warships and kept the South free of British control. The British did not capture the fort until 1780, by marching overland rather than attacking from the sea.

The original Revolutionary War fort, built of sand and spongy palmetto logs, no longer exists. The fort was rebuilt several times and was blockaded by the British during the War of 1812, although privateers managed to slip through the blockade. After Federal troops withdrew from Fort Moultrie during the Civil War, Confederate troops took over and held the fort to the end of the war.

Visitor center, exhibits, tours. Free.

CONFEDERATE MUSEUM, 188 Meeting St.

Military articles relating to the Charleston–Fort Sumter area. Mar. 15–Oct. 15. Wed., Fri., Saturday. Free.

HUNLEY MUSEUM, 50 Broad and Church Sts.

Confederate Naval history museum, which includes a replica of the Confederate submarine, *Hunley,* the first submarine to sink a surface vessel in combat. The *Hunley,* because of the dangerous duty in which it was engaged, was called the "peripatetic coffin."

Free.

# EXPLORING MILITARY AMERICA

THE CITADEL ARCHIVES-MUSEUM, Ashley Ave. to Hampton Park and Moultrie St.

Exhibits in the museum of this historic military school (1842) deal mainly with the military history of South Carolina and The Citadel itself. The cadet corp of The Citadel fought as a unit in the Civil War. Free.

CHARLESTON NAVAL BASE, n. of Charleston off the Sprull Ave. exit off I-26.

During afternoon tours on Saturday and Sunday, visitors may board a destroyer, survey a submarine, or walk the decks of a minesweeper.
Free.

THE PATRIOTS POINT NAVAL AND MARITIME MUSEUM ABOARD THE U.S.S. YORKTOWN, 2 mi. n. of Charleston on US 17 in Mt. Pleasant.

The "Fighting Lady" of World War II, the famous aircraft carrier *Yorktown* is the only aircraft carrier that may be toured by the public. Exhibits of aircraft, tours. Admission.

## COLUMBIA

SOUTH CAROLINA CONFEDERATE RELIC ROOM AND MUSEUM, 920 Sumter St.

South Carolina's military history from colonial times to the present day. Closed weekends. Free.

FORT JACKSON MUSEUM, Fort Jackson, Jackson Blvd., off Route 76, within Columbia.

The museum traces the history of the modern United States Army and includes memorabilia from the life of President Andrew Jackson, for whom the fort is named. President Jackson's military career included Indian fighting east of the Mississippi and the War of 1812. Free.

# SOUTH CAROLINA

## EUTAWVILLE

EUTAW BATTLEFIELD, 3 mi. e. on SC 6.
 This was the last major battle of the Revolutionary War in South Carolina. The American Continentals defeated a British force, leaving the Americans in possession of the interior of South Carolina. Interpretive markers. Free.

## FLORENCE

FLORENCE AIR AND MISSILE MUSEUM, US 301 and 76 at north airport entrance.
 Outdoor display of missiles, rockets and aircraft from World War I through the Space Age. Museum has memorabilia relating to military aviation. Admission.

## GAFFNEY

COWPENS NATIONAL BATTLEFIELD, 11 mi. n.w. of Gaffney and 18 mi. n.e. of Spartanburg, ¼ mi. w. of junction of SR 11 and 110.
 After the American victory at Kings Mountain in the American Revolution, Colonel Daniel Morgan marched against the British fort at Ninety-Six. The British troops, outnumbering the colonists, clashed with Morgan's backwoods militia at a small cattle grazing area, called Cowpens, in January 1781. Morgan's brilliant tactics sent the British into disorganized retreat; a major victory for the Americans.
 Battlefield, visitor center and exhibits. Free.

## KINGS MOUNTAIN

KINGS MOUNTAIN NATIONAL MILITARY PARK, 5 mi. s. of Kings Mountain off I-85, or n.w. of Bethany on SR 161.
 By 1780, the British controlled most of North and South Carolina except for the southern Appalachians. When British Major Ferguson attacked a mountain town in September 1780, threatening to "Lay the country waste with fire and sword," the frontiersmen, along with

# EXPLORING MILITARY AMERICA

Virginia and North Carolina militia, struck back. Advancing stubbornly against repeated bayonet charges, the outnumbered Americans took the ridge where the British troops were entrenched. The battle forced the British to withdraw from North Carolina and gave the Americans time to create an army that fought later at Cowpens and Guilford Courthouse.

Battlefield, visitor center, museum, tours. Free.

## NINETY-SIX

NINETY-SIX NATIONAL HISTORIC SITE, SC 246, s. of Ninety-Six.

The village of Ninety-Six was fortified during the Cherokee Indian outbreak of 1759 and was Tory in sympathy at the time of the American Revolution. The first battle of the war in South Carolina took place here when Patriots and Tories clashed for three days in November 1775. The Tories were defeated but later established the star fort at Ninety-Six, which the Americans attacked unsuccessfully.

Ruins of earthworks and interpretive markers at battle site. Free.

Also at Ninety-Six is the BURT-STARK HOUSE on North Main and Greenville Sts. Jefferson Davis disbanded the armies of the Confederacy at this house on May 4, 1865. Legend has it that remnants of the Confederate army took with it millions in gold bullion, which mysteriously disappeared at the same time.

Hours vary. Admission.

## SANTEE

FORT WATSON, 3 mi. n. of Santee on US 301 and 15.

During the Revolutionary War, the British occupied a huge Indian mound, which gave them command of the area. The Americans, in retaliation, built a wooden tower higher than the mound and forced the British to surrender. Observation Point. Free.

# South Dakota

A French claim to the South Dakota area was made in 1743, but fur trappers from St. Louis and Canada were the first Europeans to appear in large numbers. The Lewis and Clark Expedition later explored the region on their way west. In 1823, the agricultural Arikara Indians, who had held their land for centuries, were defeated in battle with fur traders, soldiers and Sioux Indians. American military expeditions into South Dakota in 1824 brought peace with the Sioux tribes, but Fort Pierre, originally a fur-trading post, became military in 1855. By the late 1870s, gold was found in the Black Hills. Although the land had been granted to the Sioux, miners and settlers rushed into the area despite the Army's attempts to keep them out. War developed with the Sioux; the Sioux victory at Little Bighorn in 1876 in Montana only delayed their inevitable final defeat at Wounded Knee.

★ ★ ★

# EXPLORING MILITARY AMERICA

## CUSTER

CRAZY HORSE MOUNTAIN MEMORIAL, 5 mi. n. of Custer on US 16 (22 mi. from Mount Rushmore).

A statue of Chief Crazy Horse astride his stallion is being carved in a granite mountain by sculptor Korczak Ziolkowski. When completed, the statue in the round will be over 500 feet high and 600 feet long, the largest piece of sculpture in the world. Chief Crazy Horse was a brilliant military leader of the Teton Sioux from 1865 to 1877. He defeated Custer at Little Bighorn and was killed resisting arrest at Fort Robinson in 1877. The statue shows the chief with his arm pointing to the east, the direction from which the white invaders came, and the inscription on the base of the statue will read, "My lands are where my dead are buried." A nearby museum houses a display of Indian art and artifacts. Museum hours vary with season. Admission.

## LAKE CITY

FORT SISSETON STATE PARK, 10 mi. s.w. of Lake City.

A well-preserved stone fort built for protection during the Sioux uprisings in the 1860s.

Fort, museum. May–September. Free.

## MOBRIDGE

SITTING BULL MONUMENT AND MEMORIAL SITE, 6 mi. w. on US 12 then 4 mi. on paved road.

Chief Sitting Bull was killed here in 1890, along with his son and bodyguard, by Indian policemen. It was feared that the Chief would join the Ghost Dance uprising.

## PICKSTOWN

FORT RANDALL, w. of Fort Randall Dam, near Pickstown.

All that remains of this once-important frontier fort is the ruins of a stone chapel. Interpretive marker. Free.

# SOUTH DAKOTA

## PIERRE

FORT SULLY SITE, Farm Island Visitor Center, Farm Island State Recreation area, 4 mi. e. of Pierre, SR 34.

Military and Indian relics from Fort Sully, built during General Sully's Indian campaign, then abandoned, are preserved at Farm Island Visitor Center. May–Sept. Free.

SOLDIERS AND SAILORS MEMORIAL HALL, opposite the capitol on Capital Ave.

Dedicated to servicemen and women from South Dakota who lost their lives in America's wars. The State Historical Society, with Indian exhibits from the Sioux Wars, is also in this building. Also at Pierre is the ROBINSON MUSEUM, with Sioux Indian artifacts. Free.

## PINE RIDGE

BATTLE OF WOUNDED KNEE, 8 mi. e. of Pine Ridge on US 18, then 7 mi. n. to Wounded Knee, following signs.

In the Wounded Knee Massacre on December 29, 1890, the Seventh Cavalry under Colonel Forsyth attempted to disarm a Sioux encampment. Firing broke out, and before the bitter hand-to-hand fighting and artillery barrage finished, 146 known Indian men, women and children died. This was the last armed conflict between the Sioux and the U.S. Army. The spread of the Ghost Dance religion and the death of Sitting Bull contributed to the final defeat of the Sioux.

Descriptive marker at site of battle; monument marks Indian graves. Oglala Sioux Tribal Museum, edge of industrial park in Pine Ridge. Admission to museum.

## SIOUX FALLS

U.S.S. SOUTH DAKOTA BATTLESHIP MEMORIAL, 2 mi. w. on SR 42 at Kiwanis Ave.

Memorial to a noted World War II battleship.

Museum. Memorial Day–Labor Day, rest of year by appt. Free.

# EXPLORING MILITARY AMERICA

## STURGIS

BEAR BUTTE STATE PARK, on SR 344 and SR 79.

Considered a sacred mountain by the Cheyenne, many notable Indian leaders met here in 1857 to "council" for resistance to further white encroachment upon their lands. Tours of trails. Free.

OLD FORT MEADE CAVALRY POST and MUSEUM, 1½ mi. e. on SR 34 and SR 79.

This fort was built in 1878 to control the Sioux and to protect the Black Hills miners. It was a key command post during the Sioux struggle. The famous Seventh Cavalry was stationed here, and it was at Fort Meade that Major Reno, whose command was detached from Custer's at the Little Bighorn, was court martialed. The only cavalry survivor of the Battle of Little Bighorn was a horse named Comanche, who lived his remaining years at the fort.

Fort buildings, cemetery, museum. Memorial Day–Labor Day. Free.

# Tennessee

The Spanish explored the area in the mid-1500s, followed by the English and French who arrived in the 1600s. In 1756, the English built Fort Loudoun on the Tennessee River, and although the British prohibited settlements west of the Appalachians, the richness of the land brought in settlers, who leased land from the Indians. The Revolutionary War brought Indian attacks; and Tennessee troops participated in the victory at King's Mountain, South Carolina in 1780. In the War of 1812, large numbers of volunteers fought against the Creek Indians as well as in the battles of Pensacola and New Orleans. Tennessee's supply of soldiers in the Mexican War earned it the nickname of the "Volunteer State." In the Civil War, the state was divided in its sympathies; of its 145,000 soldiers, 30,000 went to the Union. More than 400 battles or skirmishes were fought within the state.

★ ★ ★

# EXPLORING MILITARY AMERICA

## CAMDEN

NATHAN BEDFORD FORREST MEMORIAL PARK, off US 70, 8 mi. e.

Park overlooks site where General Forrest's cavalry destroyed a large number of Federal naval vessels and supply base at Johnsonville in late 1864.

Interpretive markers, Monument on Pilot Knob. Free.

## CHATTANOOGA

CHICKAMAUGA-CHATTANOOGA NATIONAL MILITARY PARK. Visitors center 9 mi. s. of Chattanooga on US 27 near n. end of park. Lookout Mountain accessible by SR 58 and 148.

The important Civil War battles of Lookout Mountain, Chickamauga and Missionary Ridge were all fought near Chattanooga. In September 1863, Union forces captured the city but then were defeated at Chickamauga Creek. After retreating to Chattanooga, they endured a month-long siege. In November, reinforced, the Union forces attacked again and drove the Confederates to the base of Lookout Mountain (also called the Battle above the Clouds) and the Battle of Missionary Ridge. The Confederates were finally dislodged from all strategic points above the city of Chattanooga.

The oldest and largest of the national military parks, the battlefields covered are divided between Georgia and Tennessee, with the woods and fields maintained as much as possible in their wartime conditions.

Visitor center, exhibits, battle sites, historic homes. Free.

POINT PARK VISITOR CENTER on Lookout Mountain has a panoramic view of the battlefields, which may be seen from the terrace of the OCHS MEMORIAL MUSEUM. Park and museum free.

CRAVENS HOUSE, off US 41 and 11, via SR 148.

During the "Battle above the Clouds," this house served as headquarters for both Confederate and Union forces.

Exhibits, restored historic home. March–December. Admission.

# TENNESSEE

NATIONAL CEMETERY, downtown Chattanooga, off Bailey Ave., just e. of Central Ave., and CONFEDERATE CEMETERY, between East 3rd and 5th Sts., n. of University of Tennessee.

James A. Andrews and seven of the "Andrews Raiders" are buried in the National Cemetery with a monument replica of *The General* locomotive used in their raid. Andrews and his men were the first Americans awarded the Congressional Medal of Honor. Free.

## CUMBERLAND

CUMBERLAND GAP NATIONAL HISTORIC PARK.
See Kentucky.

## DOVER

FORT DONELSON NATIONAL MILITARY PARK, 1 mi. w. on US 79.

General Grant's first major victory in the Civil War, in February 1862, occurred at Fort Donelson on the Cumberland River. After several days siege, the Confederates in the fort requested a truce, and Grant issued his famous ultimatum, "No terms except unconditional and immediate surrender."

Battlefield, visitor center, exhibits, tours. Free.

## ELIZABETHTON

FORT WATAUGA, SR 321, 2 mi. w. of Elizabethton on Watauga River.

At this 1775 fort, settlers took refuge from sieges led by Chief Dragging Canoe. Also, from this point in 1780, Tennessee mountain men marched to the Kings Mountain battle in South Carolina.

Visitor center, exhibits, tours. Free.

## FRANKLIN

FRANKLIN BATTLEFIELD, S. of Franklin on US 31.

At Franklin, in November 1864, the defeat of Confederate General Hood's Army of Tennessee led to his final defeat at Nashville.

# EXPLORING MILITARY AMERICA

The area south of town where the battle took place is largely unchanged. Free.

WINSTEAD HILL, 2 mi. s. of Franklin.

From this knoll, General Hood surveyed Federal troops occupying Franklin. Interpretive marker and map. Free.

FORT GRANGER, off Liberty Pike.

Federal troops camped at the earthen fort here and intermittently bombarded the town of Franklin for two years, to control troop movements north.

Site under excavation. Free.

CARTER HOUSE on US 31, Franklin, s. of Courthouse Square.

Six Confederate generals died in the Battle of Franklin. The Carter House was in the center of the heaviest fighting and a command post for the Union Army during the battle. Also found mortally wounded near the house after the battle was Tod Carter, a Confederate soldier and the Carters' youngest son.

Restored house, museum. Admission.

BATTLE-O-RAMA, 1143 Columbia Ave.

History of the Battle of Franklin may be seen here. Admission.

## KNOXVILLE

JAMES WHITE FORT, e. end of Hill Ave. Bridge, downtown Knoxville.

Palisaded fort (1786) built to protect settlers and travelers. In 1791, William Blount, Governor of Southwest Territory, signed treaty here with the Cherokee Indians. Open weekdays and Sunday afternoons. Closed Dec. 15–Feb. 1. Admission.

CONFEDERATE MEMORIAL HALL, 2¼ mi. s.w. on US 11 and 70.

During siege of Knoxville in 1863, this hall was General Longstreet's headquarters and came under constant enemy fire. Nearly every wall in the house had bullet marks.

Museum of Civil War relics. Afternoons only. Admission.

# TENNESSEE

## MEMPHIS

CONFEDERATE PARK, W. side of Front St. between Court and Jefferson Ave.

Confederate ramparts may still be seen here. Citizens of Memphis watched the Civil War naval battle from this point in 1862.
Free.

## MURFEESBORO

OAKLANDS MANSION, 900 N. Maney Ave.

Occupied at various times by both Confederate and Union troops, the house witnessed the surrender of Murfeesboro to Confederate General Nathan Bedford Forrest in 1862. Museum. Admission.

## NASHVILLE

FORT NASHBOROUGH, 170 First Ave., n. of Broadway.

Log fort (1780) erected on bluff overlooking Cumberland River as protection for settlers against Indian attacks.

Reconstructed fort, exhibits. Closed Sundays, except June 1–Aug. 31. Free.

BATTLE OF NASHVILLE.

The battle of Nashville, December 15–16, 1864, is well marked throughout the city with descriptive plaques. The BELLE MEADE mansion, 7 mi. s.w. of Nashville on US 70S was headquarters for Confederates during the battle, a portion of which took place on the front lawn. Admission. Also TRAVELLERS REST, 6 mi s. of Nashville on I-65 (use exit 78, then 3 mi. s. on US 31) was site of the Battle of Peach Orchard Hill. Museum. Admission.

STONES RIVER NATIONAL BATTLEFIELD, 27 mi. s.e. of Nashville on US 41/70S.

The night before this battle, the two armies serenaded each other with their army bands. At dawn, December 31, 1862, the Confederates attacked, driving the Union army back, but on January 2, Union

# EXPLORING MILITARY AMERICA

artillery forced Confederates to withdraw, with both sides claiming victory.

Battlefield, visitor center, exhibits, tours. Free.

WAR MEMORIAL BUILDING, 7th Ave., facing Capitol Plaza.

Memorial to soldiers and sailors of Tennessee who died in World War I. Free.

## SAVANNAH

SHILOH NATIONAL MILITARY PARK, 12 mi. s.w. of Savannah via US 64 and SR 22.

The Battle of Shiloh (also called Pittsburg Landing) was the first major battle of Grant's western campaign, following his decisive victory at Fort Donelson. In April 1862, 90,000 untrained soldiers from the North and South met at Pittsburg Landing, and after a two-day battle, almost 24,000 were wounded or killed. The Confederates withdrew to Corinth. The large Northern losses brought an outcry for Grant's dismissal. Lincoln replied, "I can't spare this man. He fights."

Battlefield, visitor center, exhibits, tours. Free.

## SMYRNA

SAM DAVIS HOME, 1¼ mi. n.e. of Smyrna on SR 102.

Spies were used successfully on both sides during the Civil War, from glamorous women espionage agents as Pauline Cushman for the North and Belle Boyd in the South, to an unassuming 21-year-old Confederate spy, Sam Davis. Caught behind Federal lines, Davis refused to reveal the names of his fellow spies in order to save his life, insisting heroically, "I would die a thousand deaths before I would betray a friend."

Restored home, museum. Admission.

## VONORE

FORT LOUDOUN, off US 411, s. of bridge over Little Tennessee River near Vonore. Vonore is between Maryville and Madisonville.

## TENNESSEE

English outpost (1756) built against the French. Nine Cherokee towns bordered the river near the fort. Incited by the French, the Cherokees cut off the fort's supply lines and starved the garrison into surrender. Although promised safe conduct to Fort Prince George, the soldiers and their families were attacked after they left the fort, with 26 killed and others imprisoned.

Reconstructed fort, exhibits, tours. Admission.

# Texas

Indians, Spanish, French, Mexicans, Texans, Americans —all fought hard for Texas. The Spanish first explored the country in 1519, followed by the French in 1682; both battled hostile Indians. The Mexican people began their revolt against Spain in 1810, achieving freedom even while Americans were settling Mexican-claimed Texas. Texans fought for their independence from Mexico in 1836 and were annexed by the United States in 1845. The annexation brought about the Mexican War of 1845, the first battles of which were fought on Texas soil. In the Civil War, most Texans took the Confederate side. Meanwhile, during and after the war, the Indians maintained a fierce resistance to white settlements. At one time one-fifth of the U.S. Army was garrisoned in Texas, fighting Kiowa and Comanche Indians, a warfare that didn't cease until the 1880s.

★ ★ ★

# TEXAS

## ABILENE

FORT PHANTOM HILL, 10 mi. n. via SR 600.
Only ruins and a few scattered stone buildings are left of this fort, which was built in 1851. One of the most desolate forts in the west, desertions were frequent.
Interpretive signs. Free.

## ALBANY

FORT GRIFFIN STATE HISTORIC PARK, 15 mi. n. on US 283 at Clear Fork of the Brazos River.
Ruins of several old fort buildings with interpretive markers. Admission to park.

## AUSTIN

DAUGHTERS OF THE CONFEDERACY AND DAUGHTERS OF THE REPUBLIC OF TEXAS MUSEUM, Capitol Grounds at Brazos at Austin.
Relics from the military history of early Texas; also portrays the role of Texans in the Civil War.
Closed weekends. Free.

## BROWNSVILLE

FORT BROWN, terminus of Taylor Ave.
Established 1846 by General Zachary Taylor, the fort housed troops in the Mexican and Civil War and is also noted for the work of William Crawford Gorgas against yellow fever. At one staging point during the Mexican War, yellow fever killed over half of the troops waiting to go into battle. During the Civil War, Sheridan's occupation army of 25,000 men was headquartered at the fort.
Partially restored fort, museum. Free.

RESACA DE LA PALMA BATTLE SITE, n. edge of Brownsville on Paredes Line Road.

# EXPLORING MILITARY AMERICA

One of the first battles of the Mexican War took place here on May 9, 1846. The Mexicans were forced to retreat back across the Rio Grande with about 1100 casualties. Interpretive markers. Free.

PALMITO HILL BATTLEFIELD, 12 mi. e. of Brownsville on SR 4.

A battle sometimes called the "Last battle of the War Between the States" took place here, ironically one month after Lee's surrender at Appomattox. Interpretive markers. Free.

## BURNET

FORT CROGHAN, on SR 29 w.

Constructed in 1849, this stone fort was abandoned in 1855. Partially restored fort, museum. May 30–Labor Day. Admission.

## CAMP VERDE

CAMP VERDE, 2 mi. w. on SR 689 near Bryan.

Home of the first and last U.S. Army attempt to employ camels as a means of transportation in the West. Interpretive markers.

## CANYON

PALO DURO BATTLE, Palo Duro Canyon State Park, 12 mi. e. via SR 217 and Park Rd.

The last great Indian battle in Texas was fought in 1874 in Palo Duro Canyon between Fourth Cavalry troops from Fort Richardson and Comanches; the Indians were forced to move to reservations in Oklahoma.

Interpretive center. Admission.

## COMFORT

COMFORT MONUMENT, High St.

A monument in memory of 28 Northern sympathizers, originally from Germany, who were killed by Confederates when they attempted

# TEXAS

to enlist in the Union cause. COMFORT HISTORICAL MUSEUM at 838 High St. has information on the German settlement in the Comfort area. Hours vary. Free.

## EAGLE PASS

FORT DUNCAN PARK, Adams St., US 277.

Built in 1849 on the Rio Grande, the fort was garrisoned by Confederates in the Civil War.

Partially restored fort, museum. Summers, weekends only in winter. Free.

## EL PASO

SAN ELIZARIO PRESIDIO, FM 258 s.

Founded in 1777 to serve a Spanish military garrison, this 200-year-old chapel is still in use as a museum. Weekends. Free.

FORT BLISS REPLICA MUSEUM, Pleasanton Road, facing the main parade ground of Fort Bliss. From I-10, take Fort Bliss exit.

The original adobe post was built in 1854 for protection against the Apaches and Comanches. It was burned by the Confederates as they retreated in 1862. A new fort was built and then abandoned in 1877. Finally the Army built a permanent installation at what is now the U.S. Army Air Defense Center at Fort Bliss. It was from Fort Bliss that General Pershing led forces against Pancho Villa in Mexico in 1916.

Military artifacts on display cover period 1848–1948. Free.

THIRD ARMORED CAVALRY REGIMENT MUSEUM, Bldg. 2407, Fort Bliss.

Memorabilia from the proud history of "The Regiment of Mounted Riflemen" who fought in Indian and Mexican Wars. Free.

AIR DEFENSE ARTILLERY MUSEUM, Pleasanton Rd., Bldg. 5000, Fort Bliss.

History of air defense from days of coast artillery to present sophisticated air defense artillery weaponry. Free.

# EXPLORING MILITARY AMERICA

CAVALRY MUSEUM, 15 mi. s.e. of El Paso on US 80 and I-10, via Ave. of the Americas exit.
Artifacts from the history of U.S. Cavalry in the Southwest, as well as items from Spanish Conquistadors to Pancho Villa. Free.

## FORT DAVIS

FORT DAVIS, n. on SR 17 and 118.
Built in 1854 to defend west Texas against Comanches and Apaches, this frontier fort is one of the best preserved of the southwest forts. The Confederates occupied it in 1861, but then the fort was deserted to Apaches for five years. After the Civil War, buffalo soldiers garrisoned the fort for 18 years, engaging in many clashes with the Indians, including a campaign against Chief Victorio's Apaches.
Fort, visitor center, exhibits, music recreation of 1875 military retreat. Admission.

## FORT McKAVETT

FORT MCKAVETT STATE HISTORIC SITE.
Built in 1852 on the San Saba River, the fort was abandoned when Indian troubles diminished, then reestablished after the Civil War when Indian raids increased. Unlike many frontier posts in west Texas, Fort McKavett is relatively untouched by time, and several of the original buildings still stand, rubbing elbows with modern dwellings. Marked sites, historic buildings. Free.

## FORT STOCKTON

OLD FORT STOCKTON, Williams St.
A typical frontier post built in 1859 as a defense against Comanche raids. Several adobe and limestone buildings remain, including an old guard house with dungeon and leg irons. Free.

# TEXAS

## FREDERICKSBURG

ADMIRAL NIMITZ CENTER.
Exhibits on the Pacific Theater in World War II and the life of Admiral Nimitz, naval leader in that war. Free.

## GALVESTON

U.S.S. CAVALLA, Sea Wolf Park.
Visitors may tour this World War II submarine, holder of four battle stars, and the destroyer escort *Stewart*. Admission.

## GOLIAD

PRESIDIO LA BAHIA, 2 mi. s. on US 77A and US 183, immediately s. of San Antonio River.
Built in 1749, the Presidio was one of the most important forts on the Spanish frontier and the finest example of a Spanish presidio (fort) in Texas. In 1812 and 1817, Mexicans struggled with Spanish troops over the presidio. In 1821 Mexico took over from Spain. The first Texas flag waved over La Bahia, and it was at this presidio that Fannin's men were imprisoned and massacred by General Santa Anna during the Texas Revolution.
Restoration, museum. Admission.

GOLIAD STATE HISTORICAL PARK, on US 77A and 183, adjoining Goliad.
Museum with artifacts commemorating Texans slain at Goliad during Texas Revolution. Admission to park.

FANNIN'S GRAVE, 2 mi. s. of Goliad of US 183, s. of Presidio La Bahia.
Monument to and gravesite of Colonel Fannin and 342 men who surrendered to Mexicans and were massacred at order of General Santa Anna on March 27, 1836. Shrine. Free.

# EXPLORING MILITARY AMERICA

## GONZALES

GONZALES FIRST SHOT MONUMENT, 7 mi. s. on SR 97 and GONZALES MEMORIAL MUSEUM, 414 Smith St.

Gonzales has been called the "Lexington of Texas" because the first battle of the Texas Revolution was fought here in October, 1835. The monument and museum honor the Texans who first fought the Mexicans and the 32 patriots who volunteered to join Travis at the Alamo.

Museum. Free.

## GROESBECK

FORT PARKER, 3 mi. n. on SR 14.

Privately built by the Parker family in 1833, the fort with its stockade resembles eastern military forts. It was from this fort that Cynthia Ann Parker was kidnapped in 1836 by Comanche and Kiowa warriors. After living with the Indians for 24 years and rearing an Indian son, Cynthia was rescued but was unable to adjust to white society. Her son, Quannah Parker, became a famous chief.

Restored fort. Admission.

## HARLINGEN

CONFEDERATE AIR FORCE FLYING MUSEUM, 3 mi. n. at Harlingen Industrial Airport.

Interpretive museum of World War II aviation, with World War II aircraft maintained in flying condition for flight demonstrations.

Admission.

## HILLSBORO

CONFEDERATE RESEARCH CENTER AND GUN MUSEUM, Hill Junior College.

Devoted to Civil War memorabilia, especially Hood's Texas Brigade. Free.

# TEXAS

## HOUSTON

SAN JACINTO BATTLEGROUND PARK, 21 mi. e. on SR 225, then 3 mi. n. on SR 134.

The final battle that resulted in Texas Independence took place at San Jacinto, April 21, 1836, when General Sam Houston and his Texans overwhelmingly defeated the army of Mexican General Santa Anna.

Monument and museum. Free.

U.S.S. TEXAS, moored adjacent to San Jacinto Battleground.

Veteran of two world wars and flag ship on 1944 D Day invasion of Europe in World War II, the *U.S.S. Texas* is the only survivor of the dreadnought class of battleship that may be toured by the public.

Admission.

## HUNTSVILLE

SAM HOUSTON MEMORIAL MUSEUM AND PARK, ½ mi. s. on the w. side of US 75 business route.

The museum contains belongings of Sam Houston, hero of San Jacinto and the first president of the Republic of Texas, along with memorabilia of the Texas Revolution. Free.

## JACKSBORO

FORT RICHARDSON STATE HISTORIC PARK, 1 mi. s.w. off US 281.

Fort Richardson was home base of the famous Indian fighter, General Ronald MacKenzie. Two bloody battles were fought by soldiers of Fort Richardson. One battle, between 56 soldiers and 250 Comanches, occurred at Little Wichita River in July 1870, and for it 13 Medals of Honor for valor were awarded. The second celebrated battle was the Salt Creek Massacre led by Chief Satana. General MacKenzie captured Satana, and for the first time an Indian was tried in a white man's court. Satana was paroled but finally died in prison after leading an Indian raid into Texas. General MacKenzie's policy of destroying the Indian camps and supplies finally made the frontier of Texas relatively secure.

Restored fort, interpretive center. Admission.

## KILLEEN

FORT HOOD, adjacent to Killeen, Route 190.

FIRST CAVALRY DIVISION MUSEUM, Bldg. 2218 on Headquarters Ave.

History of famous First Cavalry Division from 1855 to present with indoor and outdoor displays. Free.

SECOND ARMORED DIVISION MUSEUM, Bldg. 418 on Battalion Ave.

History of the noted Second Armored Division, including armored vehicles from twentieth-century wars. Free.

## LA GRANGE

MONUMENT HILL STATE HISTORIC SITE AND PARK, Courthouse Square, 2 mi. s.w. on US 77.

Offers story of Dawson Massacre and the Mier expedition, which took place in 1842–3 in the continued hostilities between Texas and Mexico after the Battle of San Jacinto. Admission.

## LAREDO

FORT MCINTOSH, foot of Washington St.

Established in 1848 during the Mexican War, this fort was one of a series of border defenses—along with Fort Brown at Brownsville, Ringgold Barracks at Rio Grande City, and Fort Duncan at Eagle Pass. The fort was occupied by Confederates in the Civil War and reoccupied and expanded by Union forces in 1865. It was further expanded during the Mexican Revolution of 1910 and World War I. One of first airfields was built here in 1910.

# TEXAS

Several post buildings form Nuevo Santander Museum, which interprets military history of area. Free.

## MASON

FORT MASON, 5 blocks s. of courthouse.

Men from this cavalry post took part in several Indian actions; the post was the last command of Robert E. Lee in the U.S. Army.

Partially reconstructed. Free.

## MENARD

REAL PRESIDIO DE SABA, 2 mi. w. off SR 29.

A year after its construction in 1758, the presidio was destroyed by Indian attack, but continued as a frontier post for ten years more, under almost constant Indian attack. Abandoned 1769.

Archaeological excavations. Free.

## NACOGDOCHES

OLD STONE FORT, campus Stephen F. Austin State University.

Eight flags have flown over this area. In November, 1806, an agreement signed here averted war between Spain and United States. Nearby, the Mexican forces of Bustamente and Santa Anna fought the Battle of Nacogdoches in 1832. In 1836, the fort offered safety from Indian attack. Davy Crockett and Jim Bowie were here before the Alamo.

Rebuilt fort now a museum. Free.

## NAVASOTA

WASHINGTON ON THE BRAZOS STATE HISTORICAL PARK, 7 mi. s.w. off SR 105 (at Washington).

Replica of site of Texas Declaration of Independence. Museum. Free.

# EXPLORING MILITARY AMERICA

## NEWCASTLE

FORT BELKNAP, 3 mi. s. on SR 251.

Built in 1851, this was one of the largest posts in Texas prior to the Civil War and was occupied by Texas Frontier Regulars during the Civil War.

Restored buildings, museum. Free.

## OZONA

FORT LANCASTER STATE HISTORIC SITE, 33 mi. w. on US 290.

Established in 1855 to protect wagon trains on San Antonio to El Paso Road.

Ruins, visitor center. Free.

## PRESIDIO

FORT LEATON STATE PARK, 4 mi. s.e. on SR 170.

Built in 1848 by frontiersman Ben Leaton, who traded with the Army and the Indians, the fort was often used by Army scouting patrols.

Restored fort, exhibits. Admission.

## RIO GRANDE CITY

FORT RINGGOLD, off US 83 at e. limits of city.

One of best preserved of old military posts established after the Mexican War. Portions of the fort are now part of Rio Grande School system. Free.

## SABINE PASS

SABINE PASS BATTLEGROUND HISTORIC PARK, SR 87, Dowling Point.

The Confederates defended this pass near the Gulf of Mexico against Union troops in September, 1863, capturing 3 Union gunboats. No further attempt was made to invade Texas by way of the pass.

# TEXAS

Statue memorial. Also at nearby PORT ARTHUR is historical museum with relics from battle. Free.

## SAN ANGELO

FORT CONCHO, 213 East Ave.

One of the best-preserved of the nineteenth-century western forts, Fort Concho has fourteen of its original buildings still standing and looks much as it did in 1887. The black soldiers who served here earned a remarkable record as Indian fighters and scouts, taking part in campaigns against the Kiowas and Comanches.

Fort, museum, tours. Admission.

## SAN ANTONIO

THE ALAMO, downtown San Antonio, near the river.

The Alamo, a Spanish mission and fortress established in 1718, had already seen several battles under Spanish rule before the Texas Revolution and the famous two-week siege of the Alamo by Santa Anna's Mexican Army of 3,000 men in 1836. All of Colonel Travis' 187 men in the Alamo refused to surrender and died in the final assault on the fort. The brave defense of the Alamo delayed Santa Anna's invasion and gave Texans valuable time to rally to their own defense. In 1842 and again during the Civil War, the Alamo came under attack.

Historic presidio, exhibits, tours. Free.

REMEMBER THE ALAMO THEATER AND MUSEUM, opposite the Alamo with multimedia production on the battle. Admission.

FORT SAM HOUSTON, between I-35 and Wurzback Hwy, within city limits of San Antonio (2 mi. n.e. of the Alamo.)

The present buildings of Fort Sam Houston were built in 1879, although an earlier fort had been built in 1845. The historic quadrangle of the fort has played an important role in Texas military history. Geronimo and his Apache warriors were confined here in 1886 and the famous Rough Riders were outfitted at the fort for the

# EXPLORING MILITARY AMERICA

Spanish-American War. The fort was a staging point for Pershing's 1916 punitive expedition into Mexico. For many years, Fort Sam Houston acted as a supply depot for posts throughout Texas. Today, the fort is headquarters for the Fifth Army.

Historic quadrangle, military museum at Bldg. 123 on S-4 Rd. Free.

U.S. ARMY MEDICAL MUSEUM, at Fort Sam Houston.

History of the Army Medical Department with most of the exhibits dating from its early primitive days but medical equipment from later wars also on display. Closed weekends. Free.

BROOKS AIR FORCE BASE, on Military Dr. near Intersection of Loop 410 S. and I-37. EDWARD H. WHITE II HANGAR 9 MEMORIAL MUSEUM.

Aviation artifacts from beginning of manned flight to the present, housed in 1918 World War I hangar. Closed weekends. Free.

LACKLAND AIR FORCE BASE, intersection of R. 90 W and Loop 410. AIR FORCE MILITARY TRAINING CENTER HISTORY AND TRADITIONS MUSEUM.

Outdoor displays of military aircraft from JN-4 Jenny to F-104 Starfighter and F-80, first jet plane used in aerial combat. Inside the museum are exhibits on aerial warfare, including reconnaissance balloons used during Civil War. Free.

SAN JOSE MISSION HISTORICAL SITE, 6539 San Jose Dr., San Antonio.

1720 mission with soldiers' barracks preserved. Admission.

## SIERRA BLANCA

FORT QUITMAN, 18 mi. w. on I-10 at SR 34.

Adobe replica of original fort showing the primitive conditions under which frontier soldiers lived. Admission.

## WACO

TEXAS RANGER HALL OF FAME AND MUSEUM, Fort Fisher Park, adjacent to I-35 on Lake Brazos in Waco.

# TEXAS

Although not a military organization, the Texas Rangers often worked with the military in maintaining law and order in Texas. During the Mexican War, the Rangers were sent out to eliminate Mexican "banditos" who preyed on military supply trains.
Admission.

## WECHES

MISSION SAN FRANCISCO DE LOS TEJAS STATE HISTORIC PARK, S.W. off SR 21.

Replica of first Spanish mission in east Texas, built in 1690 to stem tide of French settlements. Also in the park is Rice Stagecoach Inn, along the Royal Highway, a victim of early Indian attacks.
Replica of fort, exhibits. Admission.

## WICHITA FALLS

HERITAGE HALL, 3701 Armory Rd.

World War II artifacts from Pacific Campaign with emphasis on the "Lost Battalion" of the 131st Field Artillery. Free.

# Utah

The Spanish explored the area in the late 1700s and were followed by Canadian and American fur trappers. American military leaders Captains Bonneville and Fremont led expeditions into the area in 1833–34 and 1843–45. In 1847 the Mormons founded Salt Lake City, one year before Mexico ceded the Utah area to the United States. Clashes between Mormons and non-Mormons over plural marriages and religious control in politics brought about strained relations with the United States government. Troops were kept at Camp Floyd and Fort Douglas to watch the Mormons as well as guard against troubles with the Utes. These erupted into the Blackhawk War of 1865. By 1890, the Mormon Church had discontinued sanction of plural marriages and the Indian troubles had ended.

★ ★ ★

# UTAH

## BEAVER

OLD COVE FORT, 20 mi. n. of Beaver, SR 4 via US 91.

Built of volcanic rock in 1864 after the Ute Indian Rebellion broke out, a large bell in front of fort warned of Indian attacks.

State monument with museum. Free.

## FAIRFIELD

CAMP FLOYD STATE HISTORIC SITE, ½ mi. w. on SR 73.

In 1857 President Fillmore appointed a non-Mormon governor of the Utah territory to replace Mormon Governor Brigham Young. A military expedition was sent to Utah to enforce his appointment, and the result was the Utah War of 1857–59. The Mormons burned trading posts and destroyed military supply trains in front of the advancing troops. However, before open hostilities developed, a reconciliation was effected, and Army troops established Camp Floyd forty miles from Salt Lake City. The camp was abandoned at the start of the Civil War.

Remains of stagecoach inn, army commissary and cemetery. Mar. 15–Nov. 15. Free.

## OGDEN

JOHN M. BROWNING ARMORY, 450 E. 5100 St.

Called "the father of modern firearms," John Browning invented more than 80 distinct firearm models, including the Winchester, Colt, Remington and the semi-automatic pistol, 30-caliber machine gun and Browning Automatic Rifle. Many of Browning's weapons became standard equipment for the U.S. Army, and in the Indians Wars in the West often made the difference between victory and defeat. Exhibit hall of original models of firearms. Admission.

## SALT LAKE CITY

FORT DOUGLAS MILITARY MUSEUM. Entrance at intersection of Wasatch St. and Hempstead Rd. Museum in Bldg. 32.

# EXPLORING MILITARY AMERICA

The fort was built during the Civil War to protect the vital overland mail route. Numerous conflicts flared up between the Mormon pioneers and the non-Mormon troops at the fort. In addition, there were periodic outbreaks between the Army and the Ute Indians. In 1863 at the Battle of the Bear, troops from the fort wiped out a party of 300 Indians. Unlike many other forts on the frontier, Fort Douglas was not abandoned at the end of the Indian troubles. The post sent troops to the Philippines, and in World War I, it also served as a POW camp. During World War II, the fort was the military nerve center of the western United States.

Original fort buildings, museum, tours. Free.

# Vermont

From 1609 until 1724, the French tried to conquer the Vermont area, building forts against the Iroquois. Later, the Indians joined the French against the English settlements, which began with Fort Dummer in 1724, site of present day Brattleboro. After the French and Indian War, the British controlled the Vermont area, with the land claimed by the British colonies of New York and New Hampshire.

There was only one Revolutionary War battle on Vermont soil, but Vermont's Green Mountain Boys were important participants in the capture of Fort Ticonderoga and the Battle of Bennington. In the War of 1812, Vermont sent a raiding party into Canada, although there was strong sentiment against that war and the Mexican War of 1845. Strongly anti-slavery, almost 35,000 Vermonters joined the Union cause in the Civil War. Major General John Sedgwick's order at Gettysburg was: "Put the Vermonters ahead and keep the column well closed up."

★ ★ ★

# EXPLORING MILITARY AMERICA

## BENNINGTON

BENNINGTON BATTLE MONUMENT, on SR 9, 1 mi. w. of jct. with US 7, then n. to end of Monument Ave.

It was at this site that General John Stark said, "There are the Red Coats and they are ours or this night Molly Stark sleeps a widow." American General Stark and his forces defeated two detachments of British General Burgoyne's invading army in August 1777, near Bennington. The battle took place about 2 mi. w. of the monument, near Wallomsac Heights (now in New York State). After the first attack and British retreat, the enemy captured and wounded were taken to Bennington. In the second British attack, the Americans gave ground until a detachment of Green Mountain Boys appeared and the British retreated. The battle halted Burgoyne's plan for cutting off New England from other colonies and helped bring on his surrender at Saratoga.

Apr. 1–Nov. 1. Admission.

BENNINGTON MUSEUM, old Bennington on SR 9, Main St., just 1 mi. w. of jct. of SR 9 and US 7.

Battle of Bennington exhibits.

Museum closed Dec., Jan. and Feb. Admission.

## BURLINGTON

BATTERY PARK, downtown, foot of Pearl St.

In the War of 1812, some 4,000 troops were quartered at what is now Battery Park. From here, a raiding party went out to attack St. Armand, Quebec. In 1813, the guns at the Battery beat off three British war vessels.

Ruins of parapet along western border of park. Free.

## CASTLETON

HUBBARDTON BATTLEFIELD AND MUSEUM, 7 mi. n. of US 4 at East Hubbardton.

In one of the most successful rear-guard actions in American military history, General Arthur St. Clair, retreating from Fort

# VERMONT

Ticonderoga, left a rear guard in Hubbardton. The pursuing British troops were repulsed by the rear guard, who then retired to Monument Hill. Losses among the British troops were so great that they had to give up pursuing General St. Clair and returned to Fort Ticonderoga.

Monument, visitor center, museum. Mid-May to mid-Oct. Wed.–Sun. Free.

## NORTHFIELD

NORWICH UNIVERSITY MUSEUM, SR 12, ¼ mi. n. of jct. 12 and 12A.

A special collection of military artifacts, including personal memorabilia of Admiral George Dewey of Spanish-American War fame.

Museum open when campus in session, weekday afternoons, otherwise by appointment. Free.

## ORWELL

MOUNT INDEPENDENCE.

Opposite Fort Ticonderoga and part of its military complex, this major Revolutionary War fortification is considered the least disturbed of Revolutionary War sites. It was an essential part of American defenses against British attack from Canada. American General St. Clair, undermanned and undersupplied, with British forces cutting off his retreat, managed to move south from Mount Independence to Hubbardton. Except for a short and unsuccessful American counterattack in September, 1777, Mount Independence saw little further action. The British garrison was evacuated after the surrender of the British at Saratoga in 1777.

Several trails connect well-preserved remains of Revolutionary War fortifications. Memorial Day to mid-Oct. Free.

## WINDSOR

OLD CONSTITUTION HOUSE, N. Main St.

Items from Colonial and Civil War periods in Vermont. Mid-May to mid-Oct. Free.

# Virginia

Warfare with the Indians developed soon after the English established Jamestown in 1607. In one massacre in 1644, about 500 colonists died. More than a century later, during the French and Indian War, the Virginia militia, under George Washington, played a leading role in protecting frontier settlements. In the American Revolution, Virginia was one of the first colonies to fight for independence. Virginia frontiersmen, led by George Rogers Clark, conquered British-held posts in the Northwest Territory. The final major defeat of the British took place at Yorktown. Virginia also played a prominent role in the War of 1812 and saw her shipping destroyed and the port of Norfolk burned. In the Civil War, the capital of the Confederate States of America was located at Richmond, and major engagements of that war were fought on Virginia soil.

★ ★ ★

# VIRGINIA

## ALEXANDRIA

GADSBY'S TAVERN MUSEUM, 134 N. Royal St.

At this historic inn, now a museum, George Washington recruited troops during the French and Indian War and reviewed local troops at the end of his military career. Alexandria was headquarters for British General Braddock during the American Revolution and was captured and occupied by Federal forces during the Civil War. Walking tour of Old Town Alexandria includes Gadsby's Tavern. Admission to museum.

FORT WARD MUSEUM AND PARK, 4301 W. Braddock Rd, e. of I-395.

Fort Ward was one in a line of Federal forts built to protect Washington D.C. during the Civil War. The Union capital was only one hundred miles from the Confederate capital of Richmond and both cities lived under constant fear of enemy attack during the war. Fort Ward has been partially restored and has a museum of Civil War artifacts. Free.

## APPOMATTOX

APPOMATTOX COURT HOUSE NATIONAL HISTORIC PARK, on SR 24, 3 mi. n.e. of Appomattox.

After General Grant broke the Petersburg line and captured Richmond, General Lee withdrew to Appomattox. A week later, with the last of his Army of Northern Virginia surrounded, Lee surrendered to General Grant on Palm Sunday, April 9, 1865, ending the bloodiest war in America's history. The village where the Civil War ended has been restored to the way it looked on that historic day in 1865, including the McLean farmhouse where the surrender took place. The Court House at Appomattox now contains a museum and audiovisual presentations of the last days of the Confederacy. Admission.

## ARLINGTON

ARLINGTON NATIONAL CEMETERY, directly across the Potomac River from Washington, D.C.

# EXPLORING MILITARY AMERICA

The most cherished national shrine in America and the largest national cemetery in the United States, Arlington National Cemetery was established at the end of the Civil War for America's military dead. Some of the famous sites within the cemetery are the Tomb of the Unknown Soldier, Confederate Memorial and Tomb of the Unknown Dead of the Civil War, Arlington House, Mast of the Battleship *Maine*, Marine Corps War Memorial of the flag-raising on Iwo Jima, and the grave of John F. Kennedy. The Memorial Amphitheater has a tribute room to the unknown dead in America's wars. Conducted motorized tours provide the only transportation through the cemetery for tourists. Charge for tour.

THE OLD GUARD MUSEUM, Fort Meyer. Take SR 27 n. from I-95 to Fort Myer exit to Henry Gate.

Fort Myer was one of the forts that defended Washington, D.C., during the Civil War. Today, the post houses several elite military units, including the historic Third Infantry Regiment (The Old Guard), which guards the Tomb of the Unknown Soldier at Arlington National Cemetery twenty-four hours a day. It was the Third Infantry Regiment that made the famous bayonet charge at Chapultapec Castle during the Mexican War. Museum. Free.

## CHATHAM

CHATHAM MUSEUM, across the Rappahannock River from Fredericksburg, via SR 3 E.

Once the manor of a colonial plantation, this 1771 mansion was used by the Union army during the Civil War as a headquarters, an artillery communications center and a hospital. Museum tells the story of Chatham and its role in the Civil War. Admission.

## COLONIAL HEIGHTS

VIOLET BANK CIVIL WAR MUSEUM, Colonial Heights exit No. 4/west to SR 301, left to Arlington Ave., off I-95.

General Lee's headquarters in 1864 is now a museum of weapons

# VIRGINIA

and equipment carried by Civil War soldiers. Open summers only. Free.

## FORT BELVOIR

U.S. ARMY ENGINEER MUSEUM, Bldg. 1000, 16th St. and Belvoir Rd. Fort Belvoir is 15 mi. s. of Washington, D.C.

The museum presents memorabilia of Army Corps of Engineers from the past two centuries, ranging from maps used during the Siege of Yorktown in the Revolutionary War to satellites prepared by the Engineers in 1964. Free.

## FREDERICKSBURG

FREDERICKSBURG AND SPOTSYLVANIA NATIONAL MILITARY PARK. Visitor Center with museum is at Lafayette Blvd. (US 1) and Sunken Rd.

The park includes a portion of four great Civil War battlefields: Fredericksburg, Spotsylvania Court House, Chancellorsville and the Wilderness. All the battlefields are within a seventeen mile radius of Fredericksburg, a theater of war that cannot be matched elsewhere on the American continent. On the fields of Fredericksburg (1862) and Chancellorsville (1863), the Confederate Army dominated. However, at the Wilderness and Spotsylvania Court House (1864) a stubborn Union Army under General Grant began an advance toward Richmond that ultimately toppled the Confederacy. The great loss of men that General Grant suffered during these battles caused this campaign to be called "Grant's Funeral March." The Fredericksburg National Cemetery is next door to the visitor center. The Union lost 70,000 men in the four battles, the South, 35,000.

Included in the Military Park is the JACKSON MEMORIAL SHRINE, 15 mi. s. of Fredericksburg, reached from US 1 then SR 606 to Guinea. General Jackson was one of the South's most brilliant tacticians. He was accidentally shot by his own men during the battle of Chancellorsville and died in this house, now a shrine to his memory.

# EXPLORING MILITARY AMERICA

Park open all year; Jackson Shrine, summers, shortened hours rest of year. Free.

## FRONT ROYAL

WARREN RIFLES CONFEDERATE MUSEUM, 95 Chester St.

Museum contains artifacts of the Civil War, including memorabilia of Mosby's Rangers, Stonewall Jackson, Robert E. Lee and other Confederate heroes. Also in the collection are mementos of Belle Boyd, the famous Confederate Civil War spy who helped deliver the town of Front Royal into Confederate hands.

Open summers or by appointment. Admission.

## HAMPTON

FORT MONROE AND U.S. ARMY COAST ARTILLERY MUSEUM, US 60 on the Virginia Peninsula in Hampton, directly n. of Norfolk across Hampton Roads.

Two British forts stood here in the seventeenth and eighteenth centuries; and then in 1819, construction of Fort Monroe was begun. Upon completion, it was the largest stone fortress in North America. It was also one of the few forts in the South not captured by the Confederates at the outbreak of the Civil War. Confederate General Robert E. Lee, who had been an Engineering Officer in the U.S. Army, had helped build the fort and knew its formidable strength.

After the Civil War, Confederate President Jefferson Davis was imprisoned at Fort Monroe for two years. His cell has been restored. The Casemate Museum within the fort is the home of the U.S. Army's Coast Artillery Museum, with scale models of historic guns of the early coast artillery era. Museum, tours. Free.

Self-guided walking tours may also be taken of historic Hampton, which was settled in 1610, burned by the British in the American Revolution and by the Confederates during the Civil War.

NASA VISITOR CENTER, Langley Air Force Base, 2 mi. n. of Hampton off I-64.

# VIRGINIA

Military space and aeronautical exhibits from Kitty Hawk to outer space. Free.

## JAMESTOWN

JAMESTOWN FESTIVAL PARK, historic settlement of Jamestown, adjoining the Colonial Parkway and Route 31.

The first English fort built in America was James Fort, constructed in 1608 under the command of Captain John Smith. It was garrisoned by "poor gentlemen, tradesmen, serving-men, libertines and such like." Those who died were secretly buried at night so the Indians would not learn how weak the fort had become.

The three-cornered, wooden-palisaded fort has been reconstructed, including the eighteen wattle and daub buildings and a guardhouse. Museum, tours. Admission.

## LEXINGTON

VIRGINIA MILITARY INSTITUTE MUSEUM, Jackson Memorial Hall.

Cadets from VMI have fought in every American War since the Mexican War. The school itself was shelled and burned during the Civil War. A mural showing the young cadets' heroic charge at the Battle of New Market and items about VMI and its students are displayed at the museum. Free.

GEORGE C. MARSHALL LIBRARY AND MUSEUM, Virginia Military Institute.

General George C. Marshall of World War II fame was a graduate of VMI. His military career spanned much of the twentieth century. Museum houses his personal possessions as well as exhibits tracing the history of World War II. Free.

## MANASSAS

MANASSAS NATIONAL BATTLEFIELD PARK, n. of Manassas. Visitor Center at SR 234 between I-66 and US 29 and 211.

# EXPLORING MILITARY AMERICA

Two important battles of the Civil War took place at Manassas. The first Battle of Manassas, also called Bull Run, was the first major battle of the war and was fought in July, 1861, between untrained soldiers in what has been called "a collision between two large armed mobs." The Confederate victory sent the Union troops, and the spectators who had come out to picnic and watch the battle, retreating hastily back to Washington. The second Battle of Manassas, in August 1862, was also a Confederate victory and was the spearhead of Lee's first invasion of the North.

A stone house on the battlefield, used as a field hospital, has been renovated and is open to the public.

Visitor center, museum, tours. Free.

## MIDDLESBORO

CUMBERLAND GAP NATIONAL HISTORICAL PARK, s.e. of Middlesboro on US 25E and 58.

This historic pass, a vital strategic point, was captured by the Union Army in September, 1863. Museum near Middlesboro Visitor Center has weapons and history of Civil War era. Free.

## NEW MARKET

NEW MARKET BATTLEFIELD PARK, SR 305, 1 mi. n. of I-81, Exit 67.

Union forces tried and failed several times to win control of the Shenandoah Valley in Virginia, a vital source of food and supplies for the Confederate Army. One such attempt was made in 1864 by General Franz Siegal. His defeat at New Market was partly due to the valor of young cadets ranging in age from 14 to 20, students at the Virginia Military Institute, who were pressed into service during the battle. The Hall of Valor at the Battlefield Park is a living memorial to the cadets, and includes the Virginia Room, which displays the chronological story of all the major Civil War campaigns in Virginia.

Museum, restored Bushong farmhouse, battlefield, tours. Admission.

# VIRGINIA

## NEWPORT NEWS

WAR MEMORIAL MUSEUM OF VIRGINIA, 9285 Warwick Blvd.

Every conflict involving America from pre-Revolutionary War days through Vietnam is represented in this museum, as well as military exhibits from foreign countries. Admission.

NEWPORT NEWS DAM NO. 1 PARK, SR 143.

Two fortified dams were built in 1862 on the Warwick River to create lakes to stop the Federal forces from marching toward Richmond. Dam No. 1, Confederate gun positions and Union trenches are still visible.

Visitor center, exhibits. Free.

## NORFOLK

AMPHIBIOUS MUSEUM, Naval Amphibious Base, Little Creek.

Displays depicting evolution of amphibious warfare.

Free.

HAMPTON ROADS NAVAL MUSEUM, Pennsylvania House, Naval Base.

Norfolk was bombarded and destroyed during the Revolutionary War and again in the War of 1812. The city held a Confederate naval station during the Civil War, and the most important naval engagement of the war took place at nearby Hampton Roads: the duel of the ironclads, the *C.S.S. Virginia* (Merrimac) and the *U.S.S. Monitor*. The battle changed the course of naval history, making all wooden naval ships obsolete.

Museum contains historic naval exhibits. Free. The Norfolk Naval Base holds open house on summer weekend afternoons, providing tours of selected ships. Group tours, by appointment, of base and museum also available. Free. Information Center, 9809 Hampton Blvd.

GENERAL DOUGLAS MACARTHUR MEMORIAL MUSEUM, City Hall Ave.

Memorabilia and crypt of one of America's most controversial war heroes and military leaders, General Douglas MacArthur.

Museum. Admission.

# EXPLORING MILITARY AMERICA

**PETERSBURG**

PETERSBURG NATIONAL BATTLEFIELD. Visitor center at park entrance off SR 36.

After his defeat at the Battle of Cold Harbor, General Grant gave up attacking Richmond directly and began a ten-month siege of Petersburg in 1864. It was the longest siege in American history, taking the lives of 70,000 Americans. There were several major battles during the siege. In one battle, Union troops tunneled under the Confederate lines. However, the tunnel exploded, resulting in the disastrous Battle of the Crater, with Union and Confederate troops trapped in the crater that formed from the explosion. Petersburg finally fell one week before Lee's final surrender at Appomattox.

Visitor center, museum, tours. Free.

SIEGE MUSEUM, Bank St.

Petersburg saw action during the Revolutionary War and was headquarters for British General Cornwallis in his Yorktown Campaign during that war. The Siege Museum has displays showing the life of the ordinary Petersburg citizen during the terrible ten-month siege in the Civil War. Free.

U.S. ARMY QUARTERMASTER MUSEUM, Fort Lee, SR 36, 2 mi. e. of Petersburg.

A varied and extensive collection covering the Army Quartermaster's invaluable role in all of America's wars, ranging from a Civil War hospital wagon to the jeep General Patton used during World War II. Free.

**PORTSMOUTH**

PORTSMOUTH NAVAL SHIPYARD MUSEUM, foot of High St.

Portsmouth with its valuable Gosport Shipyard was burned twice during the Revolutionary War, once by the British and once by the traitor, Benedict Arnold. During the Civil War, the Confederates gained control of the shipyard, and it was at Portsmouth that the

# VIRGINIA

frigate *U.S.S. Merrimac* was raised, turning it into the world's first ironclad battleship, the *C.S.S. Virginia*. Free.

A COAST GUARD MUSEUM is adjacent to the Naval Shipyard Museum. Free.

## QUANTICO

U.S. MARINE CORPS AVIATION MUSEUM, off US 1 and I-95. Map at front gate.

Depicts growth of Marine aviation. Restored aircraft from WW II. Free.

## RICE

SAYLER'S CREEK BATTLEFIELD PARK, SR 617, 2 mi. n. of SR 307.

Over 6,000 Confederates, including eleven generals, were captured here on April 6, 1865, when Confederate troops became bogged down in swampy bottom land along Sayler's Creek. Audio station at battlefield describes action. Free.

## RICHMOND

BERKELEY PLANTATION, on James River, 22 mi. s.e. of Richmond via Va. 5, 6 mi. w. of Charles City.

This seventeenth-century plantation was plundered by British troops under Benedict Arnold during the American Revolution and was used by Union General McClellan as his headquarters during his Peninsula Campaign into Virginia in 1862. Admission.

RICHMOND NATIONAL BATTLEFIELD PARK, Visitor Center/Museum at 3215 E. Broad St., Chimborazo Park.

Several major drives were launched by Union troops against Richmond, the capital of the Confederate States of America. Two campaigns brought Union forces almost within sight of the city: McClellan's Peninsula Campaign of 1862, which ended in defeat in the Seven Days' Battle; and Grant's crushing campaign, which finally

# EXPLORING MILITARY AMERICA

brought about the fall of Richmond in April 1865. Black military units were given the honor of being among the first to lead the victory march into Richmond.

One of the bloodiest battles fought near Richmond was the Battle of Cold Harbor in 1864, which has been called the "worst blunder of General Grant's career." Approximately 7,000 Union soldiers fell in one thirty-minute charge during that battle, and General Grant was forced to withdraw.

The Richmond National Battlefield Park preserves the Cold Harbor Battlefield as well as landmarks of several other battle sites, including Watt House (Battle of Gaines' Mill), Malvern Hill, Fort Harrison, Fort Brady and Drewry's Bluff (Fort Darling). There is a second visitor center at Fort Harrison.

Visitor centers, museum, tours. Free.

MUSEUM OF THE CONFEDERACY, 12th and Clay Sts.

The world's newest and largest collection of Confederate memorabilia and Civil War artifacts is housed in a museum adjacent to the WHITE HOUSE OF THE CONFEDERACY. Ranging from the elegant gold-braided uniform that General Lee wore at Appomattox to dented mess kits and gleaming surgical saws, interpretive exhibits display the history of the short-lived Confederate nation. Admission.

ROBERT E. LEE HOUSE, 707 E. Franklin St.

The home in Richmond where Robert E. Lee lived during the Civil War is now a museum, featuring exhibits on civilian life in the South during the war. Admission.

BATTLE ABBEY, 428 N. Boulevard.

Memorial Hall has exhibits on the military history of Virginia. Admission.

VIRGINIA WORLD WAR II AND KOREA MEMORIAL, n. end of Robert E. Lee Bridge on US 1.

Dedicated to Virginians in all the armed forces, the memorial contains artifacts of all major land and naval engagements of World War II and the Korean War. Free.

# VIRGINIA

## WILLIAMSBURG

HISTORIC WILLIAMSBURG, Colonial Parkway

The magazine and guardhouse in historic restored Williamsburg were used to store arms and ammunition in the eighteenth century. Today, they contain exhibits of eighteenth century military life. The governor's palace at Williamsburg was destroyed by fire during the American Revolution when it was being used as a hospital for the soldiers wounded at Yorktown. Admission.

FORT CRAFFORD, on Mulberry Island Point overlooking James River, is within the FORT EUSTIS Military Reservation. Fort Eustis is 10 mi. s. of Williamsburg.

Constructed by the Confederacy during the Civil War, the pentagon-shaped fort, with a moat, is remarkably well preserved. Free.

U.S. ARMY TRANSPORTATION MUSEUM, FORT EUSTIS, 10 mi. s. of Williamsburg off I-64, SR 105 exit.

Museum covers the evolution of military transportation from horse-drawn vehicles of Revolutionary War days to the present jet age. Free.

## WINCHESTER

GEORGE WASHINGTON'S OFFICE, US 11, southbound.

Winchester played an important part in the French and Indian War. George Washington had his headquarters in this house when he was commander of the Virginia frontier. His headquarters is now a museum containing items from Washington's early military career. May 1–Oct. 31. Admission.

STONEWALL JACKSON'S HEADQUARTERS, US 11 and 415 N. Braddock St.

Winchester was the scene of six battles and numerous skirmishes during the Civil War. Once the town changed hands thirteen times in one day's fighting! It was while he had his headquarters at Winchester in 1864 that Union General Sheridan made his famous ride to rally Federal troops to victory at the Battle of Cedar Creek, south of Winchester. During one of the many battles that took place in Winchester, Confederate General Stonewall Jackson had his headquarters in the town. The house he occupied is now a museum of Jackson's personal possessions and Civil War memorabilia. Admission.

## YORKTOWN

YORKTOWN BATTLEFIELD, part of Colonial National Historical Park.
Museum is on the s.e. edge of Yorktown, at the terminus of the Colonial Parkway.

A battlefield that encompasses two wars, the Revolutionary War and the Civil War, Yorktown was fortified by British General Cornwallis in 1781. General Washington, with French and American troops, surrounded Yorktown, and a deadly siege was begun. The British forces, weakened by the constant artillery fire, surrendered on October 19, 1781, bringing the Revolutionary War to an end, although the formal peace treaty was not signed for two years. The brilliant uniforms of the British Army during the surrender ceremony were in marked contrast to the ragged uniforms of the Continental soldiers.

During the Civil War, Yorktown was again fortified, this time by the Confederates. The Union troops prepared to open a siege, much as Washington's earlier troops had done, but this time, perhaps remembering the fate of Cornwallis, the Confederate troops withdrew toward Williamsburg. The Union Army kept control of Yorktown during the rest of the Civil War.

Many sites still stand at the battlefield from the time of the Revolutionary War siege, including the entrenchments and fortifications of both armies, and Surrender Field. The site of General Washington's headquarters is also part of a self-guided battlefield tour.

Visitor center, exhibits, tours. Free.

YORKTOWN VICTORY CENTER, ¼ mi. w. of Yorktown Bridge, via Colonial Parkway or US 17.

The history of the American Revolution is traced with sound and light exhibits and a film "The Road to Yorktown." Admission.

# VIRGINIA

MOORE HOUSE, adjacent to the battlefield.

It was at Moore house that the British and American commissioners met and the articles of capitulation were negotiated. Open late spring–early fall. Free.

There are other sites of military significance which may be visited in Yorktown, including the NELSON HOUSE (summers only), used by General Cornwallis as a command post, and GRACE CHURCH, which was used by the British as a powder magazine during the Yorktown Siege.

# Washington

Spanish, British and American seafarers all laid claims to the Washington area; the 1592 claim of the Spanish explorer Juan de Fuca was the earliest. Canadian and American fur trappers set up trading posts by 1810. With the arrival of American settlers in the 1840s, boundary disputes began between the United States and Great Britain and were not completely settled until 1872, after the bloodless 1859 Pig War. In the interior, fighting with Indians over hunting grounds occurred intermittently between 1855 and 1859. Coastal fortifications were erected during the Spanish-American War and were garrisoned through World War II.

★ ★ ★

**BREMERTON**

NAVAL SHIPYARD MUSEUM, Ferry Terminal Building, SR 16 from Tacoma or take ferry from Seattle to Bremerton.

Museum contains exhibits on history of the shipyard and U.S. naval history. Afternoons. Free.

# WASHINGTON

U.S.S. MISSOURI, anchored adjacent to the naval shipyard. May be reached by bus from terminal.

The war with Japan during World War II ended on September 2, 1945, with the signing of a treaty aboard the *U.S.S. Missouri*. Visitors may board the "Mighty Mo" and see the surrender deck.

All day, Memorial day–Labor day. Afternoons, rest of year. Free.

## CHINOOK

FORT COLUMBIA STATE PARK, 1 mi. east, off US 101.

Fort Columbia is typical of the coastal artillery forts built during the Spanish-American War when protecting American harbors was a major military strategy.

Original fort, interpretive center, museum. Free.

## COUPEVILLE

FORT CASEY STATE PARK, 3 mi. south, off SR 20 on Fort Casey Road.

Built in the Spanish-American War period, the fort was part of the Puget Sound Defense System, which existed from 1900 to World War II.

Fortifications, interpretive center housed in 1890 lighthouse. Apr. 1–Sept. 30, closed Mon. and Tues. Free.

## KEYPORT

NAVAL MUSEUM OF UNDERSEA WARFARE, Industrial Area, Naval Undersea Warfare Engineering Station, Puget Sound.

A temporary museum on the history of naval undersea warfare and undersea warfare weapons will eventually be replaced by a permanent museum for the preservation and display of artifacts relating to undersea warfare.

Open Wednesdays from 11 a.m. to 12 noon. Special tours may be arranged. Free.

# EXPLORING MILITARY AMERICA

## OLYMPIA

FORT LEWIS MILITARY MUSEUM, 20 mi. e. of Olympia, Dupont/Steilacoom exit, north off I-5, or s.w. of Tacoma.

Museum displays material relating to U.S. military endeavors in the Northwest, with emphasis on Fort Lewis and the units who served at the fort. Outdoor display of military equipment.

Afternoons. Free.

## SAN JUAN ISLAND

SAN JUAN ISLAND NATIONAL HISTORIC PARK, Friday Harbor vicinity, reached by ferry from Anacortes.

A war without bloodshed occurred in 1859 when an American settler on San Juan Island shot a pig owned by the Hudson Bay Company. American troops were sent to the island, and Great Britain sent a warship, but the matter was settled peacefully and no shots were fired. Both American and British military fortifications may be seen on the island. The English camp is at Garrison Bay, 8 miles from Friday Harbor, with a blockhouse, commissary and restored barracks. The remains of the American camp is on the southeastern tip of the island, 5 miles from Friday Harbor.

Park open all year, buildings closed in winter. Free.

## SPOKANE

FORT WRIGHT COLLEGE HISTORICAL MUSEUM, West 4000 Randolph Road.

Museum shows the life style of military personnel living at Fort George Wright when it was an army post from 1899 to 1958.

Museum open weekend afternoons or by appointment. Free.

## TOPPENISH

FORT SIMCOE STATE PARK, 28 mi. w. of Toppenish.

In 1856, hostilities with the Yakima Indians resulted in the establishment of Fort Simcoe. The intrusion of miners and settlers into

# WASHINGTON

Indian lands ceded to the Yakimas in 1855 resulted in the tragic Yakima War of 1855–58.

Partially restored fort, interpretive center. Apr. 1–Oct. 15. By appointment rest of year. Free.

## VANCOUVER

FORT VANCOUVER NATIONAL HISTORIC SITE, E. Evergreen Blvd., ½ mi. e. of Vancouver, off I-5 at Mill Plain Blvd. exit.

A fur-trading post from 1824–46, Fort Vancouver in 1849 became the first U.S. military post in the Pacific Northwest.

Reconstructed fort, visitor center, museum, tours. Free.

ULYSSES S. GRANT MUSEUM, 1106 E. Evergreen Blvd.

As a young officer, General Grant served as quartermaster at Fort Vancouver. Museum has personal memorabilia of General Grant and Indian artifacts. Admission.

# West Virginia

The mountains and the Shawnee Indians formed a barrier against the settlement of western Virginia until 1726 when the first town was founded near present-day Charlestown. Indian resistance to settlers began early, continued through the French and Indian War, and did not end until the forces of Lord Dunmore, Royal Governor of Virginia, defeated the Indian nations who had combined under Chief Cornstalk. During the American Revolution, the Shawnees and British attacked the western frontier settlements. The last battle of the Revolution occurred at Fort Henry on September 11, 1782.

Western Virginia had few slaves, and John Brown's unsuccessful attempt to cause a slave uprising at Harpers Ferry in 1859 aroused little sympathy. But when Virginia seceded from the Union at the beginning of the Civil War, the area that is now West Virginia declared the secession void. After Union military successes in the area in 1861, West Virginia became a separate state.

★ ★ ★

# WEST VIRGINIA

## DROOP

DROOP MOUNTAIN BATTLEFIELD STATE PARK, on US 219, w. of Droop.

The largest Civil War battle in West Virginia took place in November of 1863 on this high mountain plateau; it ended Confederate resistance in the state.

Partially restored battlefield, markers, museum. Free.

## FAIRMONT

PRICKETTS FORT STATE PARK, off I-79 (Exit 139) 5 mi. n.

In 1772, the Shawnee Indians resisted further white settlement in their lands in western Virginia, threatening to turn the frontier "red with Long Knives' blood." Lord Dunmore, the Royal Governor of Virginia, sent militia to fortify the outposts along the Ohio River, and the war that followed with the Shawnee was called Lord Dunmore's War. One of the forts built for protection against the Indians was Pricketts Fort. Many times during the next years, settlers would seek protection within the fort as the Indians burned and plundered the Ohio Valley.

Restored fort with stockade and pioneer cabins, exhibits. May through Sept. Weekends, Apr. 16–30 and Oct. Admission.

## HARPERS FERRY

HARPERS FERRY NATIONAL HISTORIC PARK. Visitor Center on Shenandoah Street.

The Federal arsenal and armory at Harpers Ferry provided muskets for the War of 1812 as well as the Civil War. It was this important arsenal that fanatic abolitionist John Brown attempted to capture in 1859. He had hoped to arm rebellious slaves with the weapons in the arsenal. Instead he and his men were captured, tried, found guilty and hanged. Just before he was hanged, Brown warned "that the crimes of this guilty land will never be purged away but with blood." His prophecy came true with the Civil War. During the war, Harpers Ferry was almost destroyed as Federal and Confederate troops fought for control of the town and arsenal.

# EXPLORING MILITARY AMERICA

Civil War fortification, historic buildings, John Brown's Fort, visitor center, exhibits, tours. Free.

## POINT PLEASANT

POINT PLEASANT BATTLE MONUMENT, Tu-Endie-Wei Park.

During Lord Dunmore's War in October 1774, in fierce hand-to-hand combat, 1100 Virginia militia men and an equal number of Shawnee Indians, led by Chief Cornstalk, attacked and counterattacked. The Indians finally retreated to a point of land formed by the confluence of the Great Kanawha and Ohio rivers. Over fifty Virginians were killed in the all-day battle before the Indians finally withdrew. Because it was suspected that the Indians had been incited by British agents, the battle has been called by some historians the "first battle of the American Revolution." The battle did prevent a general Indian war and broke the power of the Indians in the Ohio Valley.

Monument, museum. Apr. 1–Nov. 30. Free.

## SUMMERSVILLE

CARNIFEX FERRY BATTLEFIELD STATE PARK, 10 mi. s.w.

A house known as the Patterson house was situated between Union and Confederate lines during the skirmish at Carnifex Ferry in September 1861. It has been restored as a museum containing relics from the battle.

A marker at the courthouse in the town commemorates Nancy Hart, the beautiful Confederate spy who led a surprise attack on the town, was captured, bewitched her guard, shot him and escaped.

Museum open May 1–Sept. 30. Free.

## WHEELING

FORT HENRY SITE, Main St. near Eleventh, Wheeling Hill.

In September 1777, British-allied Indians launched an unsuccessful attack against Fort Henry. Five years later, the last battle of the American Revolution was fought here when the fort was attacked

## WEST VIRGINIA

by the British and Indians. Although the war had ended, news of the peace had not yet reached Fort Henry. It was during the three-day siege, when the fort had run out of gunpowder, that courageous Betty Zane dashed to the Zane cabin in full view of the enemy and, returning with gunpowder in her apron, saved the fort.

Plaque marks site of Fort Henry. Relics from the siege are at the MANSION MUSEUM in Oglebay Park, 5 mi. n.w. of Wheeling on SR 88.

Admission to museum.

# Wisconsin

A French expedition in 1634 brought the first Europeans to the Wisconsin area. According to legend, the leader expected to find Chinese but settled for Indians and fur trade. Though French control of the area was lost at the end of the French and Indian War, French fur traders remained, under English control, until after the War of 1812. Then the United States erected forts, and treaties were made with the resentful Indians of the area—the Winnebago, Fox, Sauk, Chippewa and other tribes. Indian hostilities continued, however, until the Black Hawk War, in which the Sauks were defeated. In the Civil War, more than 90,000 Wisconsin men served in the Union army, with 11,000 giving their lives.

★ ★ ★

**GREEN BAY**

FORT HOWARD, 402 N. Chestnut Ave.

Established in 1816, this frontier fort was garrisoned through the Mexican War, but abandoned in 1852. Nearby, also within Heritage

# WISCONSIN

Hill State Park, is the 1776 TANK COTTAGE, a War of 1812 military headquarters.
Partly restored fort. Cottage. Free.

## KENOSHA

CIVIL WAR MUSEUM, Lentz Hall, Carthage College.
Mementoes of the Civil War. Wisconsin men served in every major campaign.
Weekdays only. Free.

## KING

WISCONSIN VETERANS MUSEUM, grounds of Wisconsin Veterans Home.
World War I and II exhibits. Free.

## LA POINTE

MADELINE ISLAND HISTORICAL MUSEUM
In 1693 Pierre Le Sueur and a company of soldiers built a fur trading post on Madeline Island. The fort became British, and then later, after the War of 1812, headquarters for the American Fur Company.
Reconstructed fort with stockade, museum. May 15–Oct. 15. Ferry runs hourly between Bayfield and La Pointe. Admission.

## MADISON

G.A.R. MEMORIAL HALL MUSEUM, State Capitol, 419 N. Madison.
Civil War and Spanish-American War exhibits.
Closed weekends in winter. Free.

## MANITOWOC

INTERNATIONAL SUBMARINE MEMORIAL, Manitowoc River, adjacent to the Manitowoc Maritime Museum, 809 S. 8th St.

# EXPLORING MILITARY AMERICA

A World War II submarine, the *U.S.S. Cobia,* may be toured in connection with the Maritime Museum, which has exhibits of maritime and naval history from 1847 to the present. Admission.

## PORTAGE

FORT WINNEBAGO SURGEON'S QUARTERS, 1 mi. e. on SR 33.

The Winnebago Indian uprising in Wisconsin in 1827 ended with the imprisonment and death of the Winnebago Chief at Prairie du Chien. In 1832, the Black Hawk War (see Illinois) with the Sauk and Fox Indians ended Indian resistance in Wisconsin. Black Hawk and his people were defeated at the Battle of Bad Axe River in southern Wisconsin. Troops from Fort Winnebago were active in the Indian wars in Wisconsin.

Museum in Surgeon's Quarters (only fort structure remaining). May 1–Oct. 31. Admission.

OLD INDIAN AGENCY, 1¼ mi. e. of Portage on SR 33, ½ mi. n. along the canal.

Near site of Fort Winnebago is an old Indian agency museum containing artifacts of the Winnebago Indians.

May 1–Oct. 31, other times by appointment. Admission.

## PRAIRIE DU CHIEN

VILLA LOUIS, intersection of Villa Louis Rd. and Volvin St.

During the War of 1812, the Army built Fort Shelby near the Mississippi River at Prairie du Chien. This early fort was captured and burned by the British, and Fort Crawford took its place in 1816. Later a mansion, called the Villa Louis, was built near the site of the fort. Today, a museum in the carriage house has artifacts from Fort Shelby.

May–Oct. Admission.

# Wyoming

French fur trappers were the first Europeans into Wyoming, arriving in 1742. Land claims were also made by Spain, England, Mexico, Texas and the United States. Lieutenant John Fremont and Colonel Stephen Kearny led expeditions through the area in the mid-1840s. Beginning in 1841, more than 150,000 settlers followed the Oregon and Mormon trails west across Wyoming. Indian unrest, at this influx of white settlers into their lands, turned into open warfare by the 1860s, with the Sioux, Cheyenne, Arapaho, Crow and Shoshone Indians arrayed against the American military garrisoned at isolated army forts scattered across Wyoming. The warfare did not end until the late 1870s. In 1892, the army was called in to quell the Johnson County Range War. In the Spanish-American War, the state exceeded its quota of volunteers, with a Wyoming unit reputedly raising the first American flag over Manila.

★ ★ ★

# EXPLORING MILITARY AMERICA

**BUFFALO**

FORT PHIL KEARNY SITE, 17 mi. n. off I-90 and US 87.

Today, only a reproduction of an officers' quarters and a plaque mark the site of Fort Phil Kearny, which had the bloodiest history of any fort in the west. The focal point of siege after siege during Red Cloud's War, the fort was finally abandoned, then quickly burned by the Indians in 1868. Free.

**CASPAR**

OLD FORT CASPAR, 1¼ mi. s.w. off SR 220, then 1½ mi. w. on W. 13th St. and Fort Caspar Rd.

Built in 1857 to guard the Oregon trail, several famous Indian battles were fought within earshot of the fort, which also guarded the telegraph lines across Wyoming during the Civil War.

Restored fort. May 15–Sept. 15. By appt. rest of year. Free.

**CHEYENNE**

WARREN MILITARY MUSEUM, F. E. Warren Air Force Base, adjacent to Cheyenne on I-25.

Warren Air Force Base began as Fort Russell in 1867 when the first troops of cavalry at the fort coped with freezing weather in the winter and with Indians in the spring and summer. At one time, it was the largest cavalry post in the United States. In just eighty years, the military installation moved from muskets to missiles. In 1947 the fort became Francis E. Warren Air Force Base.

Museum in old headquarters building. May to Sept., afternoons only. Sept. to May, Sun. afternoons only. Free.

**DOUGLAS**

FORT FETTERMAN, 11 mi. n.w. via the Orpha exit from I-25.

In the mid-1870s, Fort Fetterman was the jumping-off place for several major military expeditions against the Plains Indians, including General Crook's Yellowstone Expedition and Colonel MacKenzie's

# WYOMING

Cheyenne campaign. After the Indians were confined to reservations, the fort was abandoned in 1882.

Partially restored fort, museum. May 15–Sept. 15. Free.

## FORT BRIDGER

FORT BRIDGER STATE HISTORIC SITE, US 30 S at Fort Bridger.

Originally this was a fur-trading post—built in 1843 by the famous scout, Jim Bridger; the Mormon emigrants later used the fort as a supply center. When Federal troops were sent against the Mormons, the Mormons burned the fort. It was rebuilt by the Army in 1858. "Galvanized Yankees" or ex-Confederate soldiers, garrisoned the fort during the Civil War. Afterwards, the fort served as a Pony Express and Overland Stage route station.

Original fort structures, museum. Apr.–Sept. 2. Weekends Sept.–Mar. 31. Free.

## FORT LARAMIE

FORT LARAMIE NATIONAL HISTORIC SITE, 3 mi. s.w. off US 26.

Fort Laramie was a fur-trading post from 1834 to 1849 and a well-known military post on the Oregon Trail until 1890. The troops from Fort Laramie were involved in campaigns against northern Plains Indians in the 1860s and '70s, including the unsuccessful Powder River Expedition of 1865 against the Sioux and Cheyenne. Several important Indian treaties were signed at the fort before it was abandoned in 1890.

Restored fort, museum, tours. Free.

## RANCHESTER

CONNOR BATTLEFIELD (TONGUE RIVER BATTLEFIELD), City Park on the Tongue River, s. of Ranchester, or 11 mi. n. of Sheridan on I-25 and US 14.

This stretch of Tongue River bottomland was the site of the Battle of Tongue River, the single most important military engagement

# EXPLORING MILITARY AMERICA

during the Powder River Expedition of 1865. Four hundred troopers surprised a Cheyenne and Arapaho village, killing over 600 Indians.

Interpretive markers. Free.

## STORY

FETTERMAN MASSACRE MONUMENT, n. of Story on US 87, or 20 mi. s. of Sheridan, overlooking US 87.

In December, 1866, Colonel Fetterman's troop of eighty men were ambushed and killed near Fort Phil Kearny by Chief Red Cloud and a force of 2,000 Sioux, Cheyenne and Arapaho.

Monument and interpretive markers. Free.

WAGON BOX BATTLE SITE, w. off US 87 at Story, 22 mi. n. of Buffalo.

In 1866, with the help of new repeating rifles, fewer than 30 soldiers from Fort Phil Kearny stood off several hundred Sioux warriors under the command of Crazy Horse. From behind a barricade of wagons, the soldiers cut down wave after wave of Indians by the volume of fire from the rifles.

Interpretive markers. Free.

# INDEX

Air Defense Artillery Museum, 273
Air Force Armament Museum, 68
Air Force Military Training Center History and Traditions Museum, 282
Air Force Space Museum, 67
Air Museum, 45
Alabama (U.S.S.) Battleship Memorial, 32
Alabama Space and Rocket Center, 31
Alamance Battleground, 216
Alamo, 281
Altar of Peace, 228
American Society of Military History, 45
Amphibious Museum, 297
Ancient and Honorable Artillery Company of Massachusetts, 142
Anderson House, 63, 164

Andersonville National Historic Site, 74
Antietam National Battlefield, 139
Appomattox Court House National Historic Park, 291
Arizona (U.S.S.) National Memorial, 83
Arkansas Post National Memorial, 37
Arlington National Cemetery, 291
Armed Forces Medical Museum, 63
Arnold Trail, 132
Atlanta Battle Cyclorama, 74
Avery (Ebenezer) House, 56

Baltimore Maritime Museum, 136
Baltimore Seaport, 136
Batfish, U.S.S., 194, 234

# INDEX

Battery, 254
Battery Park, 288
Battery Randolph, 83
Battery Reed, 200
Battery Robinett Historic Battlefield Park, 159
Battle Abbey, 300
Battle Abbey Behind the Cabildo, 127
Battle Ground Ridge, 40
Battle Mountain State Park, 237
Battle of Baton Rouge State Monument, 125
Battle of Cooch's Bridge, 60
Battle of Corydon, 93
Battle of Kettle Creek, 80
Battle of Mine Creek, 118
Battle of Nashville, 267
Battle of Stillman's Run, 89
Battle of Washita Battleground, 232
Battle of Wounded Knee, 261
Battle-o-Rama, 266
Battle Road Visitor Center, 148
Battleship Cove, 146
Bear Butte State Park, 262
Bear Mountain Historical Museum State Park, 202
Bears Paw State Monument, 170
Beaufort Arsenal Museum, 253
Becuna, U.S.S., 244
Beecher Island Battle Site, 54
Belle Meade, 267
Bennett Place State Historic Site, 217
Bennington Battlefield, 196

Bennington Battle Monument, 288
Bennington Museum, 288
Bent (Governor) House, 188
Benton County Museum, 167
Bentonville Battleground, 218
Bent's Old Fort National Historic Site, 53
Berkeley Plantation, 299
Big Hole National Battlefield, 169
Big Shanty Museum, 78
Big Spring Battle Monument, 30
Birch Coulee Battleground Park, 155
Black Hawk State Park, 91
Black Kettle Museum, 232
Blockade Runners of the Confederacy Museum, 216
Bloody Marsh Battle Site, 75
Blue-Gray Museum, 77
Blue Licks Battlefield State Park, 120
Boston Common, 143
Boston Massacre Site, 142
Boston Tea Party Ship and Museum, 143
Braddock's Grave, 246
Bradford (David) House, 246
Bradley Air Museum, 58
Bradley (Omar N.) Museum, 240
Brandywine Battlefield Park, 240
Brice's Cross Roads Battlefield, 158

# INDEX

Brice's Cross Roads Museum, 159
Brooks Air Force Base, 282
Browning (John M.) Armory, 285
Browning (John M.) Memorial Museum, 92
Brunswick Town, 219
Bryan Station Memorial, 121
Buckman Tavern, 147
Bunker Hill Monument, 144
Burial Hill, 149
Burnham Tavern Museum, 132
Burt-Stark House, 258
Bushwhacker Museum, 165
Bushy Run Battlefield, 242
Butts Hill Fort, 250

Cahokia Courthouse Historic Site, 89
Camden Battlefield, 253
Camp Floyd State Historic Site, 285
Camp Hancock Museum, 222
Camp Tyler, 53
Campus Martius Memorial Museum, 228
Camp Verde, 272
Camp Wardwell, 53
Cantigny War Memorial, 90
Cape Canaveral Air Force Station, 67
Carnifex Ferry Battlefield State Park, 310
Carson (Kit) Museum, 53
Carter House, 266

Castillo de San Marcos National Monument, 70
Castle Clinton National Monument, 196
Castle Island, 143
Cathedral of the Pines War Memorial, 178
Cavalla, U.S.S., 275
Cavalry Museum, 274
CEC/Seabee Museum, 46
Chalmette National Historical Park, 127
Charleston Naval Base, 256
Chatham Museum, 292
Cherry Valley Museum, 192
Chickamauga–Chattanooga National Military Park, 77, 264
Chief Joseph Battlefield, 170
Cibecue Creek Battlefield, 42
Citadel Archives–Museum, 256
City Hall Museum, 197
City of Refuge, 81
Civil War, 13–15
Civil War Museum, 313
Clark House, 183
Clark (George Rogers) Memorial National Historical Park, 96
Clark (Elijah) State Park Museum, 78
Clearwater Battlefield, 86
Coast Guard Museum, 299
Cobb House, 181
Cobia, U.S.S., 314
Cochise Visitor Center and Museum, 42

# INDEX

Cole's Hill, 149
Colonial Powder Magazine, 254
Columbus-Belmont Battlefield State Park, 120
Comfort Historical Museum, 273
Comfort Monument, 272
Concord Antiquarian Museum, 146
Confederate Air Force Flying Museum, 276
Confederate Air Force Museum, 187
Confederate Memorial Hall, 266
Confederate Museum, 76, 121, 126, 255
Confederate Naval Museum, 76
Confederate Park, 267
Confederate Research Center and Gun Museum, 276
Conference House, 199
Connor Battlefield, 317
Constellation, U.S.S., 136
Constitution, U.S.S., 145
Coronado National Memorial, 39
Cowpens National Battlefield, 257
Cravens House, 164
Crazy Horse Mountain Memorial, 260
Crazy Horse Museum, 173
Croaker (U.S.S.) Submarine Memorial, 56
Crook (General George) House, 173

Cumberland Gap National Historical Park, 122, 296
Custer Battlefield National Monument, 169

Dade Battlefield State Historic Site, 67
Dandy First Museum, 243
Daughters of the American Revolution Museum, 63
Daughters of the Confederacy and Daughters of the Republic of Texas Museum, 271
Davis (Sam) Home, 268
Dawson (Hunter) Home, 166
Dearborn Historical Museum, 152
DeLord (Kent) House, 197
De Soto National Memorial, 67
Droop Mountain Battlefield State Park, 309
Drum, U.S.S., 32
Drum Barracks, 49
Drummer Boy Museum, 144

East Coast Memorial, 196
18th Field Artillery Regiment Museum, 233
Eighth Air Force Museum, 125
Eighty-second Airborne Division War Memorial Museum, 217
Elkhorn Tavern, 38
Eutah Battlefield, 257

# INDEX

Fallen Timbers Battlefield, 228
Fannin's Grave, 275
Fetterman Massacre Monument, 318
First Cavalry Division Museum, 278
First Coast Guard District Marine Exhibit, 133
First White House of the Confederacy, 32
Five Civilized Tribes Museum, 234
Florence Air and Missile Museum, 257
Florida National Guard and Militia Museum, 71
Forest City Stockade, 155
Forrest (Nathan Bedford) Memorial Park, 264
Fort Abercrombie State Historic Site, 221
Fort Abercrombie State Park, 35
Fort Adams State Park, 248
Fort Allen Park, 133
Fort Anderson, 219
Fort Anderson State Historic Site, 220
Fort Apache Site, 42
Fort Astoria, 236
Fort Atkinson Monument State Park, 99
Fort Atkinson State Historical Park, 173
Fort Bacon State Park, 216
Fort Barry, 47
Fort Bedford Museum, 239

Fort Belknap, 280
Fort Belmont, 155
Fort Benton Historic District, 170
Fort Bidwell, 44
Fort Bissell, 117
Fort Bliss Replica Museum, 273
Fort Blunder, 198
Fort Boonesborough State Park, 123
Fort Bowie National Historic Site, 40
Fort Bragg, 217
Fort Bridger State Historic Site, 317
Fort Brown, 271
Fort Buford State Historic Site, 224
Fort Campbell Museum, 120
Fort Carillon, 200
Fort Caroline National Memorial, 68
Fort Carson Museum of the Army in the West, 51
Fort Casey State Park, 305
Fort Chartres Historic Site, 91
Fort Chickamauga, 232
Fort Christina Site, 61
Fort Churchill Historic State Monument, 175
Fort Clatsop National Memorial, 236
Fort Clinch State Park, 68
Fort Clinton, 202
Fort Collins Museum, 52
Fort Columbia State Park, 305

# INDEX

Fort Concho, 281
Fort Conde, 31
Fort Constitution, 177
Fort Crafford, 301
Fort Crailo, 198
Fort Croghan, 272
Fort Cronkhite, 47
Fort Crown Point State Historical Site, 192
Fort Cumberland Trail and George Washington's Headquarters, 138
Fort Dalles Museum, 236
Fort Davidson Historic Site, 166
Fort Davis, 274
Fort Dayton, 193
Fort Defiance, 48, 226
Fort Delaware, 195
Fort Delaware State Park, 60
Fort De Russy, 63
Fort de Soto, 71
Fort Devens Museum, 147
Fort Dobbs, 219
Fort Dodge Historical Museum Fort and Stockade, 99
Fort Donelson National Military Park, 265
Fort Douglas Military Museum, 285
Fort Duncan Park, 273
Fort Edgecomb Memorial, 134
Fort Eustis, 301
Fort Fetterman, 316
Fort Fisher, 218
Fort Foster Historic Site, 72
Fort Frederica National Monument, 75

Fort Frederick, 253
Fort Frederick State Park, 137
Fort Gadsden Historic Site, 71
Fort Gaines, 30
Fort Gaines Outpost Replica, 77
Fort George, 130
Fort Gibson, 232
Fort Gorges, 133
Fort Granger, 266
Fort Griffin State Historic Park, 271
Fort Griffith, 131
Fort Griswold State Park, 56
Fort (Nathan) Hale, 57
Fort Halifax, 134
Fort Hall Replica, 87
Fort Hamilton, 191
Fort Hancock, 178
Fort Harker Guard House Museum, 115
Fort (Benjamin) Harrison Museum, 94
Fort Harrod, 121
Fort Hartsuff State Historical Park, 172
Fort (Benjamin) Hawkins, 78
Fort Hays Frontier Historical Park, 115
Fort (William) Henry, 194
Fort (William) Henry Memorial, 132
Fort Henry Site, 310
Fort Hood, 278
Fort (Sam) Houston, 281
Fort Howard, 213
Fort Huachuca, 41

324

# INDEX

Fort Humbug Memorial Park, 128
Fort Independence, 44
Fort Jackson, 79, 125
Fort Jackson Museum, 256
Fort Jefferson, 68
Fort Jefferson State Memorial, 227
Fort Jesup State Commemorative Area, 126
Fort Johnson Powder Magazine, 254
Fort Kaskaskia State Historic Site, 89
Fort (Phil) Kearny Site, 316
Fort Kent State Memorial, 131
Fort King George Historic Site, 77
Fort Klamath Park, 237
Fort Klock, 199
Fort Knox State Memorial, 130
Fort Lancaster State Historic Site, 280
Fort Lapwai, 86
Fort Laramie National Historic Site, 317
Fort Larned National Historic Site, 116
Fort Laurens State Memorial, 226
Fort Leaton State Park, 280
Fort Leavenworth, 116
Fort LeBoeuf Museum, 247
Fort Lee Historic Park, 180
Fort Lewis Military Museum, 306
Fort Ligonier, 242

Fort (Abraham) Lincoln State Park, 223
Fort Livingston, 125
Fort Loudoun, 268
Fort Lowell Museum, 42
Fort Lyon, 53
Fort Machias, 132
Fort Macon State Park, 216
Fort Madison, 131
Fort Mandan, 224
Fort Mason, 279
Fort Mason Historic District, 47
Fort Massachusetts, 64, 159
Fort Massac Museum, 91
Fort Matanzas National Monument, 70
Fort McAllister, 79
Fort McClary Memorial, 131
Fort McClellan, 30
Fort McHenry, 136
Fort McIntosh, 278
Fort McKavett State Historic Site, 274
Fort (Lesley J.) McNair, 63
Fort (George G.) Meade Army Museum, 138
Fort Meigs, 229
Fort Miami, 94
Fort Michilimackinac National Historic Landmark, 153
Fort Mifflin, 243
Fort Miller Blockhouse Museum, 44
Fort Monroe, 294
Fort Montgomery, 198
Fort Morgan, 31

325

## INDEX

Fort Morgan Library and Museum Complex, 52
Fort Mott State Park, 183
Fort Moultrie, 255
Fort Mount Hope, 201
Fort Nashborough, 267
Fort Necessity National Battlefield, 245
Fort O'Brien, 132
Fort Ontario State Historic Site, 197
Fort Ord, 45
Fort Osage, 164
Fort Ouiatenon, 95
Fort Parker, 276
Fort Phantom Hill, 271
Fort Phoenix, 146
Fort Pickens State Park, 69
Fort Pickering, 150
Fort Pike State Commemorative Area, 127
Fort Pitt Museum, 245
Fort Plain Museum, 193
Fort Polk Military Museum, 126
Fort Popham Memorial, 133
Fort Pownall, 134
Fort Pulaski National Monument, 79
Fort Quitman, 282
Fort Raleigh National Historic Site, 219
Fort Randall, 260
Fort Recovery, 227
Fort Rice, 223
Fort Richardson State Historic Park, 277

Fort Richmond, 200
Fort Ridgely, 157
Fort Riley, 117
Fort Ringgold, 280
Fort Robinson State Park, 172
Fort Ross State Historic Park, 44
Fort St. Clair State Memorial, 226
Fort St. Joseph Museum, 153
Fort Scott National Historic Park, 115
Fort Screven, 80
Fort Sedgwick-Julesburg Museum, 53
Fort Sewall, 148
Fort (William H.) Seward, 35
Fort Sheridan Museum, 90
Fort Sill Military Reservation, 233
Fort Sill Museum, 233
Fort Simcoe State Park, 306
Fort Sisseton State Park, 260
Fort Smith National Historic Site, 36
Fort Stanwix National Monument, 198
Fort Stephenson Museum, 227
Fort Stevens, 64
Fort Stevens State Park, 236
Fort Sully Site, 261
Fort Sumner, 186
Fort Sumter National Monument, 254
Fort Taber, 148
Fort Tejon State Historic Park, 45

# INDEX

Fort Ticonderoga, 200
Fort Totten Historic Site, 222
Fort Toulouse, 32
Fort Towson, 232
Fort Trumbull, 57
Fort Union National Monument, 189
Fort Vallonia Museum, 96
Fort Vancouver National Historic Site, 307
Fort Verde State Historic Park, 40
Fort Wallace Memorial Museum, 118
Fort Ward Museum and Park, 291
Fort Washington, 139, 144
Fort Washita, 233
Fort Watauga, 265
Fort Watson, 258
Fort Wayne, 94
Fort Western, 129
Fort Wilkins State Park, 152
Fort Winchester, 225
Fort Winnebago Surgeon's Quarters, 314
Fort (Leonard) Wood Museum, 167
Fort Wright College Historical Museum, 306
Fort Yamhill Blockhouse, 236
Fort Yargo, 81
Forty-fifth Infantry Division Museum, 233
Fort Yuma Quechan Museum, 42
Franklin Battlefield, 265

Fraunces Tavern, 196
Fredericksburg and Spotsylvania National Military Park, 293
French and Indian War, 4–6
Frigate Rose, H.M.S., 249

Gadsby's Tavern Museum, 291
Gardens of the Missing Monument, 83
Gardner Log Cabin, 98
G.A.R. Hall and Museum, 155
G.A.R. Memorial Hall Museum, 313
Garst Museum, 228
Gathland State Park, 137
Georgia Veterans Memorial Museum, 76
Gettysburg Battle Theater, 242
Gettysburg National Military Park, 241
Glorieta Pass Battlefield, 188
Goddard Space Flight Center, 138
Goliad State National Park, 275
Gonzales First Shot Monument, 276
Gonzales Memorial Museum, 276
Grace Church, 303
Grand Army of the Republic Memorial, 90
Grand Gulf Military State Park, 160
Grant (Ulysses S.) Home, 91

327

# INDEX

Grant (Ulysses S.) Museum, 307
Great Lakes Indian Museum, 152
Green, the, 60
Groton Battle Monument, 56
Grouseland, 97
Guilford Courthouse National Military Park, 217

Hagley Museum, 61
Hale (Nathan) Memorial Monument, 193
Hampton Roads Naval Museum, 267
Harbor Defense Museum, 191
Harper House, 219
Harpers Ferry National Historic Park, 309
Harris-Pearson-Walker Revolutionary War Museum, 75
Hauberg Indian Museum, 92
Haverhill Historical Society Museum, 147
Heritage Gallery, 64
Heritage Hall, 283
Herkimer County Historical Society, 193
Hessian Guardhouse Museum, 240
Hessian Powder Magazine Museum, 240
Hindman Hall Museum, 37
Historical Museum of Gunn Memorial Library, 58
Historic Battlefield Park, 160
Historic Fort Snelling, 156
Historic Fort Wayne, 152
Historic Williamsburg, 301
Honey Springs Battlefield, 234
Horseshoe Bend National Military Park, 30
Houston (Sam) Memorial Museum and Park, 277
Hubbardton Battlefield and Museum, 288
Hunley Museum, 255

Inaugural #242, U.S.S., 167
Independence Hall, 244
Indiana War Memorial Monument and Museum, 95
Indian Wars, 16–20
Infantry Museum, 78
International Space Hall of Fame, 186
International Submarine Memorial, 313

Jackson Memorial Shrine, 293
Jackson's (Stonewall) Headquarters, 301
Jamestown Festival Park, 295
Jefferson Barracks Powder Magazine, 166
Jenkins Ferry Battleground, 38
Johnson Hall State Historic Site, 194
Jones (John Paul) Memorial, 131

# INDEX

Keeler Tavern, 58
Kennedy Space Center, 67
Kennesaw Mountain National Battlefield, 79
Kentucky Military History Museum, 121
Kiefner-Kane Museum, 166
Killdeer Mountain Battlefield, 223
King's Mountain National Military Park, 257
Kittery Historical and Naval Museum, 131
Klamath County Museum, 237
Knox Headquarters, 195
Korean War, 24–25
Kosciuszko House, 244

Lackland Air Force Base, 282
Lake George Battlefield Park, 195
Las Vegas Mormon Fort, 174
Lee (Robert E.) House, 300
Lee's Headquarters and Museum, 241
Lexington, U.S.S., 70
Lexington Battlefield State Historic Site, 164
Lexington Green, 147
Liberty Memorial, 164
Lighthouse Military Museum, 69
Ling (U.S.S.) New Jersey Submarine Memorial, 181
Little Rock, U.S.S., 191

Lone Jack Civil War Museum and Battlefield, 165
Louisiana Military History and State Weapons Collection Museum, 127
Lower Sioux Agency, 156

MacArthur (General Douglas) Memorial Museum, 297
MacDonough Monument, 197
Mackay House, 75
Madeline Island Historical Museum, 313
Magazine, the, 245
Manassas National Battlefield Park, 295
Mansfield State Commemorative Area, 126
March Field Museum, 46
Marine Corps Museum, 64
Marine Corps Museum and Memorial, 244
Marshall (George C.) Library and Museum, 295
Massachusetts, U.S.S., 147
Medicine Lodge Stockade, 116
Memorial Hall Museum, 146
Memorial to Black Soldiers, 250
Merrimac, U.S.S., 299
Mexican War, 11–12
Minute Man National Historical Park, 148
Minuteman Statue, 145
Missing Monument, 83

# INDEX

Mission of San Miguel of Santa Fe, 188
Mission San Francisco de Los Tejas State Historic Park, 283
Mission San Geronimo de Taos, 188
Missouri, U.S.S., 305
Monmouth Battlefield State Park, 180
Monocacy Battlefield, 138
Monument Hill State Historic Site and Park, 278
Monument House, 56
Moore House, 303
Moores Creek National Battlefield, 220
Morgan (John H.) Surrender Site, 230
Morris-Jumel Mansion, 196
Morristown National Historical Park, 181
Mount Defiance, 201
Mount Independence, 201, 289
Munroe Tavern, 148
Museum of Civil War Memorabilia, 60
Museum of History and Technology of the Smithsonian, 64
Museum of the Confederacy, 300
Museum of the Old Northwest Frontier, 229
Museum of the Plains Indians, 169

NASA Visitor Center, 294
Natchez Trace Parkway, 161
National Air and Space Museum of the Smithsonian, 64
National Atomic Museum, 186
National Cemetery, 265
National Civil War Wax Museum, 242
National Gettysburg Battlefield Tower, 241
National Guard Trophy Room, 80
National Infantry Museum, 76
National Memorial Cemetery of the Pacific, 83
Natural Bridge Battlefield Historic Site, 72
Naval Academy Museum, 135
Naval Air and Test Evaluation Museum, 139
Naval and Servicemen's Park, 191
Naval Aviation Museum, 70
Naval Museum of Undersea Warfare, 305
Naval Shipyard Museum, 304
Naval War College Museum, 250
Navy/Marine Corps Museum, 47
Navy Supply Corps Museum, 74
Nelson House, 303
Neuse, C.S.S., 218
New Hampshire Marine Memorial, 177
New Jersey Submarine Memorial, 181

330

# INDEX

New Madrid Museum, 166
New Market Battlefield Park, 296
Newport Artillery Company Armory and Museum, 250
Newport News Dam No. 1 Park, 297
New Windsor Cantonment State Historic Site, 195
New York State Military Museum, 191
Nez Perce National Historical Park, 86
Niagara, U.S.S., 240
Nimitz (Admiral) Center, 275
Ninety-Six National Historic Site, 258
North Bridge Visitor Center, 148
North Carolina (U.S.S.) Battleship Memorial, 220
Norwich University Museum, 289
Nuevo Santander Museum, 279
Nuuanu Pali Lookout, 83

Oaklands Mansion, 267
Old Arsenal Museum, 125
Old Barracks, 183
Old Cannonball House and Confederate Museum, 78
Old Chelmsford Garrison House, 145
Old Constitution House, 289
Old Cove Fort, 285
Olde Powder House, 150
Old Fort Caspar, 316
Old Fort Garland Museum, 52
Old Fort House, 192
Old Fort Johnson, 193
Old Fort Mackinac, 153
Old Fort Madison Site, 99
Old Fort Meade Cavalry Post and Museum, 262
Old Fort Museum, 37
Old Fort Niagara State Park, 202
Old Fort No. Four, 176
Old Fort Ripley, 154
Old Fort Stockton, 274
Old Guard Museum, 292
Old Indian Agency, 314
Old Jacksonport Courthouse Museum, 37
Old Joseph Monument, 237
Old Lighthouse Museum, 58
Old New-Gate Prison and Copper Mine, 54
Old North Bridge, 145
Old North Church, 143, 146
Old Pentagon Barracks, 125
Old Powder House, 148
Old South Meeting House, 142, 143
Old South Museum, 159
Old Spanish Fort, 160
Old State House, 142
Old Stone Fort, 199, 279
Old Tennent Church, 181
Olustee Battlefield State Historic Site, 69
Olympia, U.S.S., 244
109th Artillery Historical and War Museum, 242

# INDEX

Oriskany Battlefield, 198
Overland Trail Museum, 51

Pacific Submarine Museum, 84
Palmito Hill Battlefield, 272
Palo Duro Battle, 272
Parris Island Museum, 253
Patriots Point Naval and Maritime Museum, 256
Patton Museum of Cavalry and Armor, 122
Pea Ridge National Park, 38
Pemberton House, 244
Pembina State Historic Site and Museum, 223
Pennsylvania Military Museum, 239
Perry's Victory and International Peace Memorial, 229
Perryville Battlefield State Shrine, 122
Petersburg National Battlefield, 298
Picacho Peak Battleground, 41
Picatinny Arsenal Ammunition Museum, 179
Pickett's Mill Battlefield Site, 76
Pigeon Roost State Memorial, 96
Pike's Stockade, 50
Pilgrim Hall, 149
Plimoth Plantation, 149
Plymouth Rock, 149
Point Lookout State Park, 139
Point Park Visitor Center, 264

Point Pinos Lighthouse Museum, 46
Point Pleasant Battle Monument, 310
Port Johnson Powder Magazine, 254
Portsmouth Naval Shipyard Museum, 298
Prairie Grove Battlefield State Park, 37
Pratt (William) Memorial Museum, 48
Presidio Army Museum, 47
Presidio de Santa Barbara State Historic Park, 48
Presidio La Bahia, 275
Pricketts Fort State Park, 309
Princeton Battlefield State Park, 182
Providence, sloop, 249
Pueblo Museum, 54
Putnam Cottage, 56
Putnam Memorial State Park, 57
Pyramid Lake War Marker, 175

Quarai State Monument, 187

Raynham Hall, 197
Real Presidio de Saba, 279
Red Bank Battlefield, 182
Remember the Alamo Theater and Museum, 281
Requin, U.S.S., 72

# INDEX

Resaca de la Palma Battle Site, 271
Rescue Memorial Museum, 186
Revolutionary War, 6–9
Richmond National Battlefield Park, 299
Rivers Bridge Confederate Memorial State Park, 253
Rochambeau Statue and Monument, 249
Rock Island Arsenal, 92
Rogers (Edith Nourse) Museum, 30
Roop Fort, 48
Rough Riders Memorial and City Museum, 187
Roxbury High Fort, 143
Russell (Jason) House, 148

Sabine Pass Battleground Historic Park, 280
Sackets Harbor Battlefield State Historic Site, 199
Salem Maritime National Historic Site, 149
Sand Creek Massacre, 51
San Elizario Presido, 273
San Jacinto Battleground Park, 277
San Jose Mission Historical Site, 282
San Juan Bautista State Historic Park, 48
San Juan Island National Historic Park, 306
San Marcos de Apalache State Musem, 71

San Pasqual Battlefield State Historic Park, 48
Saratoga National Historical Park, 191
Savannah Volunteer Guard Museum, 80
Sayler's Creek Battlefield Park, 299
Schuyler (General Philip) House, 191
Scoper House Museum, 137
Sea and Land Survival Exhibit, 70
Second Armored Division Museum, 278
Seventh Infantry Division Museum, 45
'76 House, 200
Shaw Mansion, 57
Shaw Monument, 144
Shiloh National Military Park, 268
Ship Island, 159
Siege Museum, 298
Silversides, U.S.S., 90
Silver Wings Aviation Museum, 46
Sitka National Historical Park, 35
Sitting Bull Monument and Memorial Site, 260
Smitherman (Joseph T.) Historic Building, 33
Soldiers and Sailors Memorial Hall, 245, 261
Soldiers Memorial, 167
Soldiers' Monument, 143

# INDEX

Soldiers National Museum, 242
Sonoma Plaza, 48
South Carolina Confederate Relic Room and Museum, 256
South Dakota (U.S.S.) Battleship Memorial, 261
South River Fort, 164
Spanish-American War, 20–21
Special Warfare Museum, 217
Spirit Lake Massacre Log Cabin, 98
Springfield Armory National Historic Site, 150
State House, 177
State House Museum, 144
State of Maine, ship, 131
Stockade, 90
Stones River National Battlefield, 267
Stony Point Battlefield State Historic Site, 200
Stout Field Military Equipment Museum, 94
Strategic Air Command Museum, 172
Submarine Forces Library and Museum, 56
Sullivans, U.S.S., 191
Summit Springs Battleground, 51
Sunbury Historic Site, 79

Tank Cottage, 313
Tappan Reformed (Dutch) Church, 200

Tennent Church, 181
Texas, U.S.S., 277
Texas Ranger Hall of Fame and Museum, 282
Texas Rebellion, 11
Third Armored Cavalry Regiment Museum, 273
Thirty-eighth Infantry Division Memorial Museum, 94
Thomas Creek Battlefield, 69
Thornburgh Battlefield Site, 52
Tippecanoe Battlefield, 95
Tongue River Battlefield, 317
Torsk, U.S.S., 136
Travellers Rest, 267
Traverse des Sioux State Park, 157
Tropic Lightning Historical Center, 84
Truxton-Decatur Naval Museum, 64
Tubac Presidio State Historic Park, 41
Tupelo National Battlefield Site, 160
Twenty-eighth Division Shrine, 239
Two Lights State Park, 130
Tybee Museum, 80

U.S. Air Force Academy, 51
U.S. Air Force Museum, 226
U.S. Army Aviation Museum, 32

# INDEX

U.S. Army Coast Artillery Museum, 294
U.S. Army Communications-Electronics Museum, 180
U.S. Army Engineer Museum, 293
U.S. Army Finance Corps Museum, 94
U.S. Army Intelligence Museum, 41
U.S. Army Medical Museum, 282
U.S. Army Military Police Corps Museum, 30
U.S. Army Museum, Battery Randolph, 83
U.S. Army Museum in the Presidio of Monterey, 45
U.S. Army Ordnance Museum, 137
U.S. Army Quartermaster Museum, 298
U.S. Army Signal Museum, 75
U.S. Army Transportation Museum, 301
U.S. Cavalry Museum, 117
U.S. Coast Guard Academy, 57
U.S. Historical Aircraft Preservation Museum, 35
U.S. Marine Corps Aviation Museum, 299
U.S. Merchant Marine Academy, 194
U.S. Military Academy, 201
U.S. Naval Training Center, 46
U.S. Navy Memorial Museum, 65

Valley Forge National Historical Park, 246
Vicksburg National Military Park, 161
Vietnam War, 25–26
Village Inn, 181
Villa Louis, 314
Villa (Pancho) Museum, 186
Villa (Pancho) State Park, 186
Violet Bank Civil War Museum, 292
Virginia Military Institute Museum, 295
Virginia World War II and Korea Memorial, 300

Wagon Box Battle Site, 318
War in Georgia and Heritage Museum, 74
War Library and Museum, 244
War Memorial Building, 268
War Memorial Museum of Virginia, 297
War Memorial Room, 177
War of 1812, 9–10
Warrant Officer Candidate Hall of Fame Museum, 33
Warren Military Museum, 316
Warren Rifles Confederate Museum, 294
Washington Crossing State Park, 183, 243
Washington Headquarters State Historic Site, 195
Washington (George) Masonic Shrine, 200

# INDEX

Washington Memorial Chapel and Museum, 246
Washington on the Brazos State Historical Park, 279
Washington's (George) Headquarters, 138
Washington's (George) Office, 301
Washington Square, 243
Washington-Wilkes Historical Museum, 80
Watervliet Arsenal, 201
Wayne Blockhouse, 241
Webb (Joseph) House, 58
West Point Museum, 202
White Bird Battlefield and Hill, 85
White (James) Fort, 266
White (Edward H. II) Hangar 9 Memorial Museum, 282
White House of the Confederacy, 300
White River Museum, 54
White Sands Missile Range, 186

Whites of Their Eyes, 145
Whitestone Hill Battlefield, 222
Wilson's Creek National Battlefield, 167
Winchester Gun Museum, 56
Winsor Castle Fort, 40
Winstead Hill, 266
Wisconsin Veterans Museum, 313
Wolverine, U.S.S., 241
Women's Army Corps Museum, 30
World War I, 21–22
World War II, 22–24
Wright's Tavern, 145

Yorktown, U.S.S.. 256
Yorktown Battlefield, 302
Yorktown Victory Center, 302

Zwaanendael Museum, 60